Hello! 365 Healthy Dessert Recipes

(Healthy Dessert Recipes - Volume 1)

Best Healthy Dessert Cookbook Ever For Beginners

Ms. Hanna

Ms. Healthy

Copyright: Published in the United States by Ms. Healthy/ © MS. HEALTHY

Published on February, 05 2020

All rights reserved. No part of this publication may be reproduced, stored in retrieval system, copied in any form or by any means, electronic, mechanical, photocopying, recording or otherwise transmitted without written permission from the publisher. Please do not participate in or encourage piracy of this material in any way. You must not circulate this book in any format. MS. HEALTHY does not control or direct users' actions and is not responsible for the information or content shared, harm and/or actions of the book readers.

In accordance with the U.S. Copyright Act of 1976, the scanning, uploading and electronic sharing of any part of this book without the permission of the publisher constitute unlawful piracy and theft of the author's intellectual property. If you would like to use material from the book (other than just simply for reviewing the book), prior permission must be obtained by contacting the author at mshealthy@mrandmscooking.com

Thank you for your support of the author's rights.

Content

- **CONTENT** 3
- **INTRODUCTION** 8
- **LIST OF ABBREVIATIONS** 10
- **365 AMAZING HEALTHY DESSERT RECIPES** 11
  1. 14-karat Cake...11
  2. Almond Sunshine Citrus............................11
  3. Angel Berry Trifle......................................12
  4. Apple And Honey Sorbet..........................12
  5. Apple And Pumpkin Dessert.....................13
  6. Apple Oatmeal Crisp.................................13
  7. Apple Pie Filling II....................................14
  8. Apple Pie In A Jar.....................................14
  9. Apple Pie IV...15
  10. Apple Pie Tartlets......................................15
  11. Apple Pudding...16
  12. Apple Raisin Cakes 16
  13. Apple Skewers...17
  14. Apple-raisin Rice Dessert 17
  15. Apples By The Fire 18
  16. Applesauce Cake 18
  17. Applesauce Lattice Pie..............................19
  18. Apricot Apple Compote 19
  19. Apricot Delight..20
  20. Apricot Noodle Kugel...............................20
  21. Apricot Oat Bars 21
  22. Apricot Sundaes...21
  23. Azteca Cocoa Rice Pudding 22
  24. Baked Apple Crisp 22
  25. Baked Apple Pudding................................22
  26. Baked Banana Boats 23
  27. Baked Blueberry-peach Pound Cake 23
  28. Baked Ginger Pears 24
  29. Baked Maple Pumpkin Pie 24
  30. Baked Pumpkin Pudding...........................25
  31. Banana Chia Pudding................................25
  32. Banana Custard Scrunch...........................26
  33. Banana Honey Yogurt Ice........................26
  34. Banana Kiwi Strawberry Tart.................27
  35. Banana Oat And Bran Cookies...............27
  36. Banana Oat Bread Pudding 28
  37. Banana Spice Cake....................................28
  38. Banana Tempura..29
  39. Banana Yogurt Pie....................................29
  40. Bavarian Apple Tart.................................30
  41. Berries With Banana Cream 31
  42. Berries With Sour Cream Sauce.............31
  43. Berry Phyllo Tarts....................................31
  44. Berry Punch Parfaits 32
  45. Better-than-fruitcake Cookies.................32
  46. Bigmom's Cranberry Salad.....................33
  47. Black Bean Brownies................................33
  48. Blueberries 'n' Cream Pie 34
  49. Blueberries And Cheese Coffee Cake...34
  50. Blueberries N Cheese Coffee Cake 35
  51. Blueberry Betty...36
  52. Blueberry Crumb Pie 36
  53. Blueberry Custard Meringue Pie...........37
  54. Blueberry Pie In A Jar............................37
  55. Blueberry Quinoa With Lemon Glaze..38
  56. Bourbon Candy Apples............................38
  57. Breakfast Brownies...................................39
  58. Buttermilk Carrot Cake 39
  59. Buttermilk Chocolate Sauce....................40
  60. Cake-topped Apple Cobbler...................40
  61. Cake-topped Blueberry Dessert............41
  62. Candied Kumquat Peels..........................41
  63. Carrot Cake Cookies 42
  64. Carrot Cake II 42
  65. Carrot Chocolate Chip Cookies.............43
  66. Carrot-pineapple Gelatin Salad.............43
  67. Champagne With Strawberries...............44
  68. Cherry Angel Cake Roll.........................44
  69. Cherry Cheesecake Pie............................44
  70. Cherry Chocolate Cake............................45
  71. Cherry Chocolate Pie...............................45
  72. Cherry-almond Streusel Tart..................46
  73. Chevre Cheesecake...................................46
  74. Chewy Coconut Macaroons 47
  75. Chewy Date Cookies................................47
  76. Chewy Fudge Drop Cookies..................48
  77. Chewy Oatmeal Raisin Cookies............48

#	Title	Page
78.	Chilled Cantaloupe Soup	49
79.	Chloe's Quick Fruit Salad	49
80.	Chocolate Caramel Cheesecake	50
81.	Chocolate Cereal Bars	50
82.	Chocolate Chip Cookies	51
83.	Chocolate Chip Mint Ice Cream	51
84.	Chocolate Fudge	52
85.	Chocolate Layer Cake	52
86.	Chocolate Meringue Cups	53
87.	Chocolate Mint Eclair Dessert	54
88.	Chocolate Mint Whoopie Pies	54
89.	Chocolate Mousse	55
90.	Chocolate Pistachio Biscotti	56
91.	Chocolate Souffles	56
92.	Chocolate-filled Raspberry Meringues	57
93.	Chocolate-glazed Brownies	57
94.	Chocolate-raspberry Mousse Pie	58
95.	Chocolaty Zucchini Cake	59
96.	Chunky Banana Chip Ice Cream	59
97.	Cinnamon Peach Crisp	60
98.	Cinnamon-cranberry Oat Bars	60
99.	Citrus Meringue Pie	61
100.	Cocoa Banana Cupcakes	61
101.	Cocoa-almond Meringue Cookies	62
102.	Coconut Banana Chocolate Cream Pie	63
103.	Coconut Pineapple Pops	63
104.	Coffee Jelly	63
105.	Comforting Creamy Banana Pudding	64
106.	Cool Mandarin Dessert	64
107.	Cool Raspberry Peach Pie	65
108.	Cran-apple Crisp	65
109.	Cran-apple Praline Gingerbread	66
110.	Cranberry Apple Gelatin Mold	66
111.	Cranberry Cheesecake Bars	67
112.	Cranberry Crumb Cake	67
113.	Cranberry Fudge	68
114.	Cranberry Gelatin Salad	68
115.	Cranberry Ice	69
116.	Cranberry Oat Yummies	69
117.	Cranberry Pear Crisp Pie	70
118.	Cranberry Salad V	70
119.	Cranberry-chocolate Oatmeal Bars	71
120.	Cream-filled Strawberries	71
121.	Creamy Iced Applesauce Bars	72
122.	Crimson Crumble Bars	72
123.	Crinkle-top Chocolate Cookies	72
124.	Crispy Oat Cookies	73
125.	Crunchy Pears	73
126.	Crunchy Topped Chocolate Cake	74
127.	Dark Chocolate Layer Cake	75
128.	Dark Chocolate Sauce	75
129.	Delightful Brownies	76
130.	Deluxe Brownies	76
131.	Devil's Food Cookies	77
132.	Double Chocolate Biscotti	77
133.	Double Chocolate Cupcakes	78
134.	Double Peanut Bars	79
135.	Double-chocolate Cream Roll	79
136.	Dreamy Orange Cupcakes	80
137.	Dutch Oven Apple Crisp	81
138.	Easy Banana Ice Cream	81
139.	Easy Blueberry-lemon Parfait	81
140.	Easy Chiffon Pie	82
141.	Easy Chocolate Sherbet	82
142.	Easy Lemonade Icebox Pie	82
143.	Easy Rhubarb Pie	83
144.	Easy Vanilla Ice Cream	83
145.	Eggnog Pudding	83
146.	Elderberry Soup	84
147.	Favorite Marbled Chocolate Cheesecake Bars	84
148.	Fig Filling For Pastry	85
149.	Finnish Berry Dessert	85
150.	Flax Seed Carrot Cake	86
151.	Flourless Dark Chocolate Cake	86
152.	Fluffy Cherry Frosting	87
153.	Fluffy Orange Gelatin Pie	87
154.	Fresh Cranberry Salad	88
155.	Fresh Fruit Compote	88
156.	Fresh No-bake Fruit Pie	89
157.	Fresh Strawberry Granita	89
158.	Frosty Cantaloupe Sherbet	90
159.	Frosty Peach Pie Supreme	90
160.	Frozen Fruit Salad	90
161.	Frozen Pistachio Dessert With Raspberry Sauce	91
162.	Frozen Strawberry Torte	92
163.	Fruit-filled Angel Food Torte	92
164.	Fruit-packed Gelatin Salad	92
165.	Fruity Sherbet Dessert	93
166.	Fudgy Peanut Butter Brownies	93
167.	Fudgy White Chocolate Pudding Pie	94
168.	Ginger Thins	94
169.	Gingerbread Cookies	95

170.	Graham Cracker Banana Split Dessert.	95
171.	Graham Cracker Crust	96
172.	Grandma Moyer's Rhubarb And Strawberry Coffee Cake	96
173.	Granola Blondies	97
174.	Granola Cereal Bars	97
175.	Granola Fruit Bars	98
176.	Green Apple Sorbet With Pistachios	98
177.	Green Tomato Mincemeat	99
178.	Guava Preserves	99
179.	Guilt-free Chocolate Cake	100
180.	Harvest Snack Cake	100
181.	Healthier (but Still) The Best Rolled Sugar Cookies	101
182.	Healthier Apple Crisp II	101
183.	Healthier Apple Pie By Grandma Ople	102
184.	Healthier Award Winning Soft Chocolate Chip Cookies	102
185.	Healthier Best Big, Fat, Chewy Chocolate Chip Cookie	103
186.	Healthier Best Brownies	103
187.	Healthier Best Chocolate Chip Cookies	104
188.	Healthier Beth's Spicy Oatmeal Raisin Cookies	104
189.	Healthier Big Soft Ginger Cookies	105
190.	Healthier Cake Balls	105
191.	Healthier Chantal's New York Cheesecake	106
192.	Healthier Creamy Rice Pudding	107
193.	Healthier No Bake Cookies I	107
194.	Healthier Southern Peach Cobbler	108
195.	Healthy And Tasty Strawberry Sherbet	108
196.	Healthy Apple Cobbler	109
197.	Healthy Banana Cookies	109
198.	Healthy Blackberry Cobbler	109
199.	Holiday Baked Apples	110
200.	Homemade Lemon Cheese Pie	110
201.	Homemade Strawberry Rhubarb Sauce	111
202.	Honey Baked Apples	111
203.	Honey Bun Cake	112
204.	Honey Lemon Cookies	112
205.	Honey Spice Snack Cake	113
206.	Honeydew Blueberry Soup	113
207.	Hot Cinnamon Candy Covered Apples	114
208.	Huckleberry Buckle II	114
209.	Jo-ann's Power Bars	115
210.	Kiwi Lime Gelatin	115
211.	Lemon Blueberry Cheesecake	115
212.	Lemon Chiffon Dessert	116
213.	Lemon Cooler Cookies	117
214.	Lemon Custard Ice Cream	117
215.	Lemon Delight Cake	118
216.	Lemon Meringue Angel Cake	118
217.	Lemon Raspberry-filled Cake	119
218.	Lemon Snack Cake	120
219.	Lemon Yogurt Cream Pie	120
220.	Light Chocolate Cheesecake	121
221.	Light Lemon Cheesecake	121
222.	Light Strawberry Gelatin Pie	122
223.	Light Sweet Potato Pie	122
224.	Lime And Tequila Infused Strawberries	123
225.	Lime Frozen Yogurt	123
226.	Lime Honeydew Sorbet	123
227.	Lime Parfaits	124
228.	Low Fat Breakfast Cookies	124
229.	Low-fat Chocolate Cookies	125
230.	Mahogany Devil's Food Cake	125
231.	Make-ahead Lemon Bombe	126
232.	Makeover Chocolate Zucchini Cake	127
233.	Makeover Coconut Cookies	127
234.	Makeover Crispy Oat Cookies	128
235.	Makeover Meringue Coconut Brownies	128
236.	Makeover Peanut Butter Pie	129
237.	Makeover Pear Cheesecake	129
238.	Makeover Red Velvet Cake	130
239.	Makeover Rocky Road Fudge Brownies	131
240.	Makeover Spice Crumb Cake	131
241.	Makeover Sweet Potato Pecan Pie	132
242.	Makeover White Fruitcake	132
243.	Makeover White Layer Cake	133
244.	Maple Banana Ice Cream	134
245.	Meringue Candy Canes	134
246.	Microwave Hot Fudge Sundae Cake	135
247.	Mile-high Lime Pie	135
248.	Mixed Berry Pizza	136
249.	Mixed Berry Shortcake	136

#	Title	Page
250.	Mock Ice Cream Sandwiches	137
251.	Mock Strawberry Cheesecake Tart	137
252.	Mom's Pumpkin Pie	137
253.	Momma Lamb's Famous Fruit Salad	138
254.	No-bake Almond Bites	138
255.	No-bake Chocolate Oat Cookies	139
256.	No-bake Lemon Cheesecake	139
257.	No-fuss Rice Pudding	140
258.	No-oat Apple Crisp	140
259.	Oatmeal Fruit Cookie Mix In A Jar	140
260.	Oatmeal Peanut Butter Cookies	141
261.	Old-fashioned Fruit Soup	141
262.	One-ingredient Sorbet	142
263.	Orange Baked Alaska	142
264.	Orange Cashew Bars	143
265.	Orange Cream Pops	143
266.	Orange Delight	144
267.	Orange Dream Cups	144
268.	Orange Lime Gelatin Ring	145
269.	Orange Parfaits	145
270.	Orange Pineapple Delight	146
271.	Orange Pumpkin Gelatin	146
272.	Orange Rosemary Sorbet	147
273.	Orange Tea Cake	147
274.	Papaya Boats	148
275.	Paradise Parfaits	148
276.	Party Cranberry Salad	149
277.	Peanut Butter Bread Pudding	149
278.	Peanut Ice Cream	150
279.	Pear Cheesecake	150
280.	Pears Panos	151
281.	Peppermint-kissed Fudge Mallow Cookies	151
282.	Picnic Berry Shortcakes	152
283.	Pineapple Almond Bars	152
284.	Pineapple Orange Sherbet	153
285.	Pineapple Pecan Cake	153
286.	Pineapple Pudding	154
287.	Pineapple-coconut Angel Food Cake	154
288.	Pistachio Fluff	154
289.	Plum Clafouti	155
290.	Plum Dumplings	155
291.	Plum Flummery	156
292.	Poached Pears With Orange Cream	157
293.	Poached Pears With Wine Vinaigrette	157
294.	Power Bars	158
295.	Power Cookies	158
296.	Pretzel Strawberry Dessert	159
297.	Pudding Fruit Salad	159
298.	Pumpkin Angel Food Cake	160
299.	Pumpkin Pecan Frozen Yogurt	160
300.	Pumpkin Protein Cookies	160
301.	Quinoa Pudding	161
302.	Raspberry Cream Cake	161
303.	Raspberry Cream Pie	162
304.	Raspberry Whip	162
305.	Raspberry-filled Meringue Torte	163
306.	Raspberry-topped Cream Tarts	164
307.	Real German Baked Apples	164
308.	Red, White And Blueberry Pie	164
309.	Refreshing Cranberry Ice	165
310.	Rhubarb Shortcake Dessert	165
311.	Rich Caramel Pecan Bars	166
312.	Rich Chocolate Snack Cake	166
313.	Rosemary Pineapple Upside-down Cake	167
314.	Shudderuppers	167
315.	Silky Lemon Pie	168
316.	Simple Broiled Grapefruit	168
317.	Simple Strawberry Sherbet	169
318.	Slow Cooker Baked Apples	169
319.	Slow-cooked Bread Pudding	170
320.	Sparkling Grapefruit Pie	170
321.	Spice Bars	170
322.	Spice Crumb Cake	171
323.	Spiced Fruit Bake	172
324.	Spiced Pear Cake	172
325.	Spiced Pineapple Pumpkin Delight	173
326.	Stewed Holiday Fruit	173
327.	Strawberry Almond Pastries	174
328.	Strawberry Cheesecake Torte	174
329.	Strawberry Chiffon Pie	175
330.	Strawberry Italian Ice	175
331.	Strawberry Pie Mousse	176
332.	Strawberry Raspberry Trifle	176
333.	Strawberry Rhubarb Tart	177
334.	Strawberry Shortcake With Balsamic	177
335.	Strawberry-banana Ice Cream	178
336.	Striped Fruit Pops	178
337.	Sugarless Rice Pudding	179
338.	Summer Berry Compote	179
339.	Summer Berry Parfait With Yogurt And Granola	179
340.	Sunny Sponge Cake	180

341.	Sweet And Silky Strawberry Sorbet	181
342.	Sweet Grilled Peaches	181
343.	Sweetheart Red Cake	181
344.	Swirled Chocolate Peanut Butter Cake	182
345.	Thumbprint Cookies	183
346.	Trail Mix Clusters	183
347.	Triple Berry Sorbet	183
348.	Triple Orange Fluff	184
349.	Tropical Delight Sherbet	184
350.	Tropical Mango Mousse	185
351.	Tutti-frutti Angel Food Cake	185
352.	Ultimate Chocolate Cake	185
353.	Upside-down Peach Cake	186
354.	Valentine Strawberry Shortcake	186
355.	Vanilla Berry Parfaits	187
356.	Very Berry Parfaits	187
357.	Walnut Raisin Apple Cookies	188
358.	Walnut Streusel Coffee Cake	188
359.	Warm Banana Pudding	189
360.	Warm Blackberry Cobbler	190
361.	Warm Chocolate Almond Pudding	190
362.	Warm Chocolate Melting Cups	191
363.	Watermelon Ice Cream (sugar-free)	191
364.	White Chip Cranberry Blondies	192
365.	White Chocolate Cranberry Cookies	192

INDEX **193**

CONCLUSION **203**

Introduction

***

Hi all,

Welcome to MrandMsCooking.com — a website created by a community of cooking enthusiasts with the goal of providing books for novice cooks featuring the best recipes, at the most affordable prices, and valuable gifts.

Hats off to you for believing and trying out "Hello! 365 Healthy Dessert Recipes". The fact that you are reading this now means that you want to live a higher- quality of living and I am so thrilled for you. Living a high-quality life, both in our mind and in our body, is very beneficial for us. As an introduction, I will share with you my personal journey and the ways I attained my present quality life. Before, I was the healthy consumer I am know, I had many bad habits when it came to my choices. I did not know about the importance of taking care of myself so I ate a lot of junk foods, did not go to bed at a good time, and would sleep in late. Back then, the benefits of being healthy and the harmful effects of my unhealthy lifestyle did not occur to me, thus I remained in my bad habits for quite some time. As a result, I gained a lot of weight and my facial skin was suffering a lot too. That time in my life was very stressful and the more stressful I felt, the more I junk food I would consume. My stress eating was uncontrollable and started gaining a lot of weight. People started commenting on my appearance, and I started researching how to lose weight. Various ways are offered online, and I have learned about many of them. A lot of methods I attempted but I was not able to sustain them due to the lack of comfort they offered. But luckily, I was able to discover something that did fit me. Consuming healthy food and practicing a healthy lifestyle is something that I can do easily and efficiently every day. Until now, even after I attained my desired weight, I continue to consume healthy food because it keeps me beautiful, my body functions better, and I am more positive and have more fun. I know that it is really challenging to those of you who are used to enjoying fried/fatty foods to start consuming healthier ones. But, now is the best time to improve yourself and cleanse your body, mind and spirit. If you can regulate what you eat and what you do, then this will not be hard for you. Sleep on time and rise early in the morning, consume a heavy and healthy breakfast, and you will realize that you will have all the energy and efficiency you need to last the whole day.

Whenever you will hear the words "healthy lifestyle", your initial thought will always be about food. This is correct because as the saying goes, we are what we eat. Just by looking at someone's form and stance, I can already say if he is living a healthy life. To sustain our lives, we consume food. With this, we just need to feed on the freshest and highest quality of food to make our bodies healthy and beautiful. Most of my friends have this notion that healthy foods are not appetizing. They are also not aware that healthy foods and healthy eating are easy to do. Healthy foods are everywhere (eggs, milk, fish, meat, nuts, etc.) and are excellent for our health. Those that were processed, especially in fast food chains, are not good for our health.

So, can we process food and still retain its healthiness? Can we still produce delectable and flavorful food? These articles which I've prepared for you will provide you the answers.

My vision is to impart my knowledge about healthy living on as many people as I can reach. I have written these articles on various subjects for you to be able to select which one fits you best.

- Diabetes Diet
- Clean Eating
- ...

Every subject will contain a different style of eating; however, each one has the common goal of teaching you to eat healthy. There is a variety of styles to meet each individual's personal needs just take a look and pick the that fits you and be on your way to a higher-quality of life. Moreover, I am confident that these compilations of complete recipes will help you practice your chosen style without difficulty.

My overview is already lengthy but I would like to share more things with you later about eating healthy. For this segment, I will not be talking about the negative effects of consuming unhealthy foods because that piece is already vastly available online. Also, my expectation is that since you are reading this piece, I am assuming that you've got all the essential information as to why it is essential to live a healthy lifestyle.

Below is the recipe for a happy and healthy life:

Happy Life = Healthy Mind + Healthy Body

I really appreciate that you have selected "Hello! 365 Healthy Dessert Recipes" and for reading to the end. I anticipate that this book shall give you the source of strength during the times that you are really exhausted, as well as be your best friend in the comforts of your own home. Make it your model as you head to the kitchen to try one of these new recipes. It would also be great if you can share to me and everyone your personal journey. Send me an e-mail!

List of Abbreviations

Ms. Mr. CooKing
LIST OF ABBREVIATIONS

tbsp(s).	tablespoon(s)
tsp(s).	teaspoon(s)
c.	cup(s)
oz.	ounce(s)
lb(s).	pound(s)

365 Amazing Healthy Dessert Recipes

***

1. 14-karat Cake

""This carrot cakes satisfied my entire family.""
Serving: 18 servings. | Prep: 15m | Ready in: 45m

Ingredients

- 1-1/3 cups sugar
- 2 eggs
- 2 egg whites
- 1/2 cup unsweetened applesauce
- 1/3 cup canola oil
- 1 cup all-purpose flour
- 1 cup whole wheat flour
- 1-1/2 tsps. baking soda
- 1 tsp. salt
- 1 tsp. ground cinnamon
- 1/2 tsp. ground allspice
- 1/4 tsp. ground cloves
- 3 cups shredded carrots
- 1/2 cup golden raisins
- 6 oz. reduced-fat cream cheese
- 1 tbsp. butter, softened
- 1/2 tsp. vanilla extract
- 3 cups confectioners' sugar
- 1/4 cup chopped walnuts
- 3 tbsps. sweetened shredded coconut, toasted

Direction

- Mix together the first five ingredients in a bowl, till smooth. Mix spices, salt, baking soda and flours; include into the egg mixture; stir thoroughly. Mix in raisins and carrots. Transfer onto a 13x9-inch baking pan greased with cooking spray. Bake at 350° till a toothpick comes out clean when inserted into the center, 30-35 minutes. Allow to cool on a wire rack.
- For frosting, beat vanilla, butter and cream cheese in a bowl, till smooth. Beat in sugar. Frost the cake. Scatter with coconut and walnuts. Place in a refrigerator.

Nutrition Information

- Calories: 286 calories
- Total Carbohydrate: 49 g
- Cholesterol: 33 mg
- Total Fat: 9 g
- Fiber: 2 g
- Protein: 4 g
- Sodium: 304 mg

2. Almond Sunshine Citrus

"A dish made with a combination of tangy citrus fruits."
Serving: 4 servings. | Prep: 30m | Ready in: 30m

Ingredients

- 3 large navel oranges
- 1 medium red grapefruit
- 1 medium white grapefruit
- 1 small lemon
- 1 small lime
- 1/3 cup sugar
- 1/8 tsp. almond extract
- 2 tbsps. sliced almonds, toasted

Direction

- Great enough peel from lime, lemon, grapefruit and oranges to get a tbsp. of the mixed citrus peel, then put aside. Slice off the

- top and bottom of the lime, lemon, grapefruit and oranges thinly to section the citrus fruits. Put each fruit on a chopping board, cut side down. Take off the white pith and peel using a sharp knife. While you hold the fruit on top of a bowl, cut between the fruit and the membrane of each section, until the knife reaches the middle, then take off the sections and put it in a glass bowl. Put aside half a cup of juice.
- Mix together the reserved juice and peel and the sugar in a small saucepan, then boil. Lower the heat and let it simmer for 10 minutes without cover. Allow to cool, then mix in the extract. Pour on top of the fruit. Let it chill in the fridge overnight. Sprinkle almonds on top just prior to serving.

Nutrition Information

- Calories: 197 calories
- Total Carbohydrate: 47 g
- Cholesterol: 0 mg
- Total Fat: 2 g
- Fiber: 6 g
- Protein: 3 g
- Sodium: 1 mg

3. Angel Berry Trifle

"A lovely berry trifle."
Serving: 14 servings. | Prep: 15m | Ready in: 15m

Ingredients

- 1-1/2 cups cold fat-free milk
- 1 package (1 oz.) sugar-free instant vanilla pudding mix
- 1 cup (8 oz.) fat-free vanilla yogurt
- 6 oz. reduced-fat cream cheese, cubed
- 1/2 cup reduced-fat sour cream
- 2 tsps. vanilla extract
- 1 carton (12 oz.) frozen reduced-fat whipped topping, thawed and divided
- 2 prepared angel food cakes (8 oz. each), cut into 1-inch cubes
- 1 pint fresh blackberries
- 1 pint fresh raspberries
- 1 pint fresh blueberries

Direction

- Whisk pudding mix and milk for 2 minutes; stand for 2 minutes till soft set. Meanwhile, beat vanilla, sour cream, cream cheese and yogurt till smooth; fold 1 cup whipped topping and pudding mixture in.
- In 4-qt. trifle bowl, put 1/3 cake cubes. Put 1/3 pudding mixture, 1/3 berries then 1/2 leftover whipped topping over; repeat layers 1 time. Put leftover cake, pudding then berries over; immediately serve or refrigerate.

Nutrition Information

- Calories: 209 calories
- Total Carbohydrate: 32 g
- Cholesterol: 10 mg
- Total Fat: 6 g
- Fiber: 3 g
- Protein: 5 g
- Sodium: 330 mg

4. Apple And Honey Sorbet

"A beautiful white sorbet speckled with bright green flecks and flavored with sweet honey and piquant green apples. Using eucalyptus blossom honey is highly recommended! You can easily find it in Israel. Serve this dessert in between courses."
Serving: 8 | Prep: 1h | Ready in: 4h5m

Ingredients

- 1 1/4 lbs. Granny Smith apples, cored and thinly sliced
- 1 1/2 cups water
- 1 1/2 cups sugar
- 1 1/2 lemons, juiced
- 1 tbsp. honey

Direction

- Place apples in a big plastic resealable bag or plastic receptacle with a cover and pour in juice of 1/2 lemon. Store in the freezer overnight or at least for a few hours.
- Combine sugar and water in a small pot and cook to a boil. Turn the heat down and let it simmer for another 5 minutes. Take the pan off heat and mix in honey. Set aside to completely cool.
- In blender, combine the apples, cooled sugar syrup and squeeze in juice of 1 lemon. Pulse blender until you achieve a smooth consistency. Leave the peels of the apples on as they will prevent mixture from turning completely smooth and add texture to the sorbet.
- Pour mixture into an ice cream maker and follow instructions to freeze. Before serving, take the sorbet out and leave it for 10 minutes to soften.

Nutrition Information

- Calories: 188 calories;
- Total Carbohydrate: 50.6 g
- Cholesterol: 0 mg
- Total Fat: 0.1 g
- Protein: 0.5 g
- Sodium: 3 mg

5. Apple And Pumpkin Dessert

"This apple and pumpkin microwave dish is better and more delicious than pie. It's not only healthy, it's also very easy to make in the comfort of your own kitchen."
Serving: 1 | Prep: 5m | Ready in: 9m

Ingredients

- 2 (1 gram) packets sugar substitute
- 1 tsp. pumpkin pie spice
- 1 Granny Smith apple - peeled, cored and chopped
- 1/4 cup canned pumpkin
- 2 tbsps. water

Direction

- In a microwave-safe bowl, sprinkle 1/3 tsp. pumpkin pie spice and 1/3 packet of sugar substitute. Layer a quarter of the apple slices into the bowl; repeat to make another layer. Spread pumpkin over the apples. Take the remaining pumpkin pie spice and sugar substitute and sprinkle them on the pumpkin. Top with the rest of the apples. Pour water onto mixture.
- Place bowl inside the microwave and cook for 3 1/2 minute on high power, stirring after each minute.

Nutrition Information

- Calories: 88 calories;
- Total Carbohydrate: 23.8 g
- Cholesterol: 0 mg
- Total Fat: 0.4 g
- Protein: 1.2 g
- Sodium: 151 mg

6. Apple Oatmeal Crisp

"This dish is very easy and quick to make with just one bowl and no mess."
Serving: 8 | Prep: 20m | Ready in: 1h

Ingredients

- 1 cup brown sugar
- 1 cup rolled oats
- 1 cup all-purpose flour
- 1/2 cup butter, melted
- 3 cups apples - peeled, cored and chopped
- 1/2 cup white sugar
- 2 tsps. ground cinnamon

Direction

- Set the oven to 175°C or 350°F and coat an 8-in square pan lightly with grease.

- Mix together butter, flour, oats and brown sugar in a big bowl, then blend until crumbly. Put into pan with half of the crumb mixture, then spread evenly over crumb mixture with apples. Use cinnamon and sugar to sprinkle over and place leftover crumb mixture on top.
- In the preheated oven, bake until turn golden brown, about 40-45 minutes.

Nutrition Information

- Calories: 376 calories;
- Total Carbohydrate: 65.2 g
- Cholesterol: 31 mg
- Total Fat: 12.4 g
- Protein: 3.2 g
- Sodium: 91 mg

7. Apple Pie Filling II

"A dish made with tapioca."
Serving: 8

Ingredients

- 5 cups thinly sliced apples
- 1 cup white sugar
- 2 tbsps. quick-cooking tapioca
- 1/2 tsp. ground cinnamon
- 1 tsp. lemon juice

Direction

- In a big saucepan, mix together the sugar and apples. Combine, then allow to stand until the juice from the apples begin to release. Put it on medium-high heat and mix it often until the mixture boils. Let it boil hard for a minute and keep on mixing often.
- Combine the lemon juice, cinnamon and tapioca into the apples. Let it boil hard for another 1 minute and keep on mixing. Pack the mixture, a spoonful at a time, in a sterilized quart jar and make sure that there will be no air bubbles in the mixture. Close it securely with a sterilized lid.

- In the bottom of a big stock pot, put a rack and pour boiling water to fill it halfway. Use a holder to lower the jar carefully into the pot. If you will be processing more than 1 jar, place the jars with 2-inch spaces in between. If needed, pour in more boiling water until the water covers the tops of the jars by 2 inches. Let the water fully boil. Put on cover and process for half an hour.
- Take out the jars from the pot and put it on a wood or cloth-covered surface and place it a couple of inches apart, until it becomes cool. When it cools down, use your finger to press the top of every lid and make sure that it is tightly sealed (the lid doesn't move down or up at all). This can be kept for a maximum of 1 year.

Nutrition Information

- Calories: 145 calories;
- Total Carbohydrate: 37.7 g
- Cholesterol: 0 mg
- Total Fat: 0.1 g
- Protein: 0.2 g
- Sodium: < 1 mg

8. Apple Pie In A Jar

"Apple pie recipe."
Serving: 16

Ingredients

- 4 1/2 cups white sugar
- 1 cup cornstarch
- 2 tsps. ground cinnamon
- 1/4 tsp. ground nutmeg
- 1 tsp. salt
- 10 cups water
- 3 tbsps. lemon juice
- 7 quarts peeled, cored and sliced apples

Direction

- In the bottom of a big stock pot, put the rack and pour hot water to fill the pot. Sterilize the

7 rings, 7 lids and 7 1-qt. canning jars and put it on the rack, placing the jars upright. Boil the water; let it boil for 10 minutes. Take it out using a holder and let the jars air-dry. Set aside the water for processing the apples later.
- In a big saucepan, mix together the water, salt, nutmeg, cinnamon, cornstarch and sugar. Put it on high heat and let it cook until it becomes bubbly and thick, mixing often. Take it out of the heat and mix in lemon juice.
- Pack the apples tightly in the sterilized jars. Gradually pour the syrup on top of the apples and cover it entirely. Tap the jars gently on the countertop to let the air bubbles rise, then screw the lids to seal the jars.
- Using a holder, lower the jars carefully into the pot, then leave a 2-inch space in between the jars. If needed, pour in more boiling water until the surface of the jars are covered with water by 2 inches. Fully boil the water, then put on cover and let it process for half an hour.
- Take out the jars from the pot and put it on a wood or cloth covered surface and place it a couple of inches apart, until it cools down. When it cools, use your finger to press the top of every lid to make sure that it is tightly sealed (the lid doesn't move down or up at all). The sealed jars can be kept for a maximum of 1 year.

Nutrition Information

- Calories: 363 calories;
- Total Carbohydrate: 94.1 g
- Cholesterol: 0 mg
- Total Fat: 0.4 g
- Protein: 0.6 g
- Sodium: 153 mg

9. Apple Pie IV

"A simple apple pie with fresh apples."
Serving: 8

Ingredients

- 2 (9 inch) pie shell
- 10 apple - peeled, cored and sliced
- 1/4 cup white sugar
- 1 tbsp. ground cinnamon
- 1/2 tsp. ground nutmeg

Direction

- Set the oven to 350°F (175°C) and start preheating.
- In a large pot, put the sliced apples, then sprinkle with nutmeg, cinnamon and sugar. Stir well then cook over low heat, stir often, until apples become tender but not mushy.
- In a pastry-lined pie pan, pour apple mixture. Cover up with second pastry shell. Seal the edges and slice vents in top.
- Bake in the preheated oven for 30-40 minutes, until the crust turns golden brown.

Nutrition Information

- Calories: 279 calories;
- Total Carbohydrate: 46.5 g
- Cholesterol: 0 mg
- Total Fat: 10.7 g
- Protein: 1.9 g
- Sodium: 206 mg

10. Apple Pie Tartlets

"This tiny mouthwatering apple tart with cinnamon and sweet taste can fit well in a snack tray or a dessert buffet."
Serving: 10 servings. | Prep: 35m | Ready in: 35m

Ingredients

- 1 sheet refrigerated pie pastry
- 1 tbsp. sugar
- Dash ground cinnamon

- FILLING:
- 2 tsps. butter
- 2 cups diced peeled tart apples
- 3 tbsps. sugar
- 3 tbsps. fat-free caramel ice cream topping
- 2 tbsps. all-purpose flour
- 1/2 tsp. ground cinnamon
- 1/2 tsp. lemon juice
- 1/8 tsp. salt

Direction

- Take the pastry to a light-floured surface. Roll it out and cut into 20 2.5-inch circle. Grease miniature muffin cups with cooking spray. Press the pastry on the bottom and the up sides of the cups. Use a fork to poke the pastry. Use cooking spray to spray a thin layer on top. Mix cinnamon and sugar, dredge them on top of the pastry.
- Set the oven at 350°. Put the muffin cups in the oven and bake until the golden brown, or for 6 to 8 minutes. Let them cool for 5 minutes before moving them from the pans to wire racks.
- Melt butter in a big saucepan. Stir in apples. Cook and mix over medium heat until the apples gets crisp-tender, or for 4 to 5 minutes.
- Add in salt, lemon juice, cinnamon, flour, caramel topping and sugar, combine them together. Boil the mixture, stir and cook until the apples get tender and the sauce gets thick consistency, or for 2 minutes. Let cool for 5 minutes. Spread on tart shells with a spoon.

Nutrition Information

- Calories: 150 calories
- Total Carbohydrate: 22 g
- Cholesterol: 6 mg
- Total Fat: 6 g
- Fiber: 1 g
- Protein: 1 g
- Sodium: 126 mg

11. Apple Pudding

"Easy and simple apple pudding recipe handed down from family generations."
Serving: 6 | Prep: 15m | Ready in: 1h

Ingredients

- 6 tart apples - peeled, cored and sliced
- 1/4 cup all-purpose flour
- 1 cup sugar
- 1 pinch salt
- 2 cups milk

Direction

- Set an oven to preheat to 165°C (325°F).
- Toss the apples together with salt, sugar and flour and put it in a 9x9-inch baking dish. Put enough milk to the dish to reach nearly the surface of the apples, but don't cover it.
- Let it bake for 45 minutes in the preheated oven, until the apples become tender.

Nutrition Information

- Calories: 260 calories;
- Total Carbohydrate: 60.2 g
- Cholesterol: 7 mg
- Total Fat: 1.9 g
- Protein: 3.6 g
- Sodium: 35 mg

12. Apple Raisin Cakes

"Little cakes with applesauce."
Serving: 6 | Prep: 10m | Ready in: 17m

Ingredients

- 2 eggs, beaten
- 1 cup applesauce
- 1 tsp. ground cinnamon
- 2 tsps. white sugar
- 1 cup all-purpose flour
- 1/2 cup whole wheat flour
- 2 tsps. baking powder

- 2 tsps. vanilla extract
- 1/2 cup raisins

Direction

- Mix together the raisins, vanilla, baking powder, flour, sugar, cinnamon, applesauce and eggs in a big mixing bowl. From the batter, shape small cakes.
- Heat a nonstick griddle on medium heat, then fry the cakes for around 5-7 minutes, until it turns brown on both sides.

Nutrition Information

- Calories: 203 calories;
- Total Carbohydrate: 41.1 g
- Cholesterol: 62 mg
- Total Fat: 2.1 g
- Protein: 6.1 g
- Sodium: 189 mg

13. Apple Skewers

"These lightly spiced grilled apples are not only delicious and available all year – they are also easy to grill or broil, and cleaning up isn't a chore!"
Serving: 4 servings. | Prep: 15m | Ready in: 30m

Ingredients

- 4 medium apples, peeled and quartered
- 4 tsps. sugar
- 1-1/4 tsps. ground cinnamon

Direction

- Skewer apples on four metal or wooden skewers that have been soaked. Coat apples with a light spritz of cooking spray. Sprinkle a mixture of sugar and cinnamon over the apples. Lightly grease grates with an oil-moistened paper towel at the end of a long-handled pair of tongs. Cook on covered grill at medium heat for 6-8 minutes, until golden; flip and cook for another 8-10 minutes until tender and golden. Serve these warm.

Nutrition Information

- Calories: 80 calories
- Total Carbohydrate: 21 g
- Cholesterol: 0 mg
- Total Fat: 0 g
- Fiber: 2 g
- Protein: 0 g
- Sodium: 0 mg

14. Apple-raisin Rice Dessert

"A comforting dessert made with leftover rice, raisins, cinnamon and apples."
Serving: 10 servings. | Prep: 15m | Ready in: 01h05m

Ingredients

- 2-1/4 cups water
- 1 cup sugar
- 3 cups sliced peeled tart apples
- 3 tbsps. lemon juice
- 1 tsp. ground cinnamon
- 1/2 tsp. ground nutmeg
- 3 cups cooked long grain rice
- 1/2 cup raisins
- 2 tbsps. plus 1-1/2 tsps. butter
- 2 tsps. vanilla extract
- 1/2 cup plus 2 tbsps. reduced-fat whipped topping

Direction

- Boil water in a big saucepan, then add sugar. Let it cook and stir until the sugar has been dissolved. Mix in spices, lemon juice and apples. Lower the heat and let it simmer for 3 to 5 minutes or until the apples become tender. Mix in vanilla, butter, raisins and rice.
- Pour into a cooking spray coated 2-quart baking dish. Let it bake for 50 to 55 minutes at 350 degrees without cover, until the liquid has been absorbed. Prior to serving, allow to stand for 10 minutes. Put whipped topping on top of each serving as a garnish, then serve warm.

Nutrition Information

- Calories: 218 calories
- Total Carbohydrate: 46 g
- Cholesterol: 8 mg
- Total Fat: 4 g
- Fiber: 1 g
- Protein: 2 g
- Sodium: 32 mg

15. Apples By The Fire

"So enjoyable!"
Serving: 1 | Prep: 5m | Ready in: 15m

Ingredients

- 1 Granny Smith apple, cored
- 1 tbsp. brown sugar
- 1/4 tsp. ground cinnamon

Direction

- Fill apple core with cinnamon and brown sugar; wrap apple in big heavy foil piece, twisting extra foil into tail for handle. Put apple in campfire coals/barbeque; cook till soft for 5-10 minutes. Remove then unwrap; be careful with hot sugar.

Nutrition Information

- Calories: 114 calories;
- Total Carbohydrate: 30.9 g
- Cholesterol: 0 mg
- Total Fat: 0 g
- Protein: 0.5 g
- Sodium: 5 mg

16. Applesauce Cake

"This apple cake is very moist, sweet and delicious with low fat."
Serving: 20 servings. | Prep: 20m | Ready in: 45m

Ingredients

- 1/2 cup egg substitute
- 1-1/2 cups unsweetened applesauce
- 1 cup sugar
- 1/4 cup canola oil
- 2 cups all-purpose flour
- 2 tsps. ground cinnamon
- 1-1/2 tsps. baking soda
- 1 tsp. ground nutmeg
- 1/2 tsp. salt
- 1/2 cup raisins
- 1/2 cup chopped walnuts
- FROSTING:
- 4 oz. reduced-fat cream cheese
- 1 cup confectioners' sugar
- 1/2 tsp. vanilla extract

Direction

- Beat egg substitute in a bowl about one minute on moderate speed. Put in oil, sugar and applesauce, then blend well. Mix the dry ingredients together and put into the applesauce mixture, mixing well. Mix in walnuts and raisins.
- Remove to a 13-inch x 9-inch baking pan greased with cooking spray, then bake at 350 degrees until a toothpick pricked in the center exits clean, about 25 to 30 minutes. Allow to cool on a wire rack.
- Beat cream cheese in a bowl until fluffy. Beat in vanilla and confectioners' sugar, then frost the cake.

Nutrition Information

- Calories: 186 calories
- Total Carbohydrate: 30 g
- Cholesterol: 3 mg
- Total Fat: 6 g
- Fiber: 1 g

- Protein: 3 g
- Sodium: 124 mg

17. Applesauce Lattice Pie

"The best and yummy way to used up some extra apples."
Serving: 8 servings. | Prep: 30m | Ready in: 01h10m

Ingredients

- 1-1/2 cups all-purpose flour
- 3 tbsps. sugar
- 1/4 tsp. plus 1/8 tsp. baking powder
- 1/4 tsp. plus 1/8 tsp. salt
- 6 tbsps. cold butter, cubed
- 4 to 6 tbsps. cold water
- 4-1/2 tsps. fat-free milk
- 1-1/2 tsps. cider vinegar
- FILLING:
- 5 cups sliced peeled tart apples
- 1/4 cup raisins
- Sugar substitute equivalent to 3 tbsps. sugar
- 2 tbsps. all-purpose flour
- 4 tsps. brown sugar
- 2 tsps. ground cinnamon
- 1-1/2 cups unsweetened applesauce
- 2 tsps. butter

Direction

- Mix the salt, baking powder, sugar and flour in a big bowl; cut in the butter till mixture is similar to coarse crumbs. Mix the vinegar, milk and water; slowly put to crumb mixture, tossing using a fork till dough shapes a ball.
- With cooking spray, grease a pie plate, 9-inch in size. Reserve 1/3 of the dough. Unroll the rest of the dough to suit pie plate on a slightly floured surface. Put the pastry to a plate; clip even with edge.
- Mix raisins and apples in a big bowl. Mix cinnamon, brown sugar, flour and sugar substitute; put to the apple mixture and coat by tossing. Into the crust, scoop 3 cups; use applesauce to cover. Put the rest of apple mixture on top; scatter bits of butter.
- Unroll leftover part of dough; create a lattice crust. Clip and crimp edges. Let bake for 40 to 45 minutes at 375° or till filling is bubbly and crust is golden brown. Allow to cool on a wire rack.

Nutrition Information

- Calories: 281 calories
- Total Carbohydrate: 47 g
- Cholesterol: 26 mg
- Total Fat: 10 g
- Fiber: 3 g
- Protein: 3 g
- Sodium: 235 mg

18. Apricot Apple Compote

"Comforting compote dessert with a hint of lemon and cinnamon."
Serving: 3 servings. | Prep: 5m | Ready in: 30m

Ingredients

- 10 dried apricots, halved and sliced
- 1/2 cup water
- 4 medium apples, peeled and sliced
- 1 tbsp. sugar
- 1 tsp. lemon juice
- 1/8 tsp. grated lemon peel
- 1/8 tsp. ground cinnamon

Direction

- Soak the apricots in a bowl with water for half an hour. Let it drain and set aside 3 tbsp of the water. Mix together the reserved water, sugar, apples and apricots in a saucepan, then boil. Lower the heat, put on cover and let it simmer for 20 minutes or until the apples become tender. Take it out of the heat. Mix in cinnamon, peel and lemon juice. You may serve it either cold or warm.

Nutrition Information

- Calories: 142 calories

- Total Carbohydrate: 37 g
- Cholesterol: 0 mg
- Total Fat: 1 g
- Fiber: 4 g
- Protein: 1 g
- Sodium: 1 mg

19. Apricot Delight

"This recipe has been established years ago."
Serving: 8 servings. | Prep: 15m | Ready in: 15m

Ingredients

- 2 cans (5-1/2 oz. each) apricot nectar, divided
- 1 package (.3 oz.) sugar-free orange gelatin
- 1 package (1 oz.) sugar-free instant vanilla pudding mix
- 2/3 cup nonfat dry milk powder
- 1 carton (8 oz.) frozen reduced-fat whipped topping, thawed
- 5 cups cubed angel food cake
- 1 can (15 oz.) reduced-sugar apricot halves, drained and sliced

Direction

- Add 1 cup of apricot nectar to a microwave-safe bowl and microwave for 50-60 seconds on high until hot. Drizzle gelatin over hot nectar and whisk for approximately 5 minutes until the gelatin dissolves completely. Put aside to cool.
- Mix the remaining apricot nectar with an enough amount of water in a big bowl to measure one and a quarter cups. Stir in milk powder and pudding mix for 1-2 minutes. Stir in cooled gelatin and fold in whipped topping and cake.
- Spread over an 11x7-inch dish. Put the dish into a refrigerator for 2-4 hrs. Use apricot slices to garnish.

Nutrition Information

- Calories: 178 calories
- Total Carbohydrate: 31 g

- Cholesterol: 1 mg
- Total Fat: 3 g
- Fiber: 1 g
- Protein: 4 g
- Sodium: 303 mg

20. Apricot Noodle Kugel

""There was no class for Kugel, yet the individuals cherished it and still needed to respect me with a strip! Expectation you appreciate it also."
Serving: 12 | Prep: 25m | Ready in: 1h10m

Ingredients

- 1 (8 oz.) package wide egg noodles
- 1/4 cup butter, softened
- 1 (3 oz.) package cream cheese, softened
- 3 eggs, beaten
- 1/2 cup white sugar
- 1 tsp. vanilla extract
- 1 cup apricot nectar
- 1 cup milk
- 1/2 cup golden raisins (optional)
- 1 1/2 cups cornflake crumbs
- 1/2 cup butter, softened
- 1/4 cup white sugar
- 1 tsp. vanilla extract
- 1 tsp. ground cinnamon

Direction

- Preheat oven to 175°C (350°F). Lightly spread cooking spray over a 9x9 inch baking pan.
- Bring a big saucepan of slightly salted water to a boil. Mix in egg noodles and cook until al dente, about 8 to 10 minutes; let dry.
- Blend vanilla, 1/2-cup sugar, eggs, cream cheese, 1/4-cup butter with egg noodles carefully in a medium bowl. Mix in milk and nectar apricot nectar. Blend in the raisins. Move to the prepared baking pan.
- Blend cinnamon, remaining vanilla, 1/4 cup sugar, 1/2 cup butter and cornflake crumbs in a separate medium bowl. Pour evenly over the egg noodle blend.

- Bake in the preheated oven until bubbly and lightly browned, about 45 minutes.

Nutrition Information

- Calories: 352 calories;
- Total Carbohydrate: 46 g
- Cholesterol: 102 mg
- Total Fat: 16.5 g
- Protein: 6.6 g
- Sodium: 219 mg

21. Apricot Oat Bars

"Chewy and sweet apricot-filled bars with oat-filled crust and topped with golden crumb."
Serving: 16 bars. | Prep: 15m | Ready in: 45m

Ingredients

- 1 cup quick-cooking oats
- 1 cup all-purpose flour
- 2/3 cup packed brown sugar
- 1/4 tsp. baking soda
- 1/4 tsp. salt
- 1/4 cup canola oil
- 3 tbsps. unsweetened apple juice
- 1 jar (10 oz.) apricot spreadable fruit

Direction

- Mix together the salt, baking soda, brown sugar, flour and oats in a big bowl. Put in apple juice and oil, then mix until it becomes moist. Reserve half a cup for the topping.
- Press the leftover oat mixture in a cooking spray coated 11x7-inch baking pan. Spread the apricot fruit spread to within a quarter inch of the edges. Sprinkle the reserved oat mixture on top and let it bake for 30 to 35 minutes at 325 degrees or until it turns golden brown in color.

Nutrition Information

- Calories: 151 calories
- Total Carbohydrate: 28 g
- Cholesterol: 0 mg
- Total Fat: 4 g
- Fiber: 1 g
- Protein: 2 g
- Sodium: 24 mg

22. Apricot Sundaes

"This dessert recipe is so refreshing and fruity."
Serving: 4 servings. | Prep: 15m | Ready in: 15m

Ingredients

- 1 can (15 oz.) reduced-sugar apricot halves
- 1/3 cup plus 2 tbsps. orange juice, divided
- 1 tsp. brown sugar
- 1-1/2 tsps. cornstarch
- 1 tsp. vanilla extract
- 2 cups fat-free sugar-free frozen vanilla yogurt

Direction

- Drain apricots, putting the juice aside. Slice apricots; put aside. In the saucepan, mix the reserved apricot juice, brown sugar and a third cup of orange juice; boil. Lower the heat; let simmer, uncovered, for 10 minutes. Mix the rest of the orange juice and cornstarch till becoming smooth; whisk into apricot juice mixture. Boil; cook and whisk till becoming thick or for 2 minutes. Whisk in the reserved apricots and vanilla. Serve on the frozen yogurt.

Nutrition Information

- Calories: 151 calories
- Total Carbohydrate: 33 g
- Cholesterol: 0 mg
- Total Fat: 0 g
- Fiber: 2 g
- Protein: 5 g
- Sodium: 84 mg

23. Azteca Cocoa Rice Pudding

"Spicy and sweet."
Serving: 8 | Prep: 15m | Ready in: 1h15m

Ingredients

- 4 cups water
- 2 cups white rice
- 2 tsps. ground cinnamon
- 2 cups milk
- 1 cup white sugar
- 1/2 cup cocoa powder
- 1 tbsp. cayenne pepper
- 1 tsp. vanilla extract

Direction

- Boil cinnamon, rice and water in a big pot. Lower heat to medium low and cover pot; simmer for 20 minutes till all water is absorbed.
- Mix vanilla extract, cayenne pepper, cocoa powder, sugar and milk into rice mixture. Put heat on high; cook, constantly mixing, for 5-10 minutes till thick.
- Take off heat. Put pudding into big glass bowl; sit before serving for 30 minutes.

Nutrition Information

- Calories: 313 calories;
- Total Carbohydrate: 68.7 g
- Cholesterol: 5 mg
- Total Fat: 2.4 g
- Protein: 6.5 g
- Sodium: 32 mg

24. Baked Apple Crisp

""This recipe is a crowd-pleaser!""
Serving: 12

Ingredients

- 1 1/2 cups Mott's® Natural Applesauce
- 8 cups thinly sliced unpeeled apples
- 2 tbsps. granulated sugar
- 4 1/2 tsps. ReaLemon® Lemon Juice
- 4 tsps. ground cinnamon, divided
- 1 cup uncooked rolled oats
- 1/2 cup firmly packed light brown sugar
- 1/3 cup all-purpose flour
- 1/3 cup evaporated skim milk
- 1/4 cup nonfat dry milk powder
- 1 cup vanilla nonfat yogurt

Direction

- Set the oven to 350°F for preheating. Grease the 2-qt casserole dish with a nonstick cooking spray. Toss the slices of apple with 2 tsp. of cinnamon, granulated sugar, and lemon juice in a large bowl. Scoop the mixture into the prepared dish. Top the apple mixture with applesauce evenly.
- Mix the brown sugar, oats, dry milk powder, evaporated milk, leftover 2 tsp. of cinnamon, and flour in a medium bowl. Spread the mixture all over the applesauce.
- Bake it for 35-40 minutes or until bubbly and browned lightly. Allow it to cool slightly. Serve this while warm with a dollop of yogurt on top.

Nutrition Information

- Calories: 169 calories;
- Total Carbohydrate: 38.7 g
- Cholesterol: 1 mg
- Total Fat: 0.7 g
- Protein: 4 g
- Sodium: 39 mg

25. Baked Apple Pudding

"Pudding that's nutty and moist and seasoned with nutmeg and cinnamon."
Serving: 12 servings. | Prep: 20m | Ready in: 55m

Ingredients

- 1/4 cup butter, softened
- 1 cup sugar

- 1 egg
- 1 cup all-purpose flour
- 1 tsp. baking soda
- 1/4 tsp. salt
- 1/4 tsp. ground nutmeg
- 1/4 tsp. ground cinnamon
- 2 cups grated peeled tart apples
- 1/4 cup chopped walnuts
- 1 tsp. vanilla extract
- 4 cups low-fat vanilla frozen yogurt

Direction

- Beat the egg, sugar and butter together in a bowl until combined. Mix together the cinnamon, nutmeg, salt, baking soda and flour in a bowl, then slowly add into the sugar mixture and stir well. Mix in the vanilla, walnuts and apples until blended well.
- Spread the mixture in a cooking spray coated 8-inch square baking dish. Let it bake for 35 to 40 minutes at 350 degrees or until the pudding bounces back once lightly pressed and turns light brown in color. Serve warm together with frozen yogurt.

Nutrition Information

- Calories: 243 calories
- Total Carbohydrate: 41 g
- Cholesterol: 31 mg
- Total Fat: 7 g
- Fiber: 1 g
- Protein: 5 g
- Sodium: 238 mg

26. Baked Banana Boats

"You can customize the toppings of these banana boats based on your preference."
Serving: 4 servings. | Prep: 10m | Ready in: 20m

Ingredients

- 4 medium bananas, unpeeled
- 1/2 cup unsweetened crushed pineapple, drained
- 1/4 cup granola without raisins
- 1/4 cup chopped pecans
- 4 tsps. miniature semisweet chocolate chips

Direction

- Slice every banana into lengthwise, approximately half an inch deep and leave both ends with half an inch uncut. In a 12-inch square of foil, put each banana, then shape and crimp the foil surrounding the bananas so that they will sit flat. Lightly pull every banana peel open to form a pocket. Fill chocolate chips, pecans, granola and pineapple on the pockets.
- Put it on a baking tray and let it bake for 10 to 12 minutes at 350 degrees, until the chips become soft.

Nutrition Information

- Calories: 220 calories
- Total Carbohydrate: 40 g
- Cholesterol: 0 mg
- Total Fat: 8 g
- Fiber: 5 g
- Protein: 4 g
- Sodium: 4 mg

27. Baked Blueberry-peach Pound Cake

"Refreshing snack packed with fresh blueberries and peaches."
Serving: 12 servings. | Prep: 15m | Ready in: 01h10m

Ingredients

- 2 tbsps. butter, softened
- 1-1/4 cups sugar
- 3 tbsps. unsweetened applesauce
- 3/4 cup egg substitute
- 1/4 cup 2% milk
- 2-1/2 cups cake flour

- 2 tsps. baking powder
- 1/4 tsp. salt
- 2-1/4 cups chopped fresh or frozen unsweetened peaches
- 2 cups fresh or frozen unsweetened blueberries
- 3/4 cup reduced-fat whipped topping

Direction

- Beat applesauce, sugar and butter in a bowl. Put in milk and egg substitute. Combine salt, baking powder and flour together; put into whipped mixture and stir until combined. Fold in blueberries and peaches. Add to a flouted tube pan of 10 inches greased with cooking spray.
- Bake at 350° till a toothpick goes out clean, about 55-60 minutes. Allow to cool for 10 minutes; and then transferring from pan to a wire rack. Garnish with whipped topping and serve.

Nutrition Information

- Calories: 225 calories
- Total Carbohydrate: 45 g
- Cholesterol: 6 mg
- Total Fat: 3 g
- Fiber: 2 g
- Protein: 4 g
- Sodium: 138 mg

28. Baked Ginger Pears

"Canned pears sweetened with s bit of brown sugar and sprinkled with ginger and pecans."
Serving: 4 servings. | Prep: 10m | Ready in: 30m

Ingredients

- 2 cans (15 oz. each) pear halves in juice
- 1/3 cup packed brown sugar
- 1/4 cup chopped pecans
- 1 tsp. lemon juice
- 1/2 tsp. ground ginger
- 4 gingersnap cookies, crumbled

Direction

- Let the pears drain, then set aside the juice. Put aside a quarter cup of juice and 8 pear halves (reserve the leftover juice and pears for later use).
- In a 5-cup baking dish that's ungreased, lay out the pear halves, cut side up. Mix together the ginger, lemon juice, pecans and brown sugar, then sprinkle on top of the pears.
- Scoop the reserved pear juice around the pears. Let it bake for 20 to 25 minutes at 350 degrees without cover, or until it becomes bubbly. Put cookie crumbs on top as a garnish.

Nutrition Information

- Calories: 114 calories
- Total Carbohydrate: 22 g
- Cholesterol: 0 mg
- Total Fat: 3 g
- Fiber: 2 g
- Protein: 1 g
- Sodium: 18 mg

29. Baked Maple Pumpkin Pie

"This great pumpkin pie has a mild maple flavor."
Serving: 8 servings. | Prep: 15m | Ready in: 01h10m

Ingredients

- 1 tbsp. sugar
- 1/2 tsp. salt
- 1/4 tsp. baking powder
- 1/3 cup canola oil
- 1-1/2 cups all-purpose flour
- 1 tsp. cider vinegar
- 2 to 4 tbsps. cold water
- FILLING:
- 1 can (15 oz.) solid-pack pumpkin
- 3/4 cup egg substitute
- 1/2 cup maple syrup
- 1 tsp. ground cinnamon
- 1/2 tsp. ground ginger
- 1/2 tsp. maple flavoring

- 1/4 tsp. ground nutmeg
- 1 cup fat-free evaporated milk

Direction

- Mix the baking powder, salt, sugar and flour in a small bowl. Mix in vinegar and oil. Slowly put water, tossing using a fork till a ball creates. Form into a 6-inches round. Roll out among 2 pieces plastic wrap to suit a pie plate 9-inch in size. Take off top piece plastic wrap; flip pastry into a 9-inch pie plate covered with cooking spray. Take off the rest of the plastic wrap. Clip pastry to half inch outside edge of plate; crimp edges. Refrigerate for 20 minutes till chilled.
- Mix nutmeg, maple flavoring, ginger, cinnamon, syrup, egg substitute and pumpkin in a big bowl; combine till just incorporated. Slowly mix in milk. Put into the pastry shell.
- Allow to bake for 10 minutes at 450°. Lower heat to 350°; let bake for 45 to 50 minutes till an inserted knife in the middle comes out clean. Cool down on a wire rack. Keep in refrigerator.

Nutrition Information

- Calories: 282 calories
- Total Carbohydrate: 42 g
- Cholesterol: 3 mg
- Total Fat: 10 g
- Fiber: 3 g
- Protein: 8 g
- Sodium: 245 mg

30. Baked Pumpkin Pudding

"This pudding is perfect to end every meal."
Serving: 5 servings. | Prep: 10m | Ready in: 50m

Ingredients

- 1/2 cup egg substitute
- 1 can (15 oz.) solid-pack pumpkin
- 3/4 cup sugar
- 1 tbsp. honey

- 1 tsp. ground cinnamon
- 1/2 tsp. ground ginger
- 1/4 tsp. ground cloves
- 1-1/2 cups fat-free evaporated milk
- 5 tbsps. reduced-fat whipped topping

Direction

- Beat spices, honey, sugar, pumpkin and egg substitute until blended in a large bowl. Beat in milk gradually. Transfer to 5 8-oz. custard cups coated with cooking spray. Put in a 13x9-in. baking pan. Add hot water to pan to create a water bath.
- Bake without a cover for 10 minutes at 425°. Lower the heat to 350°. Bake until the inserted knife in the center is clean when coming out or for 30-35 more minutes.
- Serve warm or cold. Decorate with whipped topping. Keep in the fridge.

Nutrition Information

- Calories: 245 calories
- Total Carbohydrate: 51 g
- Cholesterol: 3 mg
- Total Fat: 1 g
- Fiber: 4 g
- Protein: 10 g
- Sodium: 143 mg

31. Banana Chia Pudding

"This creamy pudding with flax milk and chia seeds become a healthy snack"
Serving: 6 | Prep: 10m | Ready in: 2h10m

Ingredients

- 1 1/2 cups vanilla-flavored flax milk
- 1 large banana, cut in chunks
- 7 tbsps. chia seeds
- 3 tbsps. honey
- 1 tsp. vanilla extract
- 1/8 tsp. sea salt

Direction

- In the blender, add these ingredients in respective order: milk, banana, chia seeds, honey, vanilla extract and sea salt; blend until mixture is smooth. Pour into a bowl and keep in refrigerator for at least 2 hours until thickened. Add mixture into small bowls. Serve.

Nutrition Information

- Calories: 112 calories;
- Total Carbohydrate: 20.5 g
- Cholesterol: 0 mg
- Total Fat: 3.4 g
- Protein: 1.6 g
- Sodium: 59 mg

32. Banana Custard Scrunch

""Simple recipe - excellent presented in a tall glass with a long spoon. Layers of bananas, yogurt custard, and honey-coated oats make this a nutritious children's favorite….even though I've known adults to ask for more!!""
Serving: 4 | Prep: 10m | Ready in: 15m

Ingredients

- 1 cup plain yogurt
- 3/4 cup prepared vanilla pudding
- 3/4 cup rolled oats
- 2 tbsps. honey
- 3 small bananas, sliced

Direction

- Combine vanilla pudding and yogurt in a small bowl. Reserve. Preheat a dry skillet over medium heat. Add in the oats, and toast until hot, for about 1 minute. Sprinkle honey over the oats and keep on whisking over medium heat until the oats are crispy at the edges.
- Separate the oats from the heat, and scoop most of them into the bottom of 4 small bowls or glasses. Set aside the rest for topping. Apply about half of the slices of banana, put a layer of sliced bananas over the oats in each bowl or glass. Pour custard over the banana slices. Put the remaining banana slices on top, then dust with the remaining toasted oats.

Nutrition Information

- Calories: 267 calories;
- Total Carbohydrate: 51.8 g
- Cholesterol: 9 mg
- Total Fat: 5.4 g
- Protein: 5.8 g
- Sodium: 110 mg

33. Banana Honey Yogurt Ice

"A healthy substitute for ice cream."
Serving: 6 | Prep: 15m | Ready in: 6h15m

Ingredients

- 4 bananas, sliced
- 1 1/4 cups Greek yogurt
- 1 tbsp. lemon juice
- 2 tbsps. honey
- 1/2 tsp. ground cinnamon

Direction

- In a blender, put the cinnamon, honey, lemon juice, yogurt and bananas, then puree until it becomes smooth. Pour it in a container that's freezer safe. Let it freeze until it becomes almost solid, then scrape it back into the blender and puree once again until it has a smooth consistency. Put it back into the freezer and let it freeze until it becomes solid.

Nutrition Information

- Calories: 147 calories;
- Total Carbohydrate: 25.8 g
- Cholesterol: 9 mg
- Total Fat: 4.4 g
- Protein: 3.4 g
- Sodium: 28 mg

34. Banana Kiwi Strawberry Tart

"With fruit toppings and custard filling, this is a tasty tart!"
Serving: 8 | Prep: 25m | Ready in: 9h

Ingredients

- 1/2 cup all-purpose flour
- 1 tbsp. light brown sugar
- 1/4 tsp. ground cinnamon
- 1/8 tsp. salt
- 2 tbsps. unsalted butter
- 1 1/2 tbsps. ice water
- 1 cup skim milk
- 3 egg whites
- 2 tbsps. white sugar
- 1/4 tsp. vanilla extract
- 1 bananas, peeled and sliced
- 1 kiwi, peeled and sliced
- 1 cup sliced fresh strawberries

Direction

- Sift salt, cinnamon, light brown sugar and flour together in a bowl. Slice in the butter until the mixture forms coarse crumbs. Scatter ice water on, toss with a fork to moisten evenly. Pat to shape a round, wrap in plastic. Chill for half an hour.
- Warm the milk in the top half of a double boiler until it starts to bubble. Whip 1 tbsp. of hot milk, sugar and egg whites in a bowl. Beat the egg white mixture into the leftover hot milk. Heat and mix about 10 mins but do not boil, until the mixture is just thick enough to coat the back of a metal spoon. Take away from the heat, mix in the vanilla. Cool until it reaches room temperature.
- Heat oven to 375°F (190°C). Grease an 8-inch tart pan with a removable bottom gently.
- Roll out to shape the tart dough to a quarter inch thick on a floured surface. Push the chilled dough into the prepared tart pan. Cut off the edges, poke the bottom with a fork. Bake in the heated oven for 15 to 18 mins until golden brown. Take out and transfer to a wire rack, cool completely.
- Scoop the filling mixture into the shell. Bake in the heated oven for 18 to 20 mins. Cool to room temperature on a wire rack. Chill for 8 hours. Put sliced strawberry, kiwi and banana on top of the filling just before serving.

Nutrition Information

- Calories: 115 calories;
- Total Carbohydrate: 18.7 g
- Cholesterol: 8 mg
- Total Fat: 3.1 g
- Protein: 3.6 g
- Sodium: 72 mg

35. Banana Oat And Bran Cookies

"This banana cookie combines bran and oats"
Serving: 12 | Prep: 5m | Ready in: 15m

Ingredients

- 2 ripe bananas, mashed
- 1/2 cup whole wheat flour
- 1/4 cup wheat bran
- 1/4 cup rolled oats
- 1/2 cup packed brown sugar
- 1/2 cup low-fat plain yogurt
- 1/8 cup real maple syrup
- 2 egg whites
- 1 tsp. ground cinnamon
- 1/2 tsp. salt
- 1/2 tsp. baking powder
- 1/2 cup raisins

Direction

- Set the oven to 350°F (175°C) and start preheating.
- Whisk cinnamon, yogurt, maple syrup, brown sugar, egg whites and mashed bananas.
- In a separate bowl, mix the rest of the dry ingredients: baking powder, salt, wheat bran,

oats and flour. Mix dry mixture with wet mixture with an electric mixer.
- Add chopped prunes, raisins, and/or nuts.
- Shape cookies into balls, put on a cookie sheet coated with cooking spray. Bake until cookies are dry and firm, about 8-12 minutes.

Nutrition Information

- Calories: 117 calories;
- Total Carbohydrate: 27.6 g
- Cholesterol: < 1 mg
- Total Fat: 0.5 g
- Protein: 2.7 g
- Sodium: 138 mg

36. Banana Oat Bread Pudding

"A delicious concoction made with oats, bananas and sugar that's ready in 40 minutes."
Serving: 16 | Prep: 15m | Ready in: 1h35m

Ingredients

- 4 slices whole wheat bread
- 1 cup rolled oats
- 2 1/2 cups lowfat milk
- 1/4 cup butter, softened
- 4 ripe bananas, sliced
- 1/3 cup brown sugar
- 1/4 cup raisins (optional)

Direction

- Break the bread to small pieces in a big bowl. Add milk and oats, then mix. Allow to stand for half an hour.
- Set an oven to preheat to 175°C (350°F). Grease an 8x8-inch baking pan lightly.
- Add raisins if preferred, brown sugar, bananas and butter into the milk mixture, then mix just to blend and pour it in the prepped pan.
- Let it bake for 45 to 55 minutes at 175°C (350°F) or until the pudding becomes set. Let it cool prior to serving.

Nutrition Information

- Calories: 132 calories;
- Total Carbohydrate: 21.4 g
- Cholesterol: 11 mg
- Total Fat: 4.3 g
- Protein: 3.3 g
- Sodium: 71 mg

37. Banana Spice Cake

"Tender and moist cake made with buttermilk and bananas."
Serving: 16 | Ready in: 1h45m

Ingredients

- 2½ cups unsifted cake flour
- 2 tsps. baking powder
- 2 tsps. baking soda
- 2 tsps. ground cinnamon
- 1 tsp. freshly grated nutmeg
- ½ tsp. ground allspice
- ½ tsp. ground ginger
- ½ tsp. ground cloves
- ½ tsp. salt
- 2 tbsps. butter
- 3 large egg whites
- ¼ tsp. cream of tartar
- 1¾ cups granulated sugar, divided
- 1 cup mashed very ripe bananas, (2 large)
- ¼ cup canola oil
- 1 tbsp. freshly grated orange zest
- 1½ tsps. vanilla extract
- 1 large egg yolk
- ¾ cup buttermilk
- Confectioners' sugar for dusting

Direction

- Set an oven to preheat to 350 degrees F. Use cooking spray to coat a 12-cup Bundt pan.
- In a bowl, sift together the salt, cloves, ginger, allspice, nutmeg, cinnamon, baking soda, baking powder and flour, then put aside.

- In a small saucepan, heat the butter on medium heat and swirl the pan until the butter turns into nuttty brown color. Pour the butter in a small bowl and allow to cool a bit.
- In a clean mixing bowl, beat the egg whites using an electric mixer on low speed just until it becomes frothy. Put in cream of tartar, then turn up the heat to medium and beat it until it forms soft peaks. Slowly beat in 3/4 cup of sugar, 2 tbsp at a time, just until it forms firm peaks, then put aside.
- In a big mixing bowl, mix together the leftover cup of sugar, reserved melted butter, egg yolk, vanilla, orange zest, oil and mashed banana, then beat to blend. Add the flour mixtures and buttermilk alternately in 2 additions each with the mixer on low speed, then beat it just until combined. Put in a heaping spoonful of the meringue and beat it for just a couple of seconds to make the batter light. Use your hand to fold the leftover meringue to the batter.
- Pour the batter in the prepped pan and let it bake for 50-60 minutes, until an inserted toothpick in the middle of the cake exits clean and the cake turns richly brown in color. Allow to cool for 10 minutes in the pan, placed on the rack, then flip it out on the rack to fully cool. Dust confectioner's sugar on the cake prior to serving.

Nutrition Information

- Calories: 235 calories;
- Total Carbohydrate: 44 g
- Cholesterol: 16 mg
- Total Fat: 6 g
- Fiber: 1 g
- Protein: 3 g
- Sodium: 333 mg
- Sugar: 24 g
- Saturated Fat: 1 g

38. Banana Tempura

"The most easy and quick fried banana recipe."
Serving: 3 | Prep: 10m | Ready in: 12m

Ingredients

- 3 cups oil for frying
- 1 1/2 cups ice-cold water
- 1 (8 oz.) package tempura batter mix
- 3 ripe bananas, cut into 5 pieces
- 1 tbsp. confectioners' sugar, or to taste

Direction

- In a big saucepan or a deep fryer, heat the oil to 175°C (350°F).
- In a big bowl, pour the water, then sprinkle the tempura batter mix over. Whisk until the big lumps have been dissolved and the mix becomes moist. The batter must be lumpy.
- Dunk 5 slices of banana in the batter. Let it fry for 2-3 minutes in hot oil until it turns light golden. Let it drain on paper towels. Redo the process with the leftover slices of banana and dust confectioner's sugar on top.

Nutrition Information

- Calories: 424 calories;
- Total Carbohydrate: 53.5 g
- Cholesterol: 0 mg
- Total Fat: 22.9 g
- Protein: 3.4 g
- Sodium: 214 mg

39. Banana Yogurt Pie

"Low in calories and fat. This is a light, snappy and fruity dessert."
Serving: 8 | Prep: 30m | Ready in: 1h

Ingredients

- 2 cups rolled oats
- 1 cup pitted dates
- 1 tsp. vanilla extract

- 2 tbsps. orange juice
- 3 tbsps. cocoa powder
- 1/4 cup boiling water
- 1 tsp. unflavored gelatin
- 2 frozen bananas, peeled and chopped
- 1 cup low-fat evaporated milk, chilled
- 1/2 tsp. vanilla extract
- 1 cup low-fat plain yogurt
- 1 banana, finely sliced
- 1/4 cup lemon juice
- 1 tsp. ground nutmeg

Direction

- In the bowl of a food processor, mix the cocoa powder, orange juice, vanilla extract, dates, and rolled oats. Process for 3 minutes or until mixture holds together. Thinly push the mixture around the base and sides of a 9 inches pie dish and chill.
- In a small bowl put the gelatin. Drizzle boiling water over gelatin, mix until dissolve, and put aside to cool.
- Put frozen bananas in blender or food processor and process until smooth. Pour milk and blend for 3-4 minutes. Put in yogurt and extra vanilla and stir well. Pour in dissolved gelatin. Put mixture into the bottom of the pie dish and refrigerate until firm.
- Plunge the extra banana in lemon juice to soak, cut and put on top of pie. Dust with nutmeg and serve.

Nutrition Information

- Calories: 227 calories;
- Total Carbohydrate: 45.4 g
- Cholesterol: 7 mg
- Total Fat: 3 g
- Protein: 8.1 g
- Sodium: 62 mg

40. Bavarian Apple Tart

"I always succeed in serving this delicious pie. Everyone loves the sweet topping, creamy filling and thin crust."
Serving: 12 servings. | Prep: 25m | Ready in: 01h05m

Ingredients

- 1/3 cup butter, softened
- 1/3 cup sugar
- 1/2 tsp. vanilla extract
- 1 cup all-purpose flour
- 1/8 tsp. ground cinnamon
- FILLING:
- 1 package (8 oz.) reduced-fat cream cheese
- 1/4 cup sugar
- 1 egg
- 1-1/2 tsps. vanilla extract
- TOPPING:
- 4 cups thinly sliced peeled tart apples (about 4 medium)
- 1/3 cup sugar
- 3/4 tsp. ground cinnamon

Direction

- Beat sugar and butter in a large bowl until they form a fluffy and light mixture. Mix in cinnamon, flour and vanilla. In a springform pan sprayed with cooking spray, press dough on onto the bottom and 1 inch up the sides.
- Beat sugar and cream cheese in a big bowl until the mixture is smooth. Blend in vanilla and egg just until incorporated. Pour onto crust.
- In a separate bowl, stir together cinnamon, sugar and apples; place onto the filling. Bake in 400-degree oven until the shell turns golden browned and apples are soft. Place on a wire rack to cool. Keep refrigerated to store.

Nutrition Information

- Calories: 213 calories
- Total Carbohydrate: 30 g
- Cholesterol: 42 mg
- Total Fat: 9 g
- Fiber: 1 g

- Protein: 4 g
- Sodium: 113 mg

41. Berries With Banana Cream

"Delicious dessert recipe made with a touch of spice and airy banana-orange cream."
Serving: 2 servings. | Prep: 10m | Ready in: 10m

Ingredients

- 1-1/2 cups sliced fresh strawberries
- 1/2 cup fresh or frozen blueberries
- 1/3 cup reduced-fat sour cream
- 1/3 cup sliced ripe banana
- 1 tbsp. orange juice concentrate
- 1 tsp. sugar
- 1/8 tsp. ground cinnamon

Direction

- Split the berries among the 2 serving bowls. Mix together the sugar, orange juice concentrate, banana and sour cream in a blender. Put on cover and process until it becomes smooth. Scoop on top of the berries and sprinkle cinnamon on top.

Nutrition Information

- Calories: 156 calories
- Total Carbohydrate: 28 g
- Cholesterol: 13 mg
- Total Fat: 4 g
- Fiber: 5 g
- Protein: 4 g
- Sodium: 30 mg

42. Berries With Sour Cream Sauce

"Wonderfully dressed-up sour cream becomes a delicious topping for fresh fruit in this dish."
Serving: 10 servings. | Prep: 10m | Ready in: 10m

Ingredients

- 1 quart fresh strawberries, halved
- 1 pint fresh raspberries
- 1 pint fresh blueberries
- 1 pint fresh blackberries
- 2 cups (16 oz.) reduced-fat sour cream
- 1/4 cup honey

Direction

- Mix together the first four ingredients in a large bowl. In another bowl, stir the sour cream and honey. Serve with berries.

Nutrition Information

- Calories: 147 calories
- Total Carbohydrate: 25 g
- Cholesterol: 15 mg
- Total Fat: 4 g
- Fiber: 6 g
- Protein: 4 g
- Sodium: 32 mg

43. Berry Phyllo Tarts

"It's quick and easy to make!"
Serving: 6 servings. | Prep: 25m | Ready in: 30m

Ingredients

- 12 sheets phyllo dough (14 inches x 9 inches)
- 3 tbsps. butter, melted
- 3 tbsps. sugar
- 1/2 tsp. grated orange zest
- FILLING:
- 1/4 cup orange marmalade
- 1 cup navel orange sections
- 1 cup sliced fresh strawberries

- 1/2 cup each fresh raspberries, blueberries and blackberries
- 1 tsp. lemon juice
- 1 tsp. lime juice
- 1/2 tsp. grated lemon zest
- 1/2 tsp. grated lime zest
- Fresh mint, optional

Direction

- Roll up the phyllo dough, divide into 1/4-inch-wide strips. Put the strips into a large bowl and mix with orange zest, butter and sugar until coated. Separate the strips into 6 portions. Form into nests on the baking sheet coated with the cooking spray. Bake for 5 to 7 mins, at 400°, until golden.
- Heat the marmalade in a small microwave-safe bowl until melted. Combine berries and oranges in the large bowl. Sprinkle with juices and marmalade. Top with lime and lemon zest; gently coat by tossing. Spoon into the nests just before using. If desired, add mint for garnishing.

Nutrition Information

- Calories: 204 calories
- Total Carbohydrate: 35 g
- Cholesterol: 16 mg
- Total Fat: 7 g
- Fiber: 3 g
- Protein: 2 g
- Sodium: 159 mg

44. Berry Punch Parfaits

""Begin your day off right with a fruity luscious parfait for breakfast. The taste will amaze you.""
Serving: 4

Ingredients

- 1 lb. strawberries
- 1/3 cup Mott's® Fruit Punch Rush
- 2 cups vanilla-flavored nonfat Greek yogurt
- 2 tbsps. Mott's® Fruit Punch Rush
- 1/4 cup your favorite granola, or more if needed

Direction

- Wash, stem, and cut the strawberries into bite-size portions.
- In a wide skillet or saucepan over medium-low heat, put 1/3 cup Mott's Fruit Punch Rush and strawberries to heat. Whisk occasionally for approximately 10 minutes until the strawberries have softened.
- Let the strawberries cool at room temperature and build the parfaits.
- In a medium bowl, mix the rest of 2 tbsps. Mott's Fruit Punch Rush and yogurt.
- Into each jar, scoop 1/4 cup yogurt, then put about 2 tbsps. cooled strawberries on top. Dust with 1 to 2 tbsps. granola.
- Continue with another layer of each ingredient per jar. Keep in the refrigerator until ready to serve.
- In each parfait, the granola will remain crunchy for up to 4 hours; then after that, it will be soggier yet still yummy.

Nutrition Information

- Calories: 192 calories;
- Total Carbohydrate: 36 g
- Cholesterol: 2 mg
- Total Fat: 2.4 g
- Protein: 8.2 g
- Sodium: 90 mg

45. Better-than-fruitcake Cookies

"Chewy and sweet clusters made with nuts and fruits."
Serving: 3 dozen. | Prep: 15m | Ready in: 30m

Ingredients

- 2 cups raisins
- 1/4 cup bourbon or unsweetened apple juice
- 2 tbsps. butter, softened
- 1/4 cup packed brown sugar
- 1 egg

- 3/4 cup all-purpose flour
- 1 tsp. ground cinnamon
- 3/4 tsp. baking soda
- 1/4 tsp. ground nutmeg
- 1/4 tsp. ground cloves
- 1 cup pecan halves
- 3/4 cup red candied cherries, halved
- 3/4 cup green candied cherries, halved

Direction

- Mix together the bourbon and raisins in a small bowl. Put on cover and allow to stand for half an hour.
- Cream the brown sugar and butter in a big bowl until combined, then beat in the egg. Mix together the cloves, nutmeg, baking soda, cinnamon and flour, then slowly beat into the creamed mixture. Mix in the raisin mixture, cherries and pecans.
- Drop it on cooking spray coated baking trays by tablespoonfuls. Let it bake for 12 to 15 minutes at 325 degrees or until it becomes firm. Let it cool for 2 minutes prior to transferring to wire racks to let it fully cool. Keep it in an airtight container.

Nutrition Information

- Calories: 93 calories
- Total Carbohydrate: 16 g
- Cholesterol: 8 mg
- Total Fat: 3 g
- Fiber: 1 g
- Protein: 1 g
- Sodium: 40 mg

46. Bigmom's Cranberry Salad

"This cranberry salad is a combination of apple, celery and pineapple."
Serving: 6 | Prep: 20m | Ready in: 2h20m

Ingredients

- 1 (12 oz.) package cranberries
- 1 (8 oz.) can crushed pineapple, drained
- 1 large apple, diced
- 2 stalks celery, diced
- 1 cup white sugar
- 1 (6 oz.) package cherry flavored Jell-O®
- 2 cups boiling water

Direction

- In a food processor, add cranberries, then process until chopped roughly. Remove cranberries to a big bowl, then stir in sugar, celery, apple and pineapple. In a separate bowl, mix together boiling water and gelatin while stirring until gelatin is dissolved. Add gelatin mixture to pineapple mixture, then stir to incorporate. Cover and chill for 2 hours, until gelatin is set.

Nutrition Information

- Calories: 304 calories;
- Total Carbohydrate: 76.6 g
- Cholesterol: 0 mg
- Total Fat: 0.2 g
- Protein: 2.7 g
- Sodium: 86 mg

47. Black Bean Brownies

"Brownie recipe made with black beans."
Serving: 16 | Prep: 10m | Ready in: 40m

Ingredients

- 1 (15.5 oz.) can black beans, rinsed and drained
- 3 eggs
- 3 tbsps. vegetable oil
- 1/4 cup cocoa powder
- 1 pinch salt
- 1 tsp. vanilla extract
- 3/4 cup white sugar
- 1 tsp. instant coffee (optional)
- 1/2 cup milk chocolate chips (optional)

Direction

- Set an oven to preheat to 175°C (350°F). Grease an 8x8 square baking dish lightly.
- In a blender, mix together the instant coffee, sugar, vanilla extract, salt, cocoa powder, oil, eggs and black beans, then blend until it becomes smooth. Pour the mixture in the prepped baking dish. Sprinkle chocolate chips on top of the mixture.
- Let it bake for about half an hour in the preheated oven, until the edges begin to pull away from the pan's sides and the surface becomes dry.

Nutrition Information

- Calories: 126 calories;
- Total Carbohydrate: 18.1 g
- Cholesterol: 35 mg
- Total Fat: 5.3 g
- Protein: 3.3 g
- Sodium: 129 mg

48. Blueberries 'n' Cream Pie

"This recipe is requested often."
Serving: 8 servings. | Prep: 15m | Ready in: 45m

Ingredients

- 1/2 cup plus 1 tbsp. fat-free milk, divided
- 3 tbsps. butter
- 1 egg
- 3/4 cup all-purpose flour
- 1 package (.8 oz.) sugar-free cook-and-serve vanilla pudding mix
- 1 tsp. baking powder
- 1/8 tsp. salt
- 2 cups fresh or frozen blueberries, thawed
- 1 package (8 oz.) reduced-fat cream cheese
- 1/2 cup sugar
- TOPPING:
- 2 tsps. sugar
- 1/8 tsp. ground cinnamon

Direction

- Beat egg, butter and half cup of milk in large bowl. Combine salt, baking powder, pudding mix and flour; stir into the egg mixture until just moistened. Transfer to the 9 inches pie plate coated with the cooking spray. Place the blueberries over the batter to within 1/2 inch of the plate edge.
- Beat remaining milk, sugar and cream cheese in large bowl until they become smooth. Spread over the blueberries to within 1 inch of edge of berry.
- To make topping, combine cinnamon and sugar; add over cream cheese mixture. Bake for 30 to 35 mins at 350°, until set. Enjoy warm. Place the leftovers in refrigerator.

Nutrition Information

- Calories: 249 calories
- Total Carbohydrate: 31 g
- Cholesterol: 60 mg
- Total Fat: 12 g
- Fiber: 1 g
- Protein: 6 g
- Sodium: 302 mg

49. Blueberries And Cheese Coffee Cake

"A little reduce fat and calories, this blueberries and coffee cheesecake is absolutely fit with your diet."
Serving: 15 servings. | Prep: 25m | Ready in: 55m

Ingredients

- 2 tbsps. butter, softened
- 3/4 cup sugar
- 1 large egg
- 2 large egg whites
- 1/4 cup unsweetened applesauce
- 2 tbsps. canola oil
- 1 tsp. grated lemon peel
- 2-1/4 cups all-purpose flour, divided
- 1-1/4 tsps. baking powder

- 1 tsp. salt
- 1/2 tsp. baking soda
- 1 cup buttermilk
- 2 cups fresh or frozen blueberries
- 1 package (8 oz.) reduced-fat cream cheese, diced
- TOPPING:
- 1/4 cup all-purpose flour
- 1/4 cup sugar
- 1 tsp. grated lemon peel
- 2 tbsps. cold butter

Direction

- In a large bowl, beat sugar and butter until crumbled. Beat in lemon peel, oil, applesauce, egg whites, and egg. Mix baking soda, salt, baking powder, and 2 cups of flour; pour to the sugar mixture alternately with buttermilk; beat well after each addition.
- In a bowl, combine the flour left and blueberries; fold into the batter with cream cheese. Transfer into a 13x9-inch baking dish greased with cooking spray.
- To make the topping, mix lemon peel, sugar, and flour in a bowl; cut in butter until the mixture resembles crumbs. Scatter over batter.
- Bake for 30 to 35 minutes at 375°, until a toothpick comes out clean when inserted in the center. Let cool fully on a wire rack.

Nutrition Information

- Calories: 224 calories
- Total Carbohydrate: 34 g
- Cholesterol: 31 mg
- Total Fat: 8 g
- Fiber: 1 g
- Protein: 5 g
- Sodium: 346 mg

50. Blueberries N Cheese Coffee Cake

"Coffee cake for any fan of coffee. It is awesome!"
Serving: 15 servings. | Prep: 20m | Ready in: 55m

Ingredients

- 1/2 cup butter, softened
- 1-1/4 cups sugar
- 2 large eggs
- 1 tsp. grated lemon peel
- 2-1/4 cups all-purpose flour, divided
- 3 tsps. baking powder
- 1 tsp. salt
- 3/4 cup whole milk
- 1/4 cup water
- 2 cups fresh or frozen blueberries
- 1 package (8 oz.) cream cheese, diced
- TOPPING:
- 1/4 cup all-purpose flour
- 1/4 cup sugar
- 1 tsp. grated lemon peel
- 2 tbsps. cold butter

Direction

- In a large bowl, cream sugar and butter. Add in eggs, one at a time, and mixing well after each addition. Mix in lemon peel. Blend salt, baking powder, and 2 cups of flour; pour to the creamed mixture alternately with water and milk. In a bowl, blend blueberries with the flour left; fold into the batter along with cream cheese. Transfer into a greased 13x9-inch baking pan.
- To make the topping, blend lemon peel, sugar, and flour in a bowl; cut in butter until the mixture looks crumbly. Spread over batter. Bake at 375° for about 35 to 40 minutes, until a toothpick comes out clean when inserted in the center. Let cool fully on a wire rack.

Nutrition Information

- Calories: 300 calories
- Total Carbohydrate: 40 g
- Cholesterol: 66 mg

- Total Fat: 14 g
- Fiber: 1 g
- Protein: 5 g
- Sodium: 396 mg

51. Blueberry Betty

"Toasted raisin bread cube with blueberry on top."
Serving: 2 servings. | Prep: 10m | Ready in: 30m

Ingredients

- 2 eggs, lightly beaten
- 3/4 cup fat-free evaporated milk
- Sugar substitute equivalent to 1/3 cup sugar
- 1 tsp. vanilla extract
- 1/2 tsp. ground cinnamon
- 1/4 tsp. salt
- 1 cup fresh or frozen blueberries
- 2 slices raisin bread, toasted and cubed
- Dash ground nutmeg

Direction

- Beat the salt, cinnamon, vanilla, sugar substitute, milk and eggs in a bowl, then mix in blueberries.
- Pour it in 2 cooking spray coated 1-cup baking dishes. Put toasted cubes on top and sprinkle nutmeg on top. Let it bake for 20 to 25 minutes at 350 degrees or until it becomes bubbly.

Nutrition Information

- Calories: 278 calories
- Total Carbohydrate: 41 g
- Cholesterol: 220 mg
- Total Fat: 6 g
- Fiber: 3 g
- Protein: 15 g
- Sodium: 583 mg

52. Blueberry Crumb Pie

"Delectable blueberry pie that you should cook and share with your family."
Serving: 8 | Prep: 30m | Ready in: 1h10m

Ingredients

- 1 (9 inch) unbaked pie crust
- 3/4 cup white sugar
- 1/3 cup all-purpose flour
- 2 tsps. grated lemon zest
- 1 tbsp. lemon juice
- 5 cups fresh or frozen blueberries
- 2/3 cup packed brown sugar
- 3/4 cup rolled oats
- 1/2 cup all-purpose flour
- 1/2 tsp. ground cinnamon
- 6 tbsps. butter

Direction

- Heat the oven to 375°F (190°C).
- In a pie plate of 9 inches, press the pie crust into the bottom and onto the sides. Mix flour and sugar together in a large bowl. Stir in lemon juice and lemon zest. Carefully mix in blueberries. Add into pie crust.
- Combine cinnamon, flour, oats and brown sugar together in a medium bowl. Stir in butter with a fork until crumbly. Spread the crumb evenly over the pie filling.
- Bake for 40 minutes, or until it is browned on top. Let cool on a wire rack.

Nutrition Information

- Calories: 461 calories;
- Total Carbohydrate: 75.6 g
- Cholesterol: 23 mg
- Total Fat: 17 g
- Protein: 4.5 g
- Sodium: 185 mg

53. Blueberry Custard Meringue Pie

"This recipe is the combination of only three basic ingredients, including fresh blueberries."
Serving: 8 servings. | Prep: 40m | Ready in: 60m

Ingredients

- 10 whole reduced-fat graham crackers, quartered
- 3 tbsps. butter, melted
- 1 large egg white
- FILLING:
- 1/2 cup sugar
- 1/4 cup cornstarch
- 1/4 tsp. salt
- 2 cups fat-free milk
- 2 large egg yolks
- 1 cup fresh blueberries
- 1/2 tsp. vanilla extract
- MERINGUE:
- 3 large egg whites
- 1/4 tsp. cream of tartar
- 6 tbsps. sugar

Direction

- Set the oven to 350° and start preheating. In a food processor, pulse crackers until forming fine crumbs. Put in egg white and melted butter; process until combined. Press the mixture onto bottom and sides of a 9-in. pie plate greased with cooking spray. Bake until set, about 7-9 minutes. Let cool on a wire rack.
- Combine salt, cornstarch and sugar together in a small heavy saucepan. Whisk in milk. Over medium heat, cook and stir until bubbly and thickened. Decrease heat to low; cook and stir for 2 more minutes. Discard from heat.
- In a small bowl, whisk a little bit of hot mixture in the egg yolks; place back to pan, whisking frequently. Let it come to a gentle boil; cook and stir in 2 minutes. Discard from heat; mix in vanilla and blueberries.
- To make meringue, beat cream of tartar and egg whites together in a bowl on medium speed until foamy. Slowly put in sugar, 1 tbsp. at a time, beating on high speed after each adding until sugar is dissolved. Keep beating until forming soft glossy peaks.
- Remove the hot filling to crust. Spread meringue evenly over the filing, sealing to the edge of crust. Bake at 350° until the meringue turns golden brown, about 16-20 minutes. Let cool on a wire for 60 mins. Cool in the fridge for 1-2 hours before serving. Keep the leftovers in the fridge.

Nutrition Information

- Calories: 212 calories
- Total Carbohydrate: 35 g
- Cholesterol: 66 mg
- Total Fat: 6 g
- Fiber: 1 g
- Protein: 5 g
- Sodium: 211 mg

54. Blueberry Pie In A Jar

"Easy and quick to make pie made with blueberries."
Serving: 42 | Prep: 20m | Ready in: 4h40m

Ingredients

- 7 quarts fresh blueberries
- 4 1/2 cups white sugar
- 3 tbsps. lemon juice
- 1 tbsp. salt
- 10 cups water, divided
- 1 cup cornstarch

Direction

- In a big, non-reactive pot, put 8 cups of water, salt, lemon juice, sugar and blueberries, then boil on high heat. In the leftover 2 cups of water, dissolve the cornstarch and mix it into the boiling blueberries until it becomes thick. Let it cook and stir for another 2 minutes.
- Ladle the mixture to seven sterilized quart jars with rings and lids. Process for 5 minutes in a pressure canner at 5 lbs. of pressure. Take out

the jars from the canner and put it on the wood or cloth-covered surface and place it a couple of inches apart, until it cools down. When it cools, use your finger to press the top of every lid and make sure that it's tightly sealed (the lid doesn't move down or up at all). You can keep the sealed jars for a maximum of 1 year.

Nutrition Information

- Calories: 160 calories;
- Total Carbohydrate: 41 g
- Cholesterol: 0 mg
- Total Fat: 0.4 g
- Protein: 0.9 g
- Sodium: 169 mg

55. Blueberry Quinoa With Lemon Glaze

"A healthy dessert recipe."
Serving: 12 | Prep: 10m | Ready in: 3h

Ingredients

- Blueberry Quinoa:
- 6 cups apple juice
- 3 cups quinoa
- 1 tbsp. vanilla extract
- 1 pint blueberries
- Lemon Glaze:
- 1 cup almond milk
- 2 tbsps. water
- 1 tbsp. cornstarch
- 1 lemon, juiced
- 1 tbsp. maple syrup

Direction

- Boil vanilla extract, quinoa and apple juice in a big pot. Lower heat to medium low and cover; simmer for 15 minutes till liquid is absorbed and quinoa is tender.
- Fold blueberries gently into hot quinoa; put blueberry mixture in 9x13-in. baking dish; cool till quinoa sets.
- Whisk cornstarch, water and almond milk on high heat in small saucepan. Add maple syrup and lemon juice; cook, constantly mixing, for 2-3 minutes till glaze is thick. To fully cover, put hot glaze on quinoa. Cool to room temperature. Use plastic wrap to cover baking dish; refrigerate for 2 hours.

Nutrition Information

- Calories: 247 calories;
- Total Carbohydrate: 48.6 g
- Cholesterol: 0 mg
- Total Fat: 3 g
- Protein: 6.4 g
- Sodium: 20 mg

56. Bourbon Candy Apples

"A delicious recipe."
Serving: 8 | Prep: 10m | Ready in: 30m

Ingredients

- 8 Granny Smith apples
- 8 wooden sticks
- 1 (16 oz.) package brown sugar
- 2/3 cup dark corn syrup
- 3/4 cup water
- 2 tbsps. bourbon whiskey

Direction

- Pierce wooden sticks 3/4 of the way into stem end of every apple; put apples onto a cookie sheet covered with aluminum foil that's lightly greased.
- Mix water, corn syrup and sugar in a big saucepan; boil on medium high heat. Lower heat to medium low; simmer till thermometer reads 143°C/290°F. Take off heat; if desired, mix in bourbon.
- Keep caramel liquid to dip apples in by leaving saucepan on low heat; dip apples

carefully in caramel quickly. Put apples onto greased aluminum foil till coating is hardened and cooled.

Nutrition Information

- Calories: 361 calories;
- Total Carbohydrate: 93.3 g
- Cholesterol: 0 mg
- Total Fat: 0 g
- Protein: 0.5 g
- Sodium: 60 mg

57. Breakfast Brownies

"This delicious, hearty, and easy-to-make breakfast brownie is both dairy and gluten free!"
Serving: 12 | Prep: 15m | Ready in: 40m

Ingredients

- 1 1/2 cups quick-cooking oats
- 3/4 cup brown sugar
- 3/4 cup flax seed meal
- 1/2 cup gluten-free all purpose baking flour
- 1 tsp. baking powder
- 1/2 tsp. ground cinnamon
- 1/4 tsp. salt
- 1 banana, mashed
- 1/4 cup rice milk
- 1 egg
- 1 tsp. vanilla extract

Direction

- Preheat the oven to 175°C or 350°Fahrenheit. Grease an 8-inch by 10-inch baking pan lightly.
- In a bowl, combine salt, oats, cinnamon, brown sugar, baking powder, flax seed meal, and flour. In another bowl, combine vanilla extract, banana, egg, and rice milk; mix with the flour mixture until well combined. Transfer batter in the greased baking pan.
- Bake brownies for 20 mins in the 350°Fahrenheit oven until an inserted skewer comes out without residue. Use a towel to

cover the pan so the moisture stays in. Let the brownies cool for a minimum of five minutes; serve.

Nutrition Information

- Calories: 129 calories;
- Total Carbohydrate: 20.9 g
- Cholesterol: 16 mg
- Total Fat: 4.1 g
- Protein: 3.3 g
- Sodium: 102 mg

58. Buttermilk Carrot Cake

"This treat has been loved for years."
Serving: 12 servings. | Prep: 30m | Ready in: 01h05m

Ingredients

- 2 cups sugar
- 3/4 cup buttermilk
- 3/4 cup vegetable oil
- 3 large eggs
- 2 tsps. vanilla extract
- 2 cups all-purpose flour
- 1 tbsp. ground cinnamon
- 2 tsps. baking soda
- 1 tsp. grated orange zest
- 1/2 tsp. salt
- 2 cups grated carrots
- 1-1/3 cups sweetened shredded coconut
- 1 cup chopped walnuts
- 1 can (8 oz.) crushed pineapple, undrained
- GLAZE:
- 1 cup sugar
- 1/2 cup butter, cubed
- 1/2 cup buttermilk
- 1 tbsp. light corn syrup
- 1/2 tsp. baking soda
- 1 tsp. vanilla extract
- FROSTING:
- 1 package (8 oz.) cream cheese, softened
- 1/2 cup butter, softened
- 1 tsp. vanilla extract

- 1 tsp. orange juice
- 1 tsp. grated orange zest
- 4 cups confectioners' sugar

Direction

- Mix the first 5 ingredients in a bowl; whisk until smooth. Combine salt, orange zest, baking soda, cinnamon and flour; add to buttermilk mixture; stir well. Stir in pineapple, nuts, coconuts and carrots. Transfer to 3 greased and floured 9-in. round baking pans. Bake at 350° 35-40 minutes until the toothpick comes out clean. Transfer pans to wire racks.
- Mix the first 5 glaze ingredients in a saucepan; bring to boiling; cook while stirring for 4 minutes. Take out of the heat; add vanilla. Spread over warm cakes. Completely cool before taking out of the pans.
- Mix the first 5 frosting ingredients in a bowl; whisk until fluffy. Whisk in sugar. Put one cake glaze side up on a serving plate; spread with 1 cup frosting. Do the same layers. Frost sides and top of the cake.

Nutrition Information

- Calories: 835 calories
- Total Carbohydrate: 108 g
- Cholesterol: 116 mg
- Total Fat: 43 g
- Fiber: 2 g
- Protein: 9 g
- Sodium: 625 mg

59. Buttermilk Chocolate Sauce

"A tasty buttermilk chocolate sauce recipe."
Serving: 3/4 cup. | Prep: 5m | Ready in: 15m

Ingredients

- 3/4 cup sugar
- 1/4 cup baking cocoa
- 1 tbsp. cornstarch
- 3/4 cup buttermilk
- 1 tsp. vanilla extract
- Reduced-fat ice cream

Direction

- Mix cornstarch, cocoa and sugar together in a small saucepan. Stir in milk. Boil on medium heat; stir continuously during the process. Lower the heat; simmer without covering for 5 to 7 minutes until thickened a little.
- Put away from the heat; mix in vanilla. Serve while still warm over ice cream. Leave the remaining in the fridge.

Nutrition Information

- Calories: 62 calories
- Total Carbohydrate: 15 g
- Cholesterol: 1 mg
- Total Fat: 0 g
- Fiber: 0 g
- Protein: 1 g
- Sodium: 16 mg

60. Cake-topped Apple Cobbler

"This sweet dessert makes me think of home. When you tap on the crunchy topping and it sounds hollow then it's done."
Serving: 9 servings. | Prep: 20m | Ready in: 60m

Ingredients

- 6 cups sliced peeled tart apples
- 1-1/2 cups sugar, divided
- 1/2 tsp. ground cinnamon
- 2 tbsps. butter, softened
- 1 egg
- 1/4 cup egg substitute
- 1 cup all-purpose flour
- 1 tsp. baking powder
- 4-1/2 cups fat-free frozen vanilla yogurt

Direction

- Put apple slices in an 8-inch square baking pan sprayed with cooking spray. Mix cinnamon and half cup sugar; scatter over apples.

- Whip leftover sugar and butter in a small bowl about 2 minutes until crumbly. Put in egg substitute and egg; stir well. Mix baking powder and flour; Put into egg mixture and whip until combined. Put by spoonful on top of the apples and evenly spread it out.
- Bake for 40-45 minutes at 350° or until golden brown. Serve while warm with frozen yogurt.

Nutrition Information

- Calories: 352 calories
- Total Carbohydrate: 72 g
- Cholesterol: 40 mg
- Total Fat: 6 g
- Fiber: 2 g
- Protein: 7 g
- Sodium: 137 mg

61. Cake-topped Blueberry Dessert

"A special food for summertime: Try to make once and you will never regret."
Serving: 9 servings. | Prep: 25m | Ready in: 55m

Ingredients

- 3 cups fresh or frozen blueberries
- 1/2 cup packed brown sugar
- 1 tbsp. butter
- 3 tbsps. shortening
- 1/2 cup sugar
- 1 large egg
- 1 tsp. grated orange zest
- 1-1/4 cups all-purpose flour
- 1-1/2 tsps. baking powder
- 1/4 tsp. salt
- 1/3 cup orange juice

Direction

- In a saucepan, blend butter, brown sugar, and blueberries; cook about 5 minutes, until saucy. Transfer into an 8-inch square baking dish oiled with cooking spray. In a bowl, cream sugar and shortening. Beat in orange zest and egg. Mix salt, baking powder, and flour; pour to the creamed mixture alternately with orange juice, whisking until just combined.
- Drop spoonfuls of the batter over the blueberry mixture. Bake at 350° about 30 to 35 minutes, until a toothpick comes out clean when inserted in the center. Serve warm.

Nutrition Information

- Calories: 241 calories
- Total Carbohydrate: 44 g
- Cholesterol: 27 mg
- Total Fat: 6 g
- Fiber: 2 g
- Protein: 3 g
- Sodium: 132 mg

62. Candied Kumquat Peels

"It helps bring out the vanilla-like flavor of kumquats."
Serving: 4 | Prep: 20m | Ready in: 8h35m

Ingredients

- 1 cup kumquat peels
- 1/2 cup white sugar
- 1/4 cup water

Direction

- In a saucepan, place the kumquat peels and cover them with water. Heat it until it boils, and then drain. Pour in enough water until they are covered and boil them once more.
- In a separate saucepan, mix 1/4 cup of water and sugar and heat the mixture until it boils; add the peels, reduce the heat to medium-low, and simmer for 10 minutes.
- Place the peels on a waxed paper and let them dry for 8 hours or overnight.

Nutrition Information

- Calories: 121 calories;
- Total Carbohydrate: 31.3 g
- Cholesterol: 0 mg

- Total Fat: 0.1 g
- Protein: 0.4 g
- Sodium: 1 mg

63. Carrot Cake Cookies

"Cookies that are similar to cake and tastes like carrot cake."
Serving: 36 | Prep: 10m | Ready in: 30m

Ingredients

- 1/2 cup butter, softened
- 1 cup brown sugar
- 2 eggs
- 1 (8 oz.) can crushed pineapple, drained
- 3/4 cup shredded carrots
- 1 cup raisins
- 2 cups all-purpose flour
- 1 tsp. baking powder
- 1/2 tsp. baking soda
- 1/2 tsp. salt
- 2 tbsps. ground cinnamon
- 1 cup chopped walnuts (optional)

Direction

- Set an oven to preheat to 175°C (350°F). Grease or line the cookie sheets with parchment paper.
- Cream together the brown sugar and butter in a big bowl, until it becomes smooth. Beat in the eggs, one by one, then mix in the raisins, carrots and crushed pineapple. Mix together the cinnamon, salt, baking soda, baking powder and flour, then mix it into the carrot mixture. If preferred, stir in the walnuts. Drop it on the prepped cookie sheets by rounded spoonfuls.
- Let it bake in the preheated oven for 15-20 minutes, until the cookies become set and the bottoms start to turn brown. Let the cookies cool for several minutes on the cookie sheets prior to transferring to wire racks to let it fully cool.

Nutrition Information

- Calories: 106 calories;
- Total Carbohydrate: 14.4 g
- Cholesterol: 17 mg
- Total Fat: 5.1 g
- Protein: 1.8 g
- Sodium: 85 mg

64. Carrot Cake II

"This recipe is so wonderful."
Serving: 18 | Prep: 20m | Ready in: 1h

Ingredients

- 6 egg whites
- 1 1/3 cups white sugar
- 1 cup applesauce
- 1/2 cup skim milk
- 1 1/2 tsps. vanilla extract
- 1/4 tsp. ground cloves
- 1/2 tsp. ground nutmeg
- 1 tbsp. ground cinnamon
- 2 tsps. baking soda
- 1 cup whole wheat flour
- 1 cup all-purpose flour
- 1 (8 oz.) can crushed pineapple with juice
- 2 cups shredded carrots
- 1/2 cup chopped walnuts
- 1/2 cup raisins

Direction

- Preheat the oven to 175 degrees C (350 degrees F). Gently grease the 9X13-in. pan with the nonfat cooking spray.
- In the big mixing bowl, whip the egg whites. Gradually whip in the sugar, then vanilla, skim milk and applesauce. Whisk in the flour, baking soda, cinnamon, nutmeg and cloves. Whisk in, 1 ingredient at once, the raisins, walnuts, carrots and pineapple along with the juice. Add to prepped pan.

- Bake in preheated oven for 35 to 40 minutes. It becomes done when the toothpick inserted into the middle exits clean.

Nutrition Information

- Calories: 167 calories;
- Total Carbohydrate: 34.1 g
- Cholesterol: < 1 mg
- Total Fat: 2.4 g
- Protein: 3.9 g
- Sodium: 171 mg

65. Carrot Chocolate Chip Cookies

"A good way for children to eat carrots."
Serving: about 7 dozen. | Prep: 20m | Ready in: 30m

Ingredients

- 1 cup packed brown sugar
- 1/3 cup canola oil
- 2 eggs
- 1/3 cup fat-free milk
- 2 cups all-purpose flour
- 1 tsp. baking powder
- 1/2 tsp. salt
- 1/2 tsp. ground cinnamon
- 1/4 tsp. baking soda
- 1/4 tsp. ground nutmeg
- 1 cup (6 oz.) semisweet chocolate chips
- 1 cup quick-cooking oats
- 1 cup grated carrots
- 1 cup raisins

Direction

- In a large bowl, beat together oil and brown sugar until incorporated. Beat in the eggs, then the milk. Combine the nutmeg, baking soda, cinnamon, salt, baking powder and flour; add to the mixture of egg slowly and combine well. Stir in the raisins, carrots, oats and chips.
- On baking sheets sprayed with cooking spray, drop heaping teaspoonfuls of the dough; slightly flatten them out. Bake until golden brown at 350° or 10-13 minutes. Transfer to wire racks to cool down.

Nutrition Information

- Calories: 197 calories
- Total Carbohydrate: 33 g
- Cholesterol: 20 mg
- Total Fat: 7 g
- Fiber: 2 g
- Protein: 3 g
- Sodium: 99 mg

66. Carrot-pineapple Gelatin Salad

"This salad is a good way to get your kids to eat vegetables and fruit. My grandma often made it for me and now I'm making it for my kids and they love it."
Serving: 4 servings. | Prep: 15m | Ready in: 15m

Ingredients

- 1 can (8 oz.) unsweetened crushed pineapple
- 1 package (.3 oz.) sugar-free lemon gelatin
- 1 cup boiling water
- 1/2 cup cold water
- 1 tsp. white vinegar
- 1/8 tsp. salt
- 2 medium carrots, grated

Direction

- Drain pineapple, saving 1/2 cup juice; put the juice and pineapple aside. Dissolve gelatin in a bowl of boiling water. Mix in the saved juice, salt, vinegar, and cold water. Refrigerate for about 45 minutes until partly thickened. Mix in the saved pineapple and carrots. Add to an oil-coated 3-cup mold. Refrigerate until firm. Remove the mold and enjoy.

Nutrition Information

- Calories: 59 calories
- Total Carbohydrate: 12 g
- Cholesterol: 0 mg
- Total Fat: 0 g

- Fiber: 2 g
- Protein: 1 g
- Sodium: 158 mg

67. Champagne With Strawberries

"An easy to make and sophisticated dessert treat."
Serving: 4 | Prep: 15m | Ready in: 15m

Ingredients

- 1 pint lemon sherbet
- 2 pints strawberries, hulled and sliced
- 2 cups champagne

Direction

- In 4 tall clear glasses, drops scoops of sherbet. Put slices of strawberry on top and pour in champagne to fill the glass.

Nutrition Information

- Calories: 281 calories;
- Total Carbohydrate: 48.1 g
- Cholesterol: 0 mg
- Total Fat: 0.5 g
- Protein: 1.3 g
- Sodium: 13 mg

68. Cherry Angel Cake Roll

"Beautiful party cake recipe made with a handful of ingredients."
Serving: 2 cakes (8 slices each). | Prep: 25m | Ready in: 35m

Ingredients

- 1 package (16 oz.) angel food cake mix
- 4 tbsps. confectioners' sugar, divided
- 1 carton (8 oz.) frozen reduced-fat whipped topping, thawed, divided
- 1 can (20 oz.) reduced-sugar cherry pie filling
- 1/4 tsp. almond extract

Direction

- Use ungreased parchment paper to line the two 15x10x1-inch baking pans. Prepare the cake batter following the package instructions, then evenly spread in the prepped pans. Let it bake for 12 to 15 minutes at 375 degrees or until the cake bounces back once lightly pressed. Allow to cool for 5 minutes.
- Turn it upside down on 2 kitchen towels that were dusted with 3 tbsp confectioner's sugar. Peel off the parchment paper gently. Roll up the cakes in the towels the jelly roll style, beginning with the short side. Allow to fully cool on a wire rack.
- Spread out the cakes, then spread a cup of whipped topping on each to within half inch of the edges. Mix together the extract and pie filling, then spread on top of the whipped topping on each of the cake. Roll it up once again. Put it on a serving plate, seam side down. Put on cover and let it chill in the fridge for an hour.
- Dust leftover confectioner's sugar on top. Cut, then put the leftover whipped topping on as a garnish.

Nutrition Information

- Calories: 175 calories
- Total Carbohydrate: 36 g
- Cholesterol: 0 mg
- Total Fat: 2 g
- Fiber: 0 g
- Protein: 3 g
- Sodium: 171 mg

69. Cherry Cheesecake Pie

"Amazing!"
Serving: 8

Ingredients

- 1 (9 inch) prepared graham cracker crust
- 1 (8 oz.) package cream cheese, softened

- 1 (14 oz.) can sweetened condensed milk
- 1 (21 oz.) can cherry pie filling, chilled
- 1/2 cup lemon juice
- 1 tsp. vanilla extract

Direction

- Beat cream cheese till fluffy in a medium bowl. Add condensed milk; thoroughly mix. Mix in vanilla and lemon juice.
- Put into crust. Chill for 2 hours. Before serving, top with cherry/other pie filling. Refrigerate.

Nutrition Information

- Calories: 493 calories;
- Total Carbohydrate: 69.1 g
- Cholesterol: 47 mg
- Total Fat: 21.5 g
- Protein: 7.6 g
- Sodium: 329 mg

70. Cherry Chocolate Cake

"This chocolate cake is super rich and moist.""
Serving: 24

Ingredients

- 1/2 cup butter
- 1 1/2 cups white sugar
- 2 eggs
- 1 tsp. almond extract
- 1/2 cup unsweetened cocoa powder
- 1 3/4 cups cake flour
- 1 1/4 tsps. baking soda
- 1 tsp. salt
- 1 (21 oz.) can cherry pie filling

Direction

- Set oven to 350°F (175°C) to preheat. Gently butter and flour a 9x13-inch baking pan.
- Beat together sugar and butter until fluffy and light. Stir in almond extract and eggs, beating until well combined. Put in cocoa powder and stir until thoroughly incorporated.
- Mix salt, baking soda, and cake flour together with your hand. Put flour mixture into the butter mixture and mix just until incorporated. Mix in cherry pie filling. Transfer batter to the prepared pan.
- Bake for 30 to 35 minutes at 175 degrees C (350 degrees F) until a toothpick comes out clean from the center. Allow cake to cool; frost cooled cake with chocolate buttercream.

Nutrition Information

- Calories: 159 calories;
- Total Carbohydrate: 28.6 g
- Cholesterol: 26 mg
- Total Fat: 4.6 g
- Protein: 1.9 g
- Sodium: 201 mg

71. Cherry Chocolate Pie

"Easy preparation with pudding mix, canned cherries and frozen crust. If you want some crunchiness, garnish them with toasted pecans."
Serving: 8 servings. | Prep: 20m | Ready in: 20m

Ingredients

- 1 can (14-1/2 oz.) pitted tart cherries in water
- 2 tbsps. sugar
- 2 cups 2% milk
- 2 packages (1.3 oz. each) sugar-free cook-and-serve chocolate pudding mix
- 1 frozen pastry shell (9 inches), baked

Direction

- Strain cherries, save the liquid. Mix sugar and cherries in a bowl; put aside. Mix the milk and saved cherry liquid in a big saucepan. Mix in pudding mix. Cook and mix over medium heat until mixture comes to a boil; cook and mix for 1 to 2 minutes more or until thickened. Mix in cherries. Spread into crust. Let cool on a wire rack. Chill leftovers.

Nutrition Information

- Calories: 169 calories
- Total Carbohydrate: 27 g
- Cholesterol: 8 mg
- Total Fat: 6 g
- Fiber: 1 g
- Protein: 4 g
- Sodium: 194 mg

72. Cherry-almond Streusel Tart

"This tart is full of fresh cherries and has a topping of crunchy streusel. It looks pretty and tastes wonderful."
Serving: 8 servings. | Prep: 20m | Ready in: 50m

Ingredients

- Pastry for single-crust pie (9 inches)
- 2/3 cup sugar
- 3 tbsps. cornstarch
- Dash salt
- 4 cups fresh tart cherries, pitted or frozen pitted tart cherries, thawed
- 1/8 tsp. almond extract
- TOPPING:
- 1/4 cup quick-cooking oats
- 3 tbsps. all-purpose flour
- 2 tbsps. brown sugar
- 1 tbsp. slivered almonds
- 2 tbsps. cold butter

Direction

- Press the pastry up the sides and onto the bottom of an unoiled 9-inch fluted tart pan that has a removable bottom, trim the edges.
- Mix salt, cornstarch and sugar together in a big saucepan. Mix in cherries, boil over medium heat, whisking continuously. Stir and cook until thickened, or about 1-2 minutes. Take away from the heat, mix in the extract. Add to the crust.
- To prepare the topping, mix together almonds, brown sugar, flour and oats. Cut in butter until the mixture looks like coarse crumbs. Sprinkle over the filling. Bake at 350° until the topping turns golden brown, or about 30-35 minutes. Put on a wire rack to cool.

Nutrition Information

- Calories: 298 calories
- Total Carbohydrate: 49 g
- Cholesterol: 13 mg
- Total Fat: 11 g
- Fiber: 2 g
- Protein: 3 g
- Sodium: 143 mg

73. Chevre Cheesecake

""This decadent New York cheesecake is made without any gluten, soy, or cow dairy products. I never use any of the classic cheesecake ingredients when I serve this at parties. I wanted to make this recipe for my husband when he told me he had never eaten a cheesecake for long because of his allergies, and this is it!""
Serving: 12 | Prep: 40m | Ready in: 7h40m

Ingredients

- 7 oz. gluten-free gingersnap cookies, finely crushed
- 1/4 cup margarine, melted
- 2 lbs. chevre (soft goat cheese) at room temperature
- 1 1/2 cups white sugar
- 4 eggs, room temperature
- 3/4 cup coconut milk
- 8 oz. cultured coconut milk (coconut milk yogurt)
- 1 tbsp. gluten-free vanilla extract
- 1/4 cup gluten-free all-purpose baking flour

Direction

- Prepare an oven by heating it to 150 degrees C or 300 degrees F. Use parchment paper to line the bottom of a 9-inch springform pan, and let it cool in the freezer.
- Mix melted margarine with gingersnap crumbs. Pressing the mixture into the

prepared pan's bottom then place in the freezer.
- In a large bowl, use a beater for the sugar and chevre until blended to a smooth texture. Add eggs individually. Let each blend well into the cheese mixture before pouring in the following egg. Pour in the coconut milk. Mix the coconut yogurt, gluten-free flour, and vanilla extract. Combine well.
- Take the chilled crust and pour in the cheesecake batter. Let it bake in the preheated oven for an hour. Switch off the oven and cool the cake inside for a minimum of two hours. Place in the fridge for another 4 to 6 hours, and serve.

Nutrition Information

- Calories: 557 calories;
- Total Carbohydrate: 43.3 g
- Cholesterol: 114 mg
- Total Fat: 34.9 g
- Protein: 19.9 g
- Sodium: 504 mg

74. Chewy Coconut Macaroons

"Chewy macaroons recipe."
Serving: 32 cookies. | Prep: 10m | Ready in: 30m

Ingredients

- 2-1/2 cups sweetened shredded coconut
- 3/4 cup all-purpose flour
- 1/8 tsp. salt
- 1 can (14 oz.) fat-free sweetened condensed milk
- 1-1/2 tsps. almond extract

Direction

- Toss the salt, flour and coconut in a bowl. Mix in the extract and milk until combined (the mixture will get sticky and thick).
- Drop it on the baking trays that were lightly greased by level tbsps. and place it 3 inches apart. Let it bake for 18 to 22 minutes at 300

degrees or just until it turns golden brown in color. Allow to cool for 2 minutes prior to taking out of the pans and transferring to wire racks.

Nutrition Information

- Calories: 83 calories
- Total Carbohydrate: 13 g
- Cholesterol: 2 mg
- Total Fat: 3 g
- Fiber: 0 g
- Protein: 1 g
- Sodium: 41 mg

75. Chewy Date Cookies

"Old-fashioned cookies with chewy dates, lemon peel, cinnamon and brown sugar."
Serving: about 2-1/2 dozen. | Prep: 15m | Ready in: 30m

Ingredients

- 1/3 cup butter, softened
- 2/3 cup packed brown sugar
- 1 egg
- 3/4 cup all-purpose flour
- 2/3 cup whole wheat flour
- 2 tsps. grated lemon peel
- 1-1/2 tsps. baking powder
- 1/2 tsp. ground cinnamon
- 1/2 tsp. ground nutmeg
- 1/4 tsp. salt
- 1/4 cup fat-free milk
- 1 cup chopped dates

Direction

- Whip butter with brown sugar in a bowl. Put in egg; stir well. Mix the salt, nutmeg, cinnamon, baking powder, lemon peel and flours; alternately put into whipped mixture with milk, mixing well after each addition. Mix in dates.
- Put by heaping tablespoonfuls 2 inches apart onto baking trays, ungreased. Bake for 13-15

minutes at 325° or until golden brown. Take out to wire racks to cool. Put in an airtight container to store.

Nutrition Information

- Calories: 77 calories
- Total Carbohydrate: 14 g
- Cholesterol: 13 mg
- Total Fat: 2 g
- Fiber: 1 g
- Protein: 1 g
- Sodium: 57 mg

76. Chewy Fudge Drop Cookies

"This chocolate recipe is so chewy and amazing."
Serving: 4 dozen. | Prep: 20m | Ready in: 30m

Ingredients

- 1 cup (6 oz.) semisweet chocolate chips, divided
- 3 tbsps. canola oil
- 1 cup packed brown sugar
- 3 egg whites
- 2 tbsps. plus 1-1/2 tsps. light corn syrup
- 1 tbsp. water
- 2-1/2 tsps. vanilla extract
- 1-3/4 cups all-purpose flour
- 2/3 cup plus 1 tbsp. confectioners' sugar, divided
- 1/3 cup baking cocoa
- 2-1/4 tsps. baking powder
- 1/8 tsp. salt

Direction

- In the microwave, melt oil and three-fourths chocolate chips; whisk till smooth. Add to big bowl; let cool down for 5 minutes.
- Whisk in brown sugar. Put in vanilla, water, corn syrup and egg whites till becoming smooth. Mix salt, baking powder, cocoa, two-thirds cup of the confectioners' square, and flour; slowly put into the chocolate mixture till mixed. Whisk in rest of the chocolate chips. The dough would be very stiff.
- Drop by tablespoonfuls, 2 inches apart, to greased baking sheets. Bake at 350 degrees till becoming set and puffed or for 8 to 10 minutes. Let cool down for 2 minutes prior to transferring onto the wire racks. Sprinkle the cooled cookies with the rest of the confectioners' sugar.

Nutrition Information

- Calories: 139 calories
- Total Carbohydrate: 26 g
- Cholesterol: 0 mg
- Total Fat: 4 g
- Fiber: 1 g
- Protein: 2 g
- Sodium: 48 mg

77. Chewy Oatmeal Raisin Cookies

"Reward yourself with this oatmeal raisin cookie anytime of the week!"
Serving: 48 | Ready in: 1h

Ingredients

- 3 cups rolled oats
- ⅓ cup chopped walnuts, or pecans
- 1 cup raisins
- 1 cup water
- 1½ cups sugar
- ½ cup apple butter
- 2 large eggs
- ¼ cup canola oil
- 1 tsp. vanilla extract
- 2 cups all-purpose flour
- 1 tsp. baking soda
- ½ tsp. baking powder
- ½ tsp. salt
- ½ tsp. ground cinnamon
- ½ tsp. ground cloves

Direction

- Preheat the oven to 375°F. Use a parchment paper to line 2 baking sheets or use a cooking spray to grease the baking sheets.
- On a baking sheet that is not greased, put in the nuts and rolled oats and spread it out in the baking sheet; allow the mixture to toast for 5-7 minutes until it turns light brown in color. Put it aside.
- In a small saucepan, mix the water and raisins together. Allow the mixture to simmer and let it cook over low heat setting for about 10 minutes until the raisins have already bulged in size. Drain the cooked raisins to get rid of the cooking liquid; put it aside.
- Use an electric mixer to whisk the eggs, sugar, vanilla, apple butter and oil together in a big mixing bowl for about 5 minutes until the mixture has a fluffy and light consistency. Sift the cinnamon, flour, baking powder, cloves, salt and baking soda directly into a separate bowl. Use a spoon to mix the sifted flour mixture into the prepared apple butter mixture. Add in the reserved toasted nuts, cooked raisins and toasted oats and thoroughly mix everything together.
- On the prepared baking sheets, put in rounded teaspoonfuls of the prepared dough about 2 inches away from each other. Put 1 baking sheet, per batch, in the preheated oven and let it bake for 8-10 minutes until it turns light brown in color. Place the baked cookies onto wire racks and let them cool down.

Nutrition Information

- Calories: 96 calories;
- Total Carbohydrate: 17 g
- Cholesterol: 8 mg
- Total Fat: 2 g
- Fiber: 1 g
- Protein: 2 g
- Sodium: 47 mg
- Sugar: 9 g
- Saturated Fat: 0 g

78. Chilled Cantaloupe Soup

"This soup is very refreshing and good for luncheons."
Serving: 6 | Prep: 20m | Ready in: 1h20m

Ingredients

- 1 cantaloupe - peeled, seeded and cubed
- 2 cups orange juice
- 1 tbsp. fresh lime juice
- 1/4 tsp. ground cinnamon

Direction

- Peel and seed the cantaloupe, then cut it into cubes.
- In a food processor or a blender, add 1/2 cup of orange juice and cantaloupe, then cover and process until smooth. Remove to a big bowl, and then stir in leftover orange juice, cinnamon and lime juice. Place a cover and chill for a minimum of 1 hour. Use mint to decorate if you want.

Nutrition Information

- Calories: 69 calories;
- Total Carbohydrate: 16.4 g
- Cholesterol: 0 mg
- Total Fat: 0.3 g
- Protein: 1.4 g
- Sodium: 16 mg

79. Chloe's Quick Fruit Salad

"This is a simple and quick to prepare fruit salad. You can replace nectarine with melon or pear or your favorite fresh fruit!"
Serving: 4 | Prep: 15m | Ready in: 45m

Ingredients

- 1 apple, cored and chopped
- 1 large orange, peeled, sectioned, and cut into bite-size
- 1/2 cup seedless grapes
- 1 nectarine, pitted and chopped

- 1/4 cup fresh orange juice
- 6 tbsps. plain low-fat yogurt

Direction

- Mix nectarine, apple, grapes, and orange in a mixing bowl. If you are adding a passion fruit, spoon the flesh out and cut.
- Add plenty of fresh juice to coat and prevent oxidation. Mix and chill.
- You can serve together with dollop of low-fat yogurt.

Nutrition Information

- Calories: 90 calories;
- Total Carbohydrate: 20.6 g
- Cholesterol: 1 mg
- Total Fat: 0.7 g
- Protein: 2.3 g
- Sodium: 17 mg

80. Chocolate Caramel Cheesecake

"A recipe that is sure to be a hit at every occasion. Decorate with chocolate sauce or caramel sauce."
Serving: 12 | Prep: 45m | Ready in: 1h30m

Ingredients

- 2 cups graham cracker crumbs
- 1/3 cup white sugar
- 1/2 cup butter, melted
- 30 individually wrapped caramels, unwrapped
- 3 tbsps. milk
- 3/4 cup chopped pecans
- 1 cup semisweet chocolate chips
- 3 (8 oz.) packages cream cheese, softened
- 3/4 cup white sugar
- 1 tsp. vanilla extract
- 3 eggs

Direction

- Mix graham cracker crumbs, melted butter and sugar in a medium bowl. Press mixture into the bottom and up sides 1 inch in a 9-in. springform pan. Spread melted caramel/pecan mixture and refrigerate for 30 minutes.
- For caramel filling: mix caramels and milk in a saucepan. Stir and cook over low heat until smooth. Add in sliced pecans. Preheat the oven to 325°F or 165°C.
- Heat chocolate on top of double boiler and stir occasionally until smooth and melted. Take away from heat and to lukewarm let cool. Mix cream cheese, vanilla and sugar in a large bowl until smooth. Add in eggs one at a time. Fold 1/3 of filling in melted chocolate. Pour chocolate mixture back in filling and beat until there are no more streaks. Spread mixture in the crust.
- Bake for 50 minutes or until the center is slightly set. Put a pan of water on the rack under the cheesecake while baking to avoid cracking. Open the door of the oven slightly to cool in the oven. Chill for 5 hours before serving.

Nutrition Information

- Calories: 624 calories;
- Total Carbohydrate: 59.8 g
- Cholesterol: 131 mg
- Total Fat: 41.1 g
- Protein: 9.3 g
- Sodium: 387 mg

81. Chocolate Cereal Bars

"Crispy yet not sticky bars."
Serving: 2 dozen. | Prep: 30m | Ready in: 30m

Ingredients

- 2 tbsps. butter
- 1 oz. unsweetened chocolate
- 1 jar (7 oz.) marshmallow creme
- 2 tbsps. baking cocoa
- 1 tsp. vanilla extract
- 6 cups crisp rice cereal

Direction

- Melt chocolate and butter in heavy saucepan on low heat; mix till smooth. Mix cocoa and marshmallow crème in; mix and cook till smooth. Take off heat; mix cereal and vanilla in. Pat into 13x9-in. pan that's coated in cooking spray. Cool; cut.

Nutrition Information

- Calories: 69 calories
- Total Carbohydrate: 13 g
- Cholesterol: 3 mg
- Total Fat: 2 g
- Fiber: 0 g
- Protein: 1 g
- Sodium: 87 mg

82. Chocolate Chip Cookies

"This version of the classic chocolate chip cookie replaces butter with reduced-fat cream cheese to lower the fat."
Serving: 30 | Ready in: 1h

Ingredients

- 1 cup all-purpose flour
- ½ tsp. baking soda
- ½ tsp. salt
- 2 tbsps. unsalted butter
- 2 oz. reduced-fat cream cheese, (Neufchâtel) (¼ cup)
- 6 tbsps. packed light brown sugar
- 6 tbsps. granulated sugar
- 1 large egg
- 1 large egg white
- 1 tsp. vanilla extract
- ½ cup semisweet chocolate chips, coarsely chopped, or mini chocolate chips

Direction

- Preheat the oven to 375 degrees F. Coat two baking sheets with cooking spray or line with parchment paper.
- In a medium bowl, mix together flour, salt and baking soda and reserve. Over low heat, melt butter in a small saucepan. Cook while swirling the pan for 30 to 60 seconds until butter turns nutty brown. Transfer to a large mixing bowl. Add granulated sugar, cream cheese and brown sugar. Use an electric mixer on low speed to beat until the resulting mixture is smooth.
- Add vanilla, egg, and egg white and beat until incorporated well. Add chocolate chips and reserved flour mixture and mix with a wooden spoon just until combined. (Batter should be runny.)
- Transfer the batter by dropping rounded tablespoonfuls onto the prepared baking sheets, two inches apart. Bake for 12 to 15 minutes, one sheet at a time, until golden. Place cookies onto racks and leave them to cool.

Nutrition Information

- Calories: 62 calories;
- Total Carbohydrate: 10 g
- Cholesterol: 9 mg
- Total Fat: 2 g
- Fiber: 0 g
- Protein: 1 g
- Sodium: 71 mg
- Sugar: 7 g
- Saturated Fat: 1 g

83. Chocolate Chip Mint Ice Cream

"Creamy and smooth treat to finish any meal."
Serving: 7 servings. | Prep: 10m | Ready in: 30m

Ingredients

- 2 cups fat-free half-and-half
- 1 can (14 oz.) fat-free sweetened condensed milk
- 1 envelope whipped topping mix (Dream Whip)
- 1/4 tsp. peppermint extract

- 2 to 3 drops green food coloring
- 1 oz. semisweet chocolate, coarsely chopped

Direction

- Whip the food coloring, extract, whipped topping mix, milk and half-and-half in a small bowl on high speed for 3 minutes. Chill, covered, overnight.
- Put into the cylinder of an ice cream freezer. Put in the freezer following the manufacturer's directions. Mix in chocolate. Let it set in the freezer for a day before serving.

Nutrition Information

- Calories: 255 calories
- Total Carbohydrate: 47 g
- Cholesterol: 4 mg
- Total Fat: 3 g
- Fiber: 0 g
- Protein: 8 g
- Sodium: 128 mg

84. Chocolate Fudge

"This easy basic fudge recipe is fun to follow."
Serving: 24

Ingredients

- 3 cups white sugar
- 1 cup evaporated milk
- 1/4 cup unsweetened cocoa powder
- 1/4 cup creamy peanut butter

Direction

- Mix cocoa, evaporated milk, white sugar in a 3 quart saucepan. Bring to a hard boil then lower to medium heat. Keep cooking till the mixture reaches 112°C (234°F). That is the soft ball stage.
- Put in peanut butter and stir till the mixture is blended well. Butter an 8x8-inch baking dish and transfer the mixture into the baking dish. Cool then divide into pieces.

Nutrition Information

- Calories: 129 calories;
- Total Carbohydrate: 27.1 g
- Cholesterol: 3 mg
- Total Fat: 2.3 g
- Protein: 1.6 g
- Sodium: 24 mg

85. Chocolate Layer Cake

""A light chocolate cake with eye-catching look.""
Serving: 12 servings. | Prep: 30m | Ready in: 50m

Ingredients

- 1 package chocolate cake mix (regular size)
- 1-1/4 cups buttermilk
- 1 large egg
- 4 large egg whites
- ORANGE FILLING:
- 1 cup cold fat-free milk
- 1 package (3.3 oz.) instant white chocolate pudding mix or 1 package (3.4 oz.) instant vanilla pudding mix
- 1/4 tsp. grated orange zest
- 1/8 tsp. orange extract
- 1/2 cup heavy whipping cream, whipped
- CHOCOLATE GLAZE:
- 3 squares (1 oz. each) semisweet chocolate, chopped
- 1 tbsp. fat-free milk
- 1-1/2 tsps. butter

Direction

- Use cooking spray to coat three 9-in. round baking pans; line with waxed paper. Use cooking spray to grease the paper and dust with flour; set aside.
- Beat together the first 4 ingredients on low speed in a large bowl for 30 seconds. Beat for 2 minutes on medium. Transfer into the prepared pans.
- Bake at 350° till a toothpick turns out clean when inserted into the center, about 20-25

minutes. Allow to cool for 10 minutes; take away and allow to cool on wire racks. Gently peel off the waxed paper.
- Whisk together the first 4 filling ingredients in a large bowl for 2 minutes (the mixture should be thick). Blend in whipped cream.
- On a serving plate, place one cake layer; spoon half of the filling over. Repeat the layers. Place the third cake layer on top. Microwave the glaze ingredients without a cover in a microwave-safe bowl at 30% power for 45 seconds; combine till smooth. Transfer over the top of the cake; spread evenly.

Nutrition Information

- Calories: 316 calories
- Total Carbohydrate: 44 g
- Cholesterol: 66 mg
- Total Fat: 13 g
- Fiber: 1 g
- Protein: 8 g
- Sodium: 559 mg

86. Chocolate Meringue Cups

"Chocolate meringue that's low in cholesterol."
Serving: 15 servings. | Prep: 30m | Ready in: 01h15m

Ingredients

- 4 egg whites
- 1 tsp. vanilla extract
- 1/2 tsp. salt
- 1/2 tsp. white vinegar
- 1 cup sugar
- 2 tbsps. baking cocoa
- CHOCOLATE MOUSSE:
- 1 cup fat-free milk
- 1 egg
- 1/4 cup plus 2 tsps. corn syrup, divided
- 1/4 cup baking cocoa
- 3 oz. semisweet chocolate
- 4 oz. reduced-fat cream cheese
- 2 tsps. unflavored gelatin
- 1/4 cup plus 1 tbsp. cold water, divided
- 1 tsp. vanilla extract
- 4 egg whites
- 3/4 cup sugar
- 1/4 tsp. cream of tartar
- 15 peppermint candies, crushed

Direction

- In a big bowl, put the egg whites, then allow to stand for half an hour at room temperature. Beat the egg whites until it becomes foamy. Beat in vinegar, salt and vanilla, then beat it on medium speed, until it forms soft peaks. Slowly add the sugar, a tbsp. at a time, and beat on high until it forms stiff peaks. Sift cocoa on top of the egg whites, then fold it into the egg whites.
- Drop fifteen heaping tablespoonfuls on the baking trays lined with parchment, then use the back of a spoon to form it into 3-inch cups. Let it bake for 45 minutes at 275 degrees or until it turns golden brown in color. Turn off the oven, then leave the meringues inside the oven for 1 1/2 hours.
- Mix together the coca, a quarter cup of corn syrup and milk in a big saucepan. Let it cook and stir on medium heat, until the metal spoon is coated with the mixture and reaches 160 degrees. Take it out of the heat, then add cream cheese and chocolate mix until it melts.
- Sprinkle gelatin on top of a quarter cup of water in a small saucepan and allow to stand for a minute. Let it cook and stir on low heat, until the gelatin dissolves. Mix vanilla and gelatin into the chocolate mixture, then let it cool.
- Mix together the water, leftover corn syrup, cream of tartar, sugar and egg whites in a heavy saucepan. Let it cook on low heat and use a hand mixer to beat it on low, until the mixture reaches 160 degrees.
- Pour it on a big bowl, then beat it on high until it forms soft peaks. Fold it into the chocolate mixture, then let it chill until the mixture mounds or for 1 to 2 hours.

- Scoop the mousse to the meringue cups just prior to serving, then sprinkle peppermint candy pieces on top.

Nutrition Information

- Calories: 201 calories
- Total Carbohydrate: 40 g
- Cholesterol: 19 mg
- Total Fat: 4 g
- Fiber: 2 g
- Protein: 5 g
- Sodium: 153 mg

87. Chocolate Mint Eclair Dessert

"I learned this pudding recipe from a friend and have tried spicing it up with different flavors ever since. Out of all, I find chocolate and mint the best flavor for the holidays."
Serving: 15 servings. | Prep: 20m | Ready in: 20m

Ingredients

- 23 whole chocolate graham crackers
- 3 cups cold fat-free milk
- 2 packages (3.3 to 3.4 oz. each) instant white chocolate or vanilla pudding mix
- 1/2 tsp. mint or peppermint extract
- 3 to 4 drops green food coloring, optional
- 1 carton (8 oz.) frozen reduced-fat whipped topping, thawed
- CHOCOLATE FROSTING:
- 1 tbsp. butter
- 2 tbsps. baking cocoa
- 2 tbsps. plus 1 tsp. fat-free milk
- 1 tsp. vanilla extract
- 1 cup confectioners' sugar

Direction

- Use cooking spray to spray a 13x9-inch dish. Break 5 whole graham crackers into halves, using 6 whole crackers and 3 halves to line the pan's bottom.
- Stir food coloring (optional), extract, pudding mix and milk in a big bowl for 2 minutes (the mixture will have a thick consistency). Fold whipped topping into the mixture.
- Spread 1/2 mixture onto the crackers. Put on top another layer of 6 whole crackers and 3 cracker halves. Spread the rest of pudding mixture and graham crackers on top (leave the rest of cracker halves for later use). Chill while covered for 2 hours.
- To make the frosting, heat butter in a saucepan until melted. Mix in milk and cocoa until combined. Take away from the heat and mix in confectioners' sugar and vanilla until forming a smooth mixture. Frost onto the pudding. Chill while covered overnight.

Nutrition Information

- Calories: 244 calories
- Total Carbohydrate: 41 g
- Cholesterol: 3 mg
- Total Fat: 7 g
- Fiber: 1 g
- Protein: 4 g
- Sodium: 296 mg

88. Chocolate Mint Whoopie Pies

"Sandwich cookies that were cute and is a great addition to holiday goodies."
Serving: 1-1/2 dozen. | Prep: 25m | Ready in: 30m

Ingredients

- 1/2 cup sugar
- 3 tbsps. canola oil
- 1 egg
- 1 cup all-purpose flour
- 1/4 cup baking cocoa
- 1/2 tsp. baking soda
- 1/4 tsp. salt
- 2 tbsps. fat-free milk
- FILLING:
- 2 tbsps. butter, softened
- 1-1/3 cups confectioners' sugar
- 1/8 tsp. mint extract
- 4 drops green food coloring, optional

- 4 tsps. fat-free milk

Direction

- Beat oil and sugar in a big bowl till crumbly. Put in egg and beat for 1 minute. Combine salt, baking soda, cocoa and flour. Mix into sugar mixture slowly. Put in milk; beat well. Dough should be sticky. Roll dough using lightly floured hands to form 3/4-in. balls.
- Put on cooking spray coated baking sheets; place them 2 in. apart.
- Use a cooking spray coated glass to flatten slightly. Bake for 4-5 minutes at 400° till tops are cracked and edges are set. Allow to cool for 2 minutes then transfer to wire racks, let cool.
- Combine confectioners' sugar and butter in a small bowl till crumbly. Beat in milk, food coloring if preferred and extract. Spread on the base of 1/2 of cookies; place leftover cookies on top.

Nutrition Information

- Calories: 122 calories
- Total Carbohydrate: 21 g
- Cholesterol: 15 mg
- Total Fat: 4 g
- Fiber: 1 g
- Protein: 1 g
- Sodium: 86 mg

89. Chocolate Mousse

"A low-calorie and low-fat mousse."
Serving: 6 | Ready in: 4h

Ingredients

- 1 tsp. unflavored gelatin
- 2 tbsps. coffee liqueur, rum or strong brewed coffee
- ¾ cup low-fat milk
- 1 large egg
- 1 cup packed light brown sugar
- ⅔ cup unsweetened cocoa powder, preferably Dutch-process
- 2 oz. bittersweet (not unsweetened) chocolate, chopped
- 2 tsps. vanilla extract
- 4 large egg whites
- ½ tsp. cream of tartar
- 3 tbsps. water

Direction

- Sprinkle gelatin on coffee/rum/liqueur in small bowl; let stand for 1 minute till softened.
- Whisk cocoa, 1/4 cup brown sugar, whole egg and milk in medium saucepan till smooth; cook on low heat for 5 minutes till thick, constantly whisking. Take off heat; add softened gelatin mixture, mixing till gelatin melts. Add vanilla and chocolate; mix till chocolate melts. Cool for 30 minutes to room temperature.
- Put 1-in. water to bare simmer in wide saucepan. Mix leftover 3/4 cup brown sugar, water, cream of tartar and egg whites in heatproof bowl big enough to fit above saucepan; put bowl above barely simmering water. Use electric mixer to beat at low speed for 3-5 minutes, constantly moving beaters around, till an instant-read thermometer reads 140°F.
- Put mixer speed on high; beat for 3 1/2 minutes on heat; take bowl off heat. Beat meringue for another 4-5 minutes till cool.
- Whisk 1/4 meringue into chocolate mixture till smooth; fold chocolate mixture back into leftover meringue using rubber spatula till incorporated completely. Put mousse in 6 dessert glasses; chill for 3 hours till set.

Nutrition Information

- Calories: 247 calories;
- Total Carbohydrate: 48 g
- Cholesterol: 34 mg
- Total Fat: 6 g
- Fiber: 4 g
- Protein: 7 g
- Sodium: 67 mg

- Sugar: 40 g
- Saturated Fat: 3 g

90. Chocolate Pistachio Biscotti

"This recipe is more nutritious when adding cranberries."
Serving: 40 cookies. | Prep: 30m | Ready in: 60m

Ingredients

- 1/3 cup butter, softened
- 1 cup plus 1 tbsp. sugar, divided
- 3 large eggs
- 2 tsps. vanilla extract
- 2-3/4 cups all-purpose flour
- 1/3 cup baking cocoa
- 2-1/2 tsps. baking powder
- 1/2 tsp. ground cinnamon
- 1 cup (6 oz.) semisweet chocolate chips
- 1/2 cup pistachios
- 1/2 cup dried cranberries

Direction

- Preheat oven to 350°. In a large bowl, cream 1 cup sugar and butter until fluffy and light. Add eggs, one at a time; after each addition, beating well. Beat in vanilla. Mix cocoa, flour, cinnamon and baking powder; add flour mixture to the creamed mixture and mix well (dough will be sticky). Mix in cranberries, pistachios and chocolate chips.
- Split dough into four portions. On ungreased baking sheets, shape portions into rectangles of 10x2-1/2-inch. Use the rest sugar to sprinkle. Bake for nearly 20 to 25 minutes or until set. Take away to wire racks carefully; allow 5 minutes for cooling.
- Place to a cutting board; cut each rectangle into 10 slices. On ungreased baking sheets, place them with cut side down. Bake for approximate 5 to 8 minutes on each side or until browned lightly. Take away to wire racks for cooling. Place in an airtight container for storing.

Nutrition Information

- Calories: 107 calories
- Total Carbohydrate: 17 g
- Cholesterol: 20 mg
- Total Fat: 4 g
- Fiber: 1 g
- Protein: 2 g
- Sodium: 48 mg

91. Chocolate Souffles

"Bake for 2-3 extra minutes if soufflé was made ahead and refrigerated. Or, rest soufflés for 1/2 hour in room temperature before baking with no extra cooking time."
Serving: Makes 6 servings

Ingredients

- 1 tbsp. unsalted butter, softened
- 10 1/2 oz. (10 squares) extra-bittersweet chocolate
- 1 1/3 cups whole milk
- 1 tbsp. cornstarch
- 3 large egg yolks, room temperature, lightly beaten
- 6 large egg whites, room temperature
- 1/3 cup sugar; more for soufflé ramekins

Direction

- Heat an oven to 400°. Butter then flour 6 6-oz. soufflé ramekins. Put on rimmed baking sheet; put aside.
- Melt chocolate till smooth in double boiler above medium heat. Take off heat; keep warm.
- Mix cornstarch and milk well to blend with a wooden spoon in a heavy-bottom medium saucepan; boil on medium heat till thick, continuously mixing.
- Take off heat; mix in warm melted chocolate. Slightly cool. Put in lightly beaten egg yolks; mix till combined well.
- Whip egg whites at medium speed till foamy in a heavy-duty mixer's bowl. Add sugar

slowly; put speed on high. Whip for 3 minutes till stiff and shiny peaks form.
- Lighten chocolate mixture with 1/3 beaten egg whites using a whisk; mix till combined well. Fold in leftover egg whites till just incorporated using a big rubber spatula.
- Put mixture in prepped soufflé ramekins; should reach ramekin's top. Put filled soufflé ramekins onto rimmed baking sheet in oven; bake for 12-15 minutes till risen. Immediately serve.

Nutrition Information

- Calories: 381
- Total Carbohydrate: 47 g
- Cholesterol: 103 mg
- Total Fat: 21 g
- Fiber: 3 g
- Protein: 9 g
- Sodium: 88 mg
- Saturated Fat: 12 g

92. Chocolate-filled Raspberry Meringues

"Meringue cups with fluffy chocolate mousse filling."
Serving: 8 servings. | Prep: 15m | Ready in: 60m

Ingredients

- 3 egg whites
- 1/4 tsp. cream of tartar
- 3 tbsps. raspberry gelatin powder
- 3/4 cup sugar
- 4 oz. German sweet chocolate, chopped
- 3 tbsps. water
- 1/2 cup cold fat-free milk
- 1-1/2 tsps. vanilla extract
- 1 envelope whipped topping mix (Dream Whip)
- 3/4 cup fresh raspberries

Direction

- In a bowl, put the egg whites and allow to stand for half an hour at room temperature. Beat the cream of tartar and egg whites on medium speed, until it forms soft peaks. Slowly beat in the gelatin. Put in sugar, a tbsp. at a time, and beat it on high until the sugar dissolves and forms stiff peaks.
- Drop the meringue to 8 mounds on the baking tray lined with parchment. Using the back of a spoon, form it into 3 1/2 cups. Let it bake for 45 minutes at 250 degrees. Turn off the oven, then leave the meringues in the oven for 1 to 1 1/2 hours.
- To make the filling, melt the chocolate with water in the microwave, then mix until it becomes smooth. Let it cool. Beat the whipped topping mix, vanilla and milk in a small bowl, until it forms soft peaks, then fold it into the melted chocolate. Scoop into the meringue cups. Let it chill in the fridge until ready to serve. Put raspberries on as garnish.

Nutrition Information

- Calories: 205 calories
- Total Carbohydrate: 39 g
- Cholesterol: 0 mg
- Total Fat: 5 g
- Fiber: 1 g
- Protein: 4 g
- Sodium: 41 mg

93. Chocolate-glazed Brownies

"Decadent but low-fat dessert."
Serving: 1 dozen. | Prep: 15m | Ready in: 35m

Ingredients

- 1/3 cup butter, softened
- 1 cup sugar
- 1 tsp. vanilla extract
- 3 large egg whites
- 2/3 cup all-purpose flour

- 1/2 cup baking cocoa
- 1/2 tsp. baking powder
- 1/4 tsp. salt
- GLAZE:
- 2/3 cup confectioners' sugar
- 2 tbsps. baking cocoa
- 1/4 tsp. vanilla extract
- 3 to 4 tsps. hot water

Direction

- Set oven to preheat at 350°. Cream together sugar and butter until fluffy and light. Beat in egg whites and vanilla, one by one. In a small bowl, whisk salt, baking powder, cocoa and flour together; add to the creamed mixture slowly. Spread out into a cooking spray-coated 8-in. square baking pan.
- Bake until tested done with a toothpick, about 20-25 minutes. Allow to cool on a wire rack thoroughly.
- Combine the glaze ingredients; spread on top of the brownies. Slice into bars.

Nutrition Information

- Calories: 180 calories
- Total Carbohydrate: 31 g
- Cholesterol: 14 mg
- Total Fat: 6 g
- Fiber: 1 g
- Protein: 3 g
- Sodium: 124 mg

94. Chocolate-raspberry Mousse Pie

"A light raspberry mousse."
Serving: 8 servings. | Prep: 25m | Ready in: 35m

Ingredients

- 10 whole reduced-fat graham crackers
- 1 egg white
- 2 tbsps. butter, melted
- 1/2 cup semisweet chocolate chips
- 1 envelope unflavored gelatin
- 1/2 cup cold water
- 2-1/2 cups fresh raspberries
- 4 oz. reduced-fat cream cheese, cubed
- 1/2 cup sugar
- 1/2 cup nonfat dry milk powder
- 1/2 cup ice-cold water
- 2 tbsps. lemon juice

Direction

- Process graham crackers till fine crumbs form in food processor, covered. Add butter and egg white; process till blended, covered. Pat up sides and bottom of 9-in. pie plate coated in cooking spray.
- Bake for 8-10 minutes at 350° or till set. Sprinkle chocolate chips; stand for 1-2 minutes then spread melted chips on crust. On wire rack, cool.
- Sprinkle gelatin on cold water in small saucepan; stand for a minute. Heat on low heat, mixing till gelatin is completely melted. Take off heat; put aside.
- In food processor, puree raspberries; strain then discard seeds. Put puree back in food processor. Add sugar and cream cheese; process till smooth, covered. Add gelatin mixture; process till blended, covered. Put in big bowl; refrigerate, covered, till partially set or for 40 minutes.
- Beat ice-cold water and milk powder on high speed for 7 minutes till soft peaks form in small bowl; beat lemon juice in. Mix 1/3 mixture into raspberry mixture; fold leftover milk mixture in. Evenly spread in crust; cover. Refrigerate for 3 hours minimum.

Nutrition Information

- Calories: 231 calories
- Total Carbohydrate: 33 g
- Cholesterol: 19 mg
- Total Fat: 10 g
- Fiber: 4 g
- Protein: 7 g
- Sodium: 170 mg

95. Chocolaty Zucchini Cake

"This chocolate cake that my mom always makes tastes wonderful. They especially come in handy when you need to use up zucchini."
Serving: 14 servings. | Prep: 15m | Ready in: 01h20m

Ingredients

- 4 eggs
- 3 cups sugar
- 1-1/2 cups vegetable oil
- 3 oz. unsweetened chocolate, melted and cooled
- 3 cups all-purpose flour
- 1-1/2 tsps. baking powder
- 1 tsp. baking soda
- 1 tsp. salt
- 3 cups shredded zucchini, squeezed dry
- 1 cup finely chopped nuts

Direction

- Beat eggs in a bowl on high until they turn into a lemon color and thick. Slowly beat in sugar. Put in chocolate and oil then beat thoroughly. Mix together salt, baking soda, baking powder and flour; pour into the beaten mixture. On low, beat the mixture just until incorporated. Mix in nuts and zucchini.
- Transfer batter to a 10-inch fluted tube pan that is already greased and floured. Bake in 350-degree oven until a toothpick is clean when coming out of the middle, or 65 to 75 minutes. Allow to cool for 10 minutes, then transfer to a wire rack and finish cooling.

Nutrition Information

- Calories: 580 calories
- Total Carbohydrate: 68 g
- Cholesterol: 61 mg
- Total Fat: 33 g
- Fiber: 2 g
- Protein: 7 g
- Sodium: 302 mg

96. Chunky Banana Chip Ice Cream

"This ice cream is very smooth with a sprinkle of semisweet chocolate chips on top."
Serving: 8 servings. | Prep: 15m | Ready in: 35m

Ingredients

- 2 cups 2% milk
- 1 can (14 oz.) fat-free sweetened condensed milk
- 1 envelope whipped topping mix (Dream Whip)
- 2 tbsps. sugar
- 2 tsps. lemon juice
- 1 tsp. vanilla extract
- 3 medium firm bananas, cut into 1-inch pieces
- 1/2 cup miniature semisweet chocolate chips

Direction

- Whisk the first 6 ingredients in a big bowl on high speed for 3 minutes. Put a cover on and chill overnight.
- Mix bananas into the milk mixture. Fill the cylinder of ice cream freezer; freeze following the manufacturer's instructions. Mix in chocolate chips. Let firm up in the fridge freezer or ripen in the ice cream freezer before enjoying, 2-4 hours.

Nutrition Information

- Calories: 301 calories
- Total Carbohydrate: 57 g
- Cholesterol: 8 mg
- Total Fat: 5 g
- Fiber: 2 g
- Protein: 7 g
- Sodium: 84 mg

97. Cinnamon Peach Crisp

"Sweet taste from fresh peaches will make you love this dish."
Serving: 6 servings. | Prep: 15m | Ready in: 55m

Ingredients

- 4 cups sliced peeled fresh peaches
- 1/2 cup orange juice
- 2 tbsps. brown sugar
- 1/2 tsp. ground cinnamon
- 1 cup all-purpose flour
- 1/3 cup sugar
- 1 tsp. baking powder
- 1 egg, lightly beaten
- 2 tbsps. butter, melted
- CINNAMON-SUGAR:
- 1-1/2 tsps. sugar
- 1/8 tsp. ground cinnamon

Direction

- Combine cinnamon, brown sugar, orange juice, and peaches in a bowl. Pour into an 8-inch square baking dish greased with cooking spray. Mix together baking powder, sugar and flour; add butter and egg; blend until crumbly. Drizzle over peaches.
- Combine cinnamon and sugar; scatter over the crumb mixture. Bake at 350 degrees till topping is golden brown and filling is bubbly, about 40-45 minutes. Serve while still warm.

Nutrition Information

- Calories: 245 calories
- Total Carbohydrate: 48 g
- Cholesterol: 46 mg
- Total Fat: 5 g
- Fiber: 3 g
- Protein: 4 g
- Sodium: 90 mg

98. Cinnamon-cranberry Oat Bars

"These kid-loving bars serve as a snack."
Serving: 16 servings. | Prep: 15m | Ready in: 20m

Ingredients

- 3 cups quick-cooking oats
- 1-1/2 cups Rice Krispies
- 1 cup dried cranberries
- 1/2 cup ground flaxseed
- 1-1/4 tsps. ground cinnamon, divided
- 1/2 tsp. ground nutmeg
- 1/2 cup packed brown sugar
- 1/2 cup light corn syrup
- 1/4 cup canola oil
- 1/4 cup honey
- 1 tsp. vanilla extract
- 1/4 tsp. salt
- 2 tsps. sugar

Direction

- In a large bowl, combine the Rice Krispies, oats, flax, cranberries, nutmeg and 1 tsp. cinnamon.
- In a large saucepan, combine the corn syrup, brown sugar, honey and oil; cook and stir over medium heat till sugar is dissolved. Take away from the heat; mix in salt and vanilla.
- Blend in oat mixture; coat by tossing. Press into a pan of 9-inch square firmly coated with cooking spray. Combine the remaining cinnamon and sugar; sprinkle over bars. Let it cool completely. Cut into bars.

Nutrition Information

- Calories: 211 calories
- Total Carbohydrate: 40 g
- Cholesterol: 0 mg
- Total Fat: 6 g
- Fiber: 3 g
- Protein: 3 g
- Sodium: 72 mg

99. Citrus Meringue Pie

"Beautiful meringue pie featuring lemon juice, orange and grapefruit."
Serving: 8 servings. | Prep: 10m | Ready in: 40m

Ingredients

- 3 large egg whites
- 6 tbsps. sugar
- 1 tbsp. water
- 1/4 tsp. plus 1/8 tsp. cream of tartar
- 1-1/2 tsps. cornstarch
- 2 tbsps. plus 1-1/2 tsps. cold water
- 1/2 tsp. vanilla extract
- 1/8 tsp. salt
- FILLING:
- 2/3 cup sugar
- 3 tbsps. cornstarch
- 1 cup grapefruit juice
- 1/2 cup water
- 1/4 cup orange juice
- 1 tbsp. lemon juice
- 1 large egg
- 1 large egg white
- 1 tsp. grated grapefruit zest
- 7 drops yellow food coloring, optional
- 1 pastry shell (9 inches), baked

Direction

- Mix together the cream of tartar, water, sugar and egg whites in a heavy saucepan, then heat it on low heat as you beat it for 1 minute on low speed using a portable mixer, then scrape down the pan's sides. Keep on beating until the mixture reaches 160 degrees. Take it out of the heat.
- Mix together the cold water and cornstarch in a small saucepan, until it becomes smooth, then boil. Let it cook and stir for 1 to 2 minutes or until it becomes thick. Take it out of the heat and let it cool for a minute. Whisk it into the egg white mixture, then add salt and vanilla. Beat it on high until it forms stiff peaks. Put aside the meringue.
- To make the filling, mix together the cornstarch and sugar in a big saucepan. Slowly add the lemon juice, orange juice, water and grapefruit juice, until it becomes smooth, then boil on medium-high heat. Let it cook and stir until it becomes thick or for 2 minutes. Take it out of the heat.
- Whisk the egg white and egg together in a small bowl, then slowly mix in half a cup of hot filling into the egg mixture, then put it all back into the pan, mixing continuously. Let it gently boil, then cook and stir for 2 minutes. Take it out of the heat and mix in food coloring, if preferred and grapefruit zest. Pour the hot filling on the crust.
- Evenly spread the meringue on top of the hot filling and seal the edges to crust. Let it boil for 30 to 60 seconds or until the meringue turns golden brown in color. Allow to cool on a wire rack. Let it chill in the fridge for a minimum of 3 hours prior to serving. Keep the leftovers in the fridge.

Nutrition Information

- Calories: 254 calories
- Total Carbohydrate: 42 g
- Cholesterol: 32 mg
- Total Fat: 8 g
- Fiber: 1 g
- Protein: 4 g
- Sodium: 173 mg

100. Cocoa Banana Cupcakes

"Adding the cocoa powder into the frosting enhances its chocolate flavor while adding the melted chocolate provides a creamy texture which makes it much easier to spread."
Serving: 1-1/2 dozen. | Prep: 25m | Ready in: 45m

Ingredients

- 2 cups all-purpose flour
- 1 cup sugar
- 1/2 cup baking cocoa
- 1 tsp. baking powder
- 1/2 tsp. each baking soda and salt
- 2 eggs

- 1-1/4 cups fat-free milk
- 1 cup mashed ripe banana (2 to 3 medium)
- 3 tbsps. canola oil
- 1 tsp. vanilla extract
- FROSTING:
- 4 oz. reduced-fat cream cheese
- 3 tbsps. fat-free milk
- 2 oz. semisweet chocolate, melted and cooled
- 1 tsp. vanilla extract
- 2 cups confectioners' sugar
- 1/3 cup baking cocoa

Direction

- Mix all the dry ingredients in a bowl. In a separate bowl, mix the vanilla, eggs, oil, milk, and banana and whisk the mixture into the dry ingredients until just moistened.
- Use the cooking spray to coat the muffin cups or paper liners to line the cups. Fill the cups with the mixture, about 3/4 full. Bake them at 375° for 18 to 20 minutes until the toothpick will come out clean. Let them cool for 5 minutes. Place them on wire racks and let them cool completely.
- Whisk the vanilla, cream cheese, chocolate, and milk until smooth. Mix the cocoa and confectioners' sugar and beat the mixture gradually into the cream cheese mixture. Use this to frost the cupcakes.

Nutrition Information

- Calories: 224 calories
- Total Carbohydrate: 40 g
- Cholesterol: 29 mg
- Total Fat: 6 g
- Fiber: 2 g
- Protein: 4 g
- Sodium: 171 mg

101. Cocoa-almond Meringue Cookies

"Delicious coconut, almond and chocolate treats."
Serving: 3 dozen. | Prep: 20m | Ready in: 01h10m

Ingredients

- 4 egg whites
- 1/2 tsp. coconut extract
- 1/4 tsp. almond extract
- 1/4 tsp. vanilla extract
- 1/4 tsp. cream of tartar
- 1/8 tsp. salt
- 1 cup sugar
- 1/4 cup plus 1 tbsp. baking cocoa, divided

Direction

- In a big bowl, put the egg whites and allow to stand for half an hour at room temperature. Add the salt, cream of tartar and extracts and beat it on medium speed, until it forms soft peaks. Slowly beat in the sugar, a tbsp. at a time, on high until the sugar dissolves and forms stiff peaks.
- Fold in a quarter cup of cocoa. In a heavy-duty resealable plastic bag or pastry bag, put the mixture, then snip off a small hole in the bag's corner. Pipe the meringue on the baking trays lined with parchment paper in 2-inch rounds. Let it bake for 50 to 60 minutes at 250 degrees or until it becomes dry and set. Turn the oven off and leave the cookies inside the oven for 1 1/2 hours.
- Dust the leftover cocoa on the cookies, then take it out from the parchment paper carefully. Keep it in an airtight container.

Nutrition Information

- Calories: 26 calories
- Total Carbohydrate: 6 g
- Cholesterol: 0 mg
- Total Fat: 0 g
- Fiber: 0 g
- Protein: 1 g
- Sodium: 14 mg

102. Coconut Banana Chocolate Cream Pie

"Easy to make and filled with amazing ingredients."
Serving: 8 servings. | Prep: 20m | Ready in: 20m

Ingredients

- 1-1/3 cups cold water
- 2/3 cup nonfat dry milk powder
- 1 package (1.4 oz.) sugar-free instant chocolate pudding mix
- 1 cup reduced-fat whipped topping, divided
- 1/2 tsp. coconut extract, divided
- 2 medium ripe bananas, cut into 1/4-inch slices
- 1 chocolate crumb crust (9 inches)
- 1 tbsp. sweetened shredded coconut, toasted

Direction

- Stir water and milk powder together in a bowl until the powder dissolves. Add pudding mix into the liquid; whisk until thickened, or for 1-2 minutes. Fold 1/4 cup whipped topping and 1/4 tsp. extract into the mixture. Layer the banana slices into the crust; add the pudding mixture on top. Cover then place in the refrigerator.
- Mix together the extract and rest of the whipped topping; spread on top of the pudding. Sprinkle coconut on top. Refrigerate, covered, for no less than 1 hour before serving.

Nutrition Information

- Calories: 172 calories
- Total Carbohydrate: 28 g
- Cholesterol: 1 mg
- Total Fat: 5 g
- Fiber: 2 g
- Protein: 4 g
- Sodium: 172 mg

103. Coconut Pineapple Pops

"Creamy, sunny and tropical frozen treats featuring coconut and pineapple for those hot days."
Serving: 14 servings. | Prep: 10m | Ready in: 10m

Ingredients

- 1-1/2 cups cold 2% milk
- 1 can (8 oz.) unsweetened crushed pineapple
- 1 can (6 oz.) unsweetened pineapple juice
- 1 tsp. coconut extract
- 1 package (3.4 oz.) instant vanilla pudding mix
- 14 freezer pop molds or 14 paper cups (3 oz. each) and wooden pop sticks

Direction

- Blend pineapple extract and juice, pineapple, and milk in a blender with cover until smooth. Move to a bowl; stir in pudding mix for 2mins.
- Scoop a quarter cup of mixture into each paper cup or mold; add holders on top. Place foil on top then put in sticks through if using cups. Place in the freezer until solid.

Nutrition Information

- Calories: 56 calories
- Total Carbohydrate: 12 g
- Cholesterol: 2 mg
- Total Fat: 1 g
- Fiber: 0 g
- Protein: 1 g
- Sodium: 96 mg

104. Coffee Jelly

"You may enjoy this yummy dessert served with chocolate sauce and frozen whipped cream, or with regular whipped cream, coffee-flavored cream or ice cream. You may either serve it in cubed pieces in bowls or set in glasses."
Serving: 4 | Prep: 5m | Ready in: 6h10m

Ingredients

- 1 (.25 oz.) package unflavored gelatin

- 2 tbsps. hot water
- 3 tbsps. white sugar
- 2 cups fresh brewed coffee

Direction

- In a small bowl, allow the gelatin to dissolve in hot water. In a saucepan, put the coffee, sugar and dissolved gelatin mixture and let the mixture boil over high heat setting. You may either transfer the prepared coffee mixture into a big pan to be sliced into cubes afterwards or into glasses for individual servings. Keep it in the fridge for 6-7 hours until it becomes solid.

Nutrition Information

- Calories: 43 calories;
- Total Carbohydrate: 9.4 g
- Cholesterol: 0 mg
- Total Fat: 0 g
- Protein: 1.6 g
- Sodium: 6 mg

105. Comforting Creamy Banana Pudding

"A comforting holiday treat."
Serving: 10 servings. | Prep: 15m | Ready in: 15m

Ingredients

- 3 cups cold fat-free milk
- 2 packages (1 oz. each) sugar-free instant vanilla pudding mix
- 1 cup (8 oz.) fat-free sour cream
- 1 carton (8 oz.) frozen fat-free whipped topping, thawed
- 34 vanilla wafers
- 3 large firm bananas, sliced

Direction

- Whisk pudding mixes and milk till slightly thick for 2 minutes in a bowl; mix in sour cream. Fold in the whipped topping till well blended. Put 1/2 vanilla wafers into 11x7-in. dish; put 1/2 pudding mixture, 1/2 bananas then leftover wafers, bananas and the pudding mixture over. Cover; refrigerate overnight.

Nutrition Information

- Calories: 210 calories
- Total Carbohydrate: 39 g
- Cholesterol: 2 mg
- Total Fat: 3 g
- Fiber: 1 g
- Protein: 5 g
- Sodium: 358 mg

106. Cool Mandarin Dessert

"This dessert looks good and tastes great."
Serving: 10 servings. | Prep: 20m | Ready in: 20m

Ingredients

- 1 can (11 oz.) mandarin oranges
- 2 packages (.3 oz. each) sugar-free orange gelatin
- 2 cups boiling water
- 1 pint orange sherbet, softened
- Fresh mint, optional

Direction

- Drain the oranges, saving juice. Pour enough water into juice to measure one cup. Place the oranges in the refrigerator.
- Dissolve gelatin in large bowl of boiling water. Mix in the reserved juice. Put in sherbet, stir until it has dissolved. Place in the refrigerator until thickened, about 60 mins.
- For garnish, keep ten orange segments refrigerated. Fold the remaining oranges into the gelatin mixture; refrigerate overnight, covered. If desired, decorate with mint and reserved oranges. Then serve.

Nutrition Information

- Calories: 134 calories
- Total Carbohydrate: 15 g

- Cholesterol: 2 mg
- Total Fat: 1 g
- Fiber: 1 g
- Protein: 7 g
- Sodium: 462 mg

107. Cool Raspberry Peach Pie

""An awesome combination of raspberries and peaches in one recipe.""
Serving: 8 servings. | Prep: 30m | Ready in: 30m

Ingredients

- 1-1/2 cups crushed reduced-fat vanilla wafers (about 45 wafers)
- 2 tbsps. sugar
- 2 tbsps. butter
- 1 egg white
- FILLING:
- 1/2 cup sugar
- 3 tbsps. cornstarch
- 1/4 cup water
- 4 cups sliced peeled fresh peaches or frozen unsweetened peach slices, thawed (about 1-1/2 lbs.)
- 3 cups fresh raspberries

Direction

- Mix butter, sugar and wafer crumbs in a food processor; pulse till blended. Put in egg white; pulse till moistened.
- Press the mixture onto the bottom and up the sides of a 9-in. pie plate. Bake at 375° till slightly browned, 8-10 minutes. Remove onto a wire rack to cool completely.
- Mix cornstarch and sugar in a large saucepan. Mix in water till smooth. Put in peaches; mix to coat. Boil the mixture; cook while stirring till thickened, 2 minutes. Take away from the heat; gently mix in raspberries. Scoop into the prepared crust. Chill till set. Chill any leftovers in a refrigerator.

Nutrition Information

- Calories: 252 calories
- Total Carbohydrate: 52 g
- Cholesterol: 8 mg
- Total Fat: 5 g
- Fiber: 5 g
- Protein: 2 g
- Sodium: 119 mg

108. Cran-apple Crisp

"This recipe will get a lot of asking for its rich flavor."
Serving: 15 servings. | Prep: 20m | Ready in: 60m

Ingredients

- 8 cups thinly sliced peeled tart apples (about 5 large)
- 3/4 cup sugar
- 1/2 cup dried cranberries
- 1/2 cup chopped walnuts
- 1/4 cup all-purpose flour
- 1-1/2 to 2 tsps. grated orange zest
- TOPPING:
- 1/2 cup packed brown sugar
- 1/3 cup whole wheat flour
- 1/3 cup nonfat dry milk powder
- 1 tsp. ground cinnamon
- 1/4 to 1/2 tsp. cloves
- 5 tbsps. cold butter, cubed
- 1/3 cup quick-cooking oats

Direction

- Preheat oven to 350°. In a large bowl, place the first six ingredients; combine by tossing. Place to a baking dish of 13x9-inch coated with cooking spray.
- Mix the first five topping ingredients; cut in butter until mixture resembles coarse crumbs. Mix in oats. Sprinkle over apple mixture.
- Bake without a cover for nearly 40-45 minutes till it has the color of golden brown and apples are soft.

Nutrition Information

- Calories: 200 calories
- Total Carbohydrate: 35 g
- Cholesterol: 10 mg
- Total Fat: 7 g
- Fiber: 2 g
- Protein: 2 g
- Sodium: 42 mg

109. Cran-apple Praline Gingerbread

"A great dessert with the complicated combination of a spice-rich batter baked atop apples and cranberries in a creamy caramel sauce."
Serving: 8 servings. | Prep: 25m | Ready in: 55m

Ingredients

- 2/3 cup fat-free caramel ice cream topping
- 2 medium tart apples, peeled and thinly sliced
- 2/3 cup fresh or frozen cranberries
- 1/4 cup butter, softened
- 1/4 cup sugar
- 1 egg
- 6 tbsps. molasses
- 1/4 cup unsweetened applesauce
- 1-1/2 cups all-purpose flour
- 3/4 tsp. baking soda
- 1/2 tsp. ground ginger
- 1/2 tsp. apple pie spice
- 1/4 tsp. salt
- 1/4 cup hot water
- YOGURT CREAM:
- 3/4 cup reduced-fat whipped topping
- 1/2 cup fat-free vanilla yogurt

Direction

- Use cooking spray to coat a 9-inch round baking pan. Drizzle pan with caramel topping and tilt to coat the bottom of pan evenly. Place a single layer of apples and cranberries over caramel.
- Beat sugar and butter in a big bowl for 2 minutes, until crumbly. Put in egg and blend well. Beat in applesauce and molasses; mixture will might look curdled. Mix together salt, pie spice, ginger, baking soda and flour, then put into the butter mixture just until moisten. Add hot water and stir.
- Drizzle over fruit and smooth the top. Bake at 350 degrees until a toothpick pricked in the center exits clean, about 30 to 35 minutes. Allow to cool about 10 minutes, then invert onto a serving plate. Mix yogurt and whipped topping together, then serve together with gingerbread.

Nutrition Information

- Calories: 289 calories
- Total Carbohydrate: 53 g
- Cholesterol: 42 mg
- Total Fat: 7 g
- Fiber: 2 g
- Protein: 4 g
- Sodium: 284 mg

110. Cranberry Apple Gelatin Mold

"You can also eat this with pork roast!"
Serving: 12 | Prep: 10m | Ready in: 8h20m

Ingredients

- 1 (16 oz.) can whole cranberry sauce
- 1 cup water
- 2 (3 oz.) packages raspberry flavored Jell-O® mix
- 1/4 tsp. salt
- 2 apples, cored and diced with peel
- 2 oranges, peeled, sectioned, and chopped
- 1/2 cup chopped walnuts
- 1 cup lemon yogurt

Direction

- In a saucepan, combine water and cranberry sauce over medium heat. Heat until the sauce is melted. Mix in gelatin until dissolved. Take

off the heat. Mix in yogurt, walnuts, oranges, and apples.
- Add the mixture into a nice bowl or a fancy gelatin mold, and chill in refrigerator overnight. Briefly dip in hot water, and flip onto a serving dish to serve.

Nutrition Information

- Calories: 180 calories;
- Total Carbohydrate: 36.7 g
- Cholesterol: < 1 mg
- Total Fat: 3.3 g
- Protein: 3.4 g
- Sodium: 122 mg

111. Cranberry Cheesecake Bars

"Great for the holidays!"
Serving: 16 | Prep: 15m | Ready in: 50m

Ingredients

- Crust:
- 1 (18.25 oz.) package butter cake mix
- 1/2 cup butter, softened
- 1 egg
- 1/4 cup chopped pecans
- Filling:
- 1 (8 oz.) package cream cheese, softened
- 1/4 cup confectioners' sugar
- 1 egg
- 1/2 tsp. vanilla extract
- 1 (16 oz.) can whole berry cranberry sauce
- 1/4 tsp. ground nutmeg

Direction

- Preheat an oven to 175°C (350°F).
- Beat 1 egg, butter and cake mix using electric mixer at low speed till crumbly in a bowl; mix in pecans. Press it into 9x13-in. baking dish.
- In preheated oven, bake for 5-8 minutes till crust is set.
- Beat vanilla extract, 1 egg, confectioners' sugar and cream cheese using an electric mixer till smooth in a bowl. Mix nutmeg and cranberry sauce in another bowl. Spread cream cheese mixture carefully onto crust; in 3 lengthwise rows, scoop cranberry sauce mixture over cream cheese mixture. Through cranberry sauce mixture, pull a knife in cream cheese mixture to make swirls.
- In preheated oven, bake for 30-40 minutes till cream cheese mixture sets; completely cool. Cut to bars.

Nutrition Information

- Calories: 294 calories;
- Total Carbohydrate: 39 g
- Cholesterol: 53 mg
- Total Fat: 14.7 g
- Protein: 2.8 g
- Sodium: 297 mg

112. Cranberry Crumb Cake

"An easy to make and light cranberry cake with streusel topping."
Serving: 9 servings. | Prep: 20m | Ready in: 55m

Ingredients

- 1 cup all-purpose flour
- 1/2 cup plus 1/3 cup sugar, divided
- 2 tsps. baking powder
- 1/2 tsp. salt
- 1 egg, lightly beaten
- 1/2 cup fat-free milk
- 1 tbsp. orange juice
- 1 tbsp. canola oil
- 1/4 tsp. almond extract
- 2 cups fresh or frozen cranberries, chopped
- TOPPING:
- 1/4 cup all-purpose flour
- 3 tbsps. sugar
- 2 tbsps. cold butter

Direction

- Mix together the salt, baking powder, half a cup of sugar and flour in a big bowl. Mix together the extract, oil, orange juice, milk and egg, then mix it into the dry ingredients. Scoop into a cooking spray coated 8-inch square baking dish. Mix together the leftover sugar and cranberries, then scoop on top of the batter.
- To make the topping, in a small bowl, mix together the sugar and flour, then slice in the butter until it becomes crumbly. Sprinkle on top of the cranberries. Let it bake for 35 to 45 minutes at 375 degrees or until the edges start to pull away from the pan's sides. Put the leftovers in the fridge.

Nutrition Information

- Calories: 212 calories
- Total Carbohydrate: 40 g
- Cholesterol: 31 mg
- Total Fat: 5 g
- Fiber: 1 g
- Protein: 3 g
- Sodium: 203 mg

113. Cranberry Fudge

"The combination of cranberries and chocolate wins every time."
Serving: 16

Ingredients

- 1 (12 oz.) package fresh or frozen cranberries
- 1/2 cup light corn syrup
- 2 cups semisweet chocolate chips
- 1/2 cup confectioners' sugar
- 1/4 cup evaporated milk
- 1 tsp. vanilla extract

Direction

- Line plastic wrap on the bottom and sides of an 8x8-inch pan. Put aside.
- Bring corn syrup and cranberries in a medium saucepan to a boil. Boil on high until liquid is reduced to three tbsps., stirring occasionally, about 5-7 minutes. Take away from the heat.
- Add the chocolate chips immediately, stirring until they are completely melted. Put in the vanilla extract, evaporated milk, and confectioner's sugar, vigorously stirring until the mixture is glossy and thick. Transfer into the pan. Chill, covered, until firm.

Nutrition Information

- Calories: 229 calories;
- Total Carbohydrate: 35.8 g
- Cholesterol: 1 mg
- Total Fat: 8.8 g
- Protein: 2.5 g
- Sodium: 11 mg

114. Cranberry Gelatin Salad

"This Jell-O salad is so delicious."
Serving: 12 | Prep: 15m | Ready in: 1day25m

Ingredients

- 1 (16 oz.) can jellied cranberry sauce
- 1 (16.5 oz.) can pitted dark sweet cherries, drained
- 10 1/2 oz. crushed pineapple with juice
- 1 (6 oz.) package cherry Jell-O®
- 2 cups boiling water
- 1 cup chopped pecans (optional)

Direction

- On low heat, melt the cranberry sauce in a medium-sized saucepan.
- Chop the cherries into pieces and place them into the melted sauce. Mix in the pineapple juice and pineapple. Take mixture out of heat.
- Add boiling water on the gelatin in a medium-sized bowl. Mix till all gelatin has dissolved.
- Pour the gelatin mixture into the cranberry mixture and mix. Mix in the optional nuts.

Add to one 9x13-inch pan and keep chilled till set.

Nutrition Information

- Calories: 206 calories;
- Total Carbohydrate: 37 g
- Cholesterol: 0 mg
- Total Fat: 6.6 g
- Protein: 2.6 g
- Sodium: 77 mg

115. Cranberry Ice

""You'd never think that frozen cranberry sorbet squares would work with turkey, but my kids adore it!""
Serving: 12

Ingredients

- 2 (12 oz.) packages fresh cranberries
- 2 cups white sugar
- 1 1/4 cups fresh orange juice
- 1 cup fresh lemon juice

Direction

- Fill a large pot with cranberries and sufficient water to cover them then boil until the cranberries start to pop. Get rid of the water and put the solids through a food mill set over a big bowl. When still warm, dissolve sugar in the warm berries. Adjust the amount of sugar based on the tartness of the berries. Keep in mind that the mixture will taste tarter after it freezes up. After the sugar dissolves in the berries, mix in fresh squeezed lemon juice and fresh squeezed orange juice. Transfer the mixture into an 8-in. or 9-in. square pan and leave it to freeze overnight. Remove it from the freezer about 5 to 10 minutes before cutting.

Nutrition Information

- Calories: 171 calories;
- Total Carbohydrate: 44.6 g
- Cholesterol: 0 mg
- Total Fat: 0.1 g
- Protein: 0.5 g
- Sodium: 2 mg

116. Cranberry Oat Yummies

"These healthier oatmeal cookies treats are better than the standard chocolate chip cookies."
Serving: 3 dozen. | Prep: 20m | Ready in: 30m

Ingredients

- 1/2 cup butter, melted
- 1/2 cup sugar
- 1 cup packed brown sugar
- 1 egg
- 1/4 cup egg substitute
- 2 tbsps. corn syrup
- 1-1/2 tsps. vanilla extract
- 3 cups quick-cooking oats
- 1 cup all-purpose flour
- 1 tsp. baking soda
- 1 tsp. ground cinnamon
- 1/2 tsp. baking powder
- 1/2 tsp. salt
- 1/8 tsp. ground nutmeg
- 1 cup dried cranberries

Direction

- In a large bowl, beat sugars and butter. Put in egg substitute, egg, vanilla and corn syrup; thoroughly mix. Combine the flour, oats, cinnamon, baking soda, baking powder, nutmeg and salt; add to egg mixture gradually and mix well. Blend in cranberries.
- On ungreased baking sheets, drop by heaping tablespoonfuls placing 2 inches apart. Bake at 375° for nearly 8 to 10 minutes or until the cookies have the color of golden brown. Allow 2 minutes to cool before taking away from pans to wire racks.

Nutrition Information

- Calories: 109 calories
- Total Carbohydrate: 19 g
- Cholesterol: 13 mg
- Total Fat: 3 g
- Fiber: 1 g
- Protein: 2 g
- Sodium: 154 mg

117. Cranberry Pear Crisp Pie

"Crumb-topped dessert filled with pears and cranberries."
Serving: 8 servings. | Prep: 25m | Ready in: 01h20m

Ingredients

- 5 cups sliced peeled fresh pears
- 1 tbsp. lemon juice
- 1 tsp. vanilla extract
- 1-2/3 cups fresh or frozen cranberries
- 1/2 cup packed brown sugar
- 1/3 cup all-purpose flour
- Pastry for single-crust pie (9 inches)
- TOPPING:
- 1/4 cup all-purpose flour
- 1/4 cup quick-cooking oats
- 3 tbsps. packed brown sugar
- 3/4 tsp. ground cinnamon
- 2 tbsps. cold butter

Direction

- In a big bowl, put the pears, then sprinkle vanilla and lemon juice on top; put in cranberries. Mix together the flour and brown sugar, then sprinkle it on top of the fruit and toss it gently until coated.
- Roll out the crust until it fits the 9-inch pie plate, then move to the pie plate. Cut the crust to half an inch far off the plate's edge, then flute the edges; add the filling.
- Mix together the cinnamon, brown sugar, oats and flour in a small bowl. Slice in the butter until it becomes crumbly. Sprinkle atop the filling.
- Let it bake for 55 to 60 minutes at 375 degrees on the lower rack of the oven, then use foil to loosely cover the edge if necessary, to avoid overbrowning, until the filling becomes bubbly. Let it cool on a wire rack.

Nutrition Information

- Calories: 332 calories
- Total Carbohydrate: 58 g
- Cholesterol: 13 mg
- Total Fat: 11 g
- Fiber: 4 g
- Protein: 3 g
- Sodium: 137 mg

118. Cranberry Salad V

" "This is a refreshing side dish!" "
Serving: 9

Ingredients

- 1 (3 oz.) package lemon flavored Jell-O® mix
- 1 cup boiling water
- 1/2 cup white sugar
- 1 (12 oz.) package fresh cranberries
- 1 cup chopped celery
- 1/2 cup chopped walnuts
- 1 (15 oz.) can crushed pineapple

Direction

- In a food processor, chop the walnuts, cranberries, and celery lightly.
- Whisk the sugar, gelatin, and water. Stir the gelatin mixture, pineapple with its juice, and cranberry mixture thoroughly. Spread the mixture into the mold. Place it inside the fridge to set.
- Serve it on a lettuce leaf and add a dollop of mayonnaise.

Nutrition Information

- Calories: 167 calories;
- Total Carbohydrate: 32.3 g

- Cholesterol: 0 mg
- Total Fat: 4.3 g
- Protein: 2.3 g
- Sodium: 63 mg

119. Cranberry-chocolate Oatmeal Bars

"You can use dried cherries for cranberries and create drop cookies instead of making bars."
Serving: 16 servings. | Prep: 10m | Ready in: 30m

Ingredients

- 2 cups quick-cooking oats
- 1/2 cup whole wheat flour
- 2 oz. semisweet chocolate, grated
- 3/4 tsp. baking soda
- 1/2 tsp. ground cinnamon
- 1/4 tsp. salt
- 1/4 tsp. ground nutmeg
- 2 eggs
- 1 egg white
- Sugar substitute equivalent to 1/2 cup sugar
- 1/2 cup unsweetened applesauce
- 1/4 cup canola oil
- 2 tsps. vanilla extract
- 3/4 cup dried cranberries

Direction

- Mix initial 7 ingredients in big bowl. Whisk vanilla, oil, applesauce, sugar substitute, egg whites and eggs; mix into dry ingredients till just moist. Mix dried cranberries in.
- Spread in square 9-in. baking pan coated in cooking spray. Bake for 17-20 minutes till set at 350°. On wire rack, cool.

Nutrition Information

- Calories: 135 calories
- Total Carbohydrate: 18 g
- Cholesterol: 27 mg
- Total Fat: 6 g
- Fiber: 2 g
- Protein: 3 g
- Sodium: 108 mg

120. Cream-filled Strawberries

"These plump berries are so elegant-looking and luscious-tasting that are excellent for holiday gatherings."
Serving: 18 strawberries. | Prep: 30m | Ready in: 30m

Ingredients

- 18 large fresh strawberries
- 1 cup cold fat-free milk
- 1 package (1 oz.) sugar-free instant vanilla pudding mix
- 2 cups reduced-fat whipped topping
- 1/4 tsp. almond extract

Direction

- Get rid of the stems from strawberries. Cut in top of each berry a deep X shape, then spread the berries apart.
- Whisk together pudding mix and milk in a big bowl about 2 minutes; fold in whipped topping and almond extract. Pipe or scoop into each berry with about 5 tsp. mixture. Refrigerate until ready to serve.

Nutrition Information

- Calories: 36 calories
- Total Carbohydrate: 6 g
- Cholesterol: 1 mg
- Total Fat: 1 g
- Fiber: 1 g
- Protein: 1 g
- Sodium: 73 mg

121. Creamy Iced Applesauce Bars

"Serve this with a spoonful of dulce de leche!"
Serving: 4 | Prep: 10m | Ready in: 1h10m

Ingredients

- 2 cups applesauce
- 1/2 cup milk
- 1/2 cup warm water
- 1/2 cup orange juice
- 1/4 cup white sugar
- 1 tbsp. poppy seeds, or more to taste
- 1 pinch ground cinnamon
- 1 pinch ground nutmeg
- 1/4 cup dulce de leche, or more to taste

Direction

- In a blender, blend nutmeg, cinnamon, poppy seeds, orange juice, warm water, milk and applesauce until smooth. Put in a loaf pan. Use plastic wrap to cover it. Freeze for a minimum of 1-2 hours until very cold. Cut to bars or squares. Top with a mound of dulce de leche.

Nutrition Information

- Calories: 203 calories;
- Total Carbohydrate: 43.7 g
- Cholesterol: 5 mg
- Total Fat: 2.8 g
- Protein: 2.8 g
- Sodium: 57 mg

122. Crimson Crumble Bars

"Enjoy these crimson crumble bars as an afternoon snack."
Serving: 2 dozen. | Prep: 20m | Ready in: 45m

Ingredients

- 1 cup sugar
- 2 tsps. cornstarch
- 2 cups fresh or frozen cranberries
- 1 can (8 oz.) unsweetened crushed pineapple, undrained
- 1 cup all-purpose flour
- 2/3 cup old-fashioned oats
- 2/3 cup packed brown sugar
- 1/4 tsp. salt
- 1/2 cup cold butter, cubed
- 1/2 cup chopped pecans

Direction

- Mix pineapple, cranberries, cornstarch and sugar in a big saucepan; boil and stir constantly. Lower the heat; simmer, covered, for 10 to 15 minutes until berries pop. Put away from the heat.
- Blend salt, brown sugar, oats and flour in a large bowl. Cut butter into the mixture until crumbly and coarse. Mix in pecans. Put aside 1.5 cups for topping.
- Spread the rest of crumb mixture to the bottom of a greased 13x9" baking pan. Bake for 8 to 10 minutes at 350 degrees until stiff; let cool for 10 minutes.
- Cover the crust with fruit filling. Add a sprinkle of crumb mixture reserved earlier. Bake until golden brown, 25 to 30 minutes more. Let cool on a wire rack.

Nutrition Information

- Calories: 152 calories
- Total Carbohydrate: 24 g
- Cholesterol: 10 mg
- Total Fat: 6 g
- Fiber: 1 g
- Protein: 2 g
- Sodium: 67 mg

123. Crinkle-top Chocolate Cookies

"Moist and fudgy cookies."
Serving: about 3-1/2 dozen. | Prep: 15m | Ready in: 25m

Ingredients

- 2 cups (about 12 oz.) semisweet chocolate chips, divided
- 2 tbsps. butter, softened

- 1 cup sugar
- 2 large egg whites
- 1-1/2 tsps. vanilla extract
- 1-1/2 cups all-purpose flour
- 1-1/2 tsps. baking powder
- 1/4 tsp. salt
- 1/4 cup water
- 1/2 cup confectioners' sugar

Direction

- Melt 1 cup chocolate chips in microwave. Mix till smooth; put aside. Beat sugar and butter for 2 minutes till crumbly. Add vanilla and egg whites; beat well. Mix melted chocolate in.
- Whisk salt, baking powder and flour in separate bowl; alternately with water, add to butter mixture slowly. Mix leftover chocolate chips in. Refrigerate for 2 hours till easy to handle, covered.
- Preheat an oven to 350°; form dough to 1-in. balls then roll in confectioners' sugar. Put on baking sheets that are coated in cooking spray, 2-in. apart. Bake for 10-12 minutes till set. Transfer to wire racks; cool.

Nutrition Information

- Calories: 85 calories
- Total Carbohydrate: 15 g
- Cholesterol: 1 mg
- Total Fat: 3 g
- Fiber: 1 g
- Protein: 1 g
- Sodium: 39 mg

124. Crispy Oat Cookies

"Tasty cookie recipe that has been the family's favorite."
Serving: 8 dozen. | Prep: 20m | Ready in: 30m

Ingredients

- 1 cup butter, softened
- 1 cup vegetable oil
- 1-1/3 cups sugar, divided

- 1 egg
- 1 tsp. vanilla extract
- 3-1/2 cups all-purpose flour
- 1 tsp. baking soda
- 1 tsp. cream of tartar
- 1 tsp. salt
- 1 cup crisp rice cereal
- 1 cup quick-cooking oats
- 1 cup sweetened shredded coconut
- 1 cup chopped walnuts

Direction

- Beat 1 cup sugar, oil and butter in a bowl and beat in the vanilla and egg. Mix together the salt, cream of tartar, baking soda and flour, then slowly add into the butter mixture. Mix in the nuts, coconut, oats and cereal.
- Roll it into 1-inch balls and roll it in some of the leftover sugar. Put it on the baking trays that were ungreased and place it two inches apart. Use a glass dipped in the leftover sugar to flatten it, then let it bake for 10 to 12 minutes at 350 degrees, until it turns light brown. Transfer to wire racks to let it cool.

Nutrition Information

- Calories: 82 calories
- Total Carbohydrate: 8 g
- Cholesterol: 7 mg
- Total Fat: 5 g
- Fiber: 0 g
- Protein: 1 g
- Sodium: 72 mg

125. Crunchy Pears

"Baked pears that are crisp-tender and coated with almond and cookie crumb."
Serving: 8 servings. | Prep: 20m | Ready in: 55m

Ingredients

- 8 large firm pears
- 1/2 cup orange juice

- 1/3 cup orange marmalade
- 1/3 cup crushed reduced-fat vanilla wafers (about 10 wafers)
- 1/3 cup finely chopped almonds
- 1 cup (8 oz.) fat-free reduced-sugar orange or plain yogurt

Direction

- Core the pears from the base and leave the stems undamaged. Take off the skin from the pears and leave a little amount of peel at the stem end. Slice a quarter inch from the base to make it level if needed. Mix together the marmalade and orange juice in a bowl, then scoop on top of the pears and let the extra drip into the bowl. Reserve for the sauce. In a big shallow dish, put the almonds and wafer crumbs. Roll the pears in the crumb mixture until the bottom 3/4 of every pear was coated.
- Put it in the cooking spray coated 13x9-inch baking dish. Let it bake for 35 to 45 minutes at 350 degrees or until it becomes tender. In the meantime, to make the sauce, mix together the reserved marmalade mixture and yogurt and let it chill in the fridge until ready to serve. Serve together with warm pears.

Nutrition Information

- Calories: 231 calories
- Total Carbohydrate: 46 g
- Cholesterol: 2 mg
- Total Fat: 5 g
- Fiber: 5 g
- Protein: 4 g
- Sodium: 55 mg

126. Crunchy Topped Chocolate Cake

"Nuts and coconut's light flavor blends perfectly with strong chocolate taste of this moist cake."
Serving: 15 servings. | Prep: 10m | Ready in: 45m

Ingredients

- 1 package chocolate cake mix (regular size)
- 1-1/4 cups water
- 1/3 cup canola oil
- 3 large egg whites
- TOPPING:
- 1/2 cup packed brown sugar
- 1/3 cup quick-cooking oats
- 3 tbsps. cold butter
- 2 tbsps. sweetened shredded coconut
- 2 tbsps. chopped pecans

Direction

- Mix together egg whites, oil, water and cake mix in a big bowl; beat for half a minute over low speed. Beat for 2 minutes over medium speed.
- Transfer to a greased broiler-proof 13x9" baking dish. Bake at 350 degrees until a toothpick slid into the middle comes out without any batter streaks, or for 30 to 35 minutes.
- Blend oats and brown sugar in a bowl to make topping; cut butter into the mixture until crumbly. Mix in pecans and coconut; scatter onto hot cake. Broil for 1 minute or 2, keeping a 4-6" distance from the heat source, or until topping forms bubbles on top. Serve while still warm.

Nutrition Information

- Calories: 245 calories
- Total Carbohydrate: 37 g
- Cholesterol: 0 mg
- Total Fat: 10 g
- Fiber: 1 g
- Protein: 2 g
- Sodium: 244 mg

127. Dark Chocolate Layer Cake

Serving: 12 servings. | Prep: 30m | Ready in: 60m

Ingredients

- 3 cups sugar
- 1-1/2 cups buttermilk
- 1-1/2 cups brewed coffee, cooled
- 3 eggs
- 3/4 cup canola oil
- 3 oz. semisweet chocolate, melted
- 3/4 tsp. vanilla extract
- 2-1/2 cups all-purpose flour
- 1-1/2 cups baking cocoa
- 2 tsps. baking soda
- 3/4 tsp. baking powder
- 1-1/4 tsp. salt
- FROSTING:
- 1 cup heavy whipping cream
- 2 tbsps. sugar
- 2 tbsps. light corn syrup
- 16 oz. semisweet chocolate, chopped
- 1/4 cup butter

Direction

- Blend well buttermilk, eggs, chocolate, vanilla, oil, coffee and sugar in a big bowl. In the separate large bowl, mix the cocoa, flour, salt, baking soda and baking powder, and then slowly add it into the buttermilk mixture. Mix it well.
- Prepare 3 floured and greased 9-inch round baking pans. Pour the mixture into them and let them bake at 350°F for 30 to 35 minutes or until a toothpick poked in the middle comes out clean. Let it cool for 10 minutes before removing from the pans. Cool it completely on wire racks.
- To make a frosting, mix sugar, corn syrup and cream in a small pot. Let it fully boil on medium heat while constantly stirring it. Take it out from the heat and mix in the butter and chocolate until they melt.
- Put in a big bowl. Place a cover on and store it in the refrigerator until consistency desired is achieved, occasionally stir. Spread the frosting on the top and sides of the cake, spread as well in between its layers then refrigerate.

Nutrition Information

- Calories: 816 calories
- Total Carbohydrate: 112 g
- Cholesterol: 93 mg
- Total Fat: 41 g
- Fiber: 11 g
- Protein: 11 g
- Sodium: 569 mg

128. Dark Chocolate Sauce

"For a quick dressing to elevate the taste of your waffles, pancakes or frozen yogurt, always have this creamy chocolate sauce ready."
Serving: 32 | Ready in: 10m

Ingredients

- 1 cup packed light brown sugar
- ⅔ cup unsweetened cocoa powder
- 1½ cups 1% milk
- 2 oz. chopped bittersweet or semisweet chocolate
- 1 tsp. vanilla extract

Direction

- In a big heavy saucepan, stir cocoa powder and brown sugar. Mix in milk, little at a time, until it forms a smooth paste. Simmer the mixture, stirring continuously. Decrease to low heat and simmer for 4 minutes, stirring continuously. Take away from the heat; put in chopped chocolate and mix until the chocolate melts. Mix in vanilla. Allow to cool a little and serve while still warm.

Nutrition Information

- Calories: 40 calories;

- Total Carbohydrate: 9 g
- Cholesterol: 1 mg
- Total Fat: 1 g
- Fiber: 1 g
- Protein: 1 g
- Sodium: 5 mg
- Sugar: 7 g
- Saturated Fat: 1 g

129. Delightful Brownies

"Moist and fudgy!"
Serving: 1 dozen. | Prep: 15m | Ready in: 45m

Ingredients

- 3 tbsps. butter, softened
- 2 egg whites
- 1 jar (4 oz.) prune baby food
- 1 tsp. vanilla extract
- 2/3 cup sugar
- 1/2 cup all-purpose flour
- 1 package (1.4 oz.) sugar-free instant chocolate pudding mix
- 1/2 tsp. baking powder
- 1/4 tsp. salt
- 3/4 cup miniature semisweet chocolate chips

Direction

- Beat egg whites and butter till blended in a bowl; beat in vanilla and baby food. Mix salt, baking powder, pudding mix, flour and sugar; add to egg mixture. Mix in chocolate chips.
- Spread into 8-in. square baking pan that's coated in cooking spray; bake it at 350° till inserted toothpick in middle exits clean for 30-35 minutes. Cool on wire rack.

Nutrition Information

- Calories: 176 calories
- Total Carbohydrate: 30 g
- Cholesterol: 8 mg
- Total Fat: 6 g
- Fiber: 2 g

- Protein: 2 g
- Sodium: 338 mg

130. Deluxe Brownies

"An easy and quick to make rich treat."
Serving: 2-1/2 dozen. | Prep: 20m | Ready in: 50m

Ingredients

- 1-1/4 cups butter, softened
- 2-1/4 cups sugar
- 5 eggs, lightly beaten
- 2 tsps. vanilla extract
- 1-1/2 cups all-purpose flour
- 2/3 cup baking cocoa
- 1 tsp. salt
- 1-1/2 cups chopped pecans
- FROSTING:
- 1 cup sugar
- 1/4 cup butter, cubed
- 1/4 cup milk
- 1/2 cup semisweet chocolate chips
- 1/2 cup miniature marshmallows

Direction

- Cream the sugar and butter in a big bowl, until it becomes fluffy and light. Beat in the vanilla and eggs. Mix together the dry ingredients, then slowly add it to the creamed mixture. Mix in the pecans.
- Spread it in a 13x9-inch baking pan that's greased. Let it bake for 30 to 35 minutes at 325 degrees or until a toothpick exits with moist crumbs attached to it. Allow to cool on a wire rack.
- Mix together the milk, butter and sugar in a small saucepan and let it cook and stir on low heat, until the sugar dissolves. Take it out of the heat and mix in marshmallows and chips until it melts. Let it chill until the mixture gets to room temperature. Beat it in a big bowl until the consistency of the frosting is spreadable. Spread it on top of the brownies.

Nutrition Information

- Calories: 265 calories
- Total Carbohydrate: 31 g
- Cholesterol: 61 mg
- Total Fat: 16 g
- Fiber: 2 g
- Protein: 3 g
- Sodium: 187 mg

131. Devil's Food Cookies

"You can freeze them well."
Serving: 24 | Ready in: 30m

Ingredients

- 1½ cups sugar
- ½ cup prune puree
- ½ cup nonfat plain yogurt
- ¼ cup canola oil
- 2 large egg whites, lightly beaten
- 1½ cups sifted cake flour
- 1 cup unsweetened cocoa powder
- ½ tsp. salt
- ½ tsp. baking soda
- ½ tsp. instant coffee granules

Direction

- Set oven to preheat at 350F. Use parchment paper to line two baking sheets or coat them using nonstick cooking spray.
- In a medium bowl, whisk together egg whites, oil, yogurt, prune puree and sugar. Mix the instant coffee, baking soda, salt, cocoa and flour together in a different medium bowl. Use a wooden spoon to mix the dry ingredients into the wet just until incorporated. On the prepared baking sheets, drop heaping tablespoonfuls of the dough about 1 1/2 inches apart from each other. Bake until when lightly touched, the tops spring back, or 12 to 14 minutes. Take the cookies out to wire racks and let cool.

Nutrition Information

- Calories: 125 calories;
- Total Carbohydrate: 25 g
- Cholesterol: 0 mg
- Total Fat: 3 g
- Fiber: 2 g
- Protein: 2 g
- Sodium: 85 mg
- Sugar: 15 g
- Saturated Fat: 0 g

132. Double Chocolate Biscotti

"Wonderful with coffee and keeps very well."
Serving: 36 | Prep: 25m | Ready in: 1h20m

Ingredients

- 1/2 cup butter, softened
- 2/3 cup white sugar
- 1/4 cup unsweetened cocoa powder
- 2 tsps. baking powder
- 2 eggs
- 1 3/4 cups all-purpose flour
- 4 (1 oz.) squares white chocolate, chopped
- 3/4 cup semisweet chocolate chips

Direction

- Use an electric mixer to cream butter and sugar in a large mixing bowl till fluffy and light. Beat cocoa and baking powder into the mix slowly. Beat for about 2 minutes. Beat the eggs, one at a time, into the mixture. Stir flour into the mix by hand. Mix the white chocolate and chocolate chips into the mixture. Cover dough and refrigerate for about 10 minutes.
- Set oven to preheat at 375°F (190°C). Split the dough into two portions and make a 9-inch long log out of each dough. Put the logs about 4 inches apart onto a lightly greased cookie sheet. Slightly flatten them out.
- Bake till tested done with a toothpick for about 20 to 25 minutes. Let it cool down on the cookie sheet for about 5 minutes, then take out

to a wire rack carefully to cool down for one hour.
- Slice each loaf into diagonal slices that are 1/2-inch wide. Put the slices onto an ungreased cookie sheet and bake for 9 minutes at 325°F (165°C). Flip the cookies and bake for 7 to 9 minutes. Let it cool down thoroughly, then keep in an airtight container.

Nutrition Information

- Calories: 99 calories;
- Total Carbohydrate: 12.7 g
- Cholesterol: 18 mg
- Total Fat: 5.1 g
- Protein: 1.5 g
- Sodium: 53 mg

133. Double Chocolate Cupcakes

"Traditional chocolate cupcakes but with whole-wheat flour and less butter. Garnish with chocolate ganache frosting."
Serving: 12 | Prep: 40m | Ready in: 1h

Ingredients

- Cupcakes
- ¾ cup cake flour
- ¾ cup whole-wheat pastry flour
- ½ cup unsweetened cocoa powder
- ½ tsp. baking soda
- ½ tsp. salt
- ¼ tsp. baking powder
- 1 cup granulated sugar
- ½ cup butter or coconut oil, softened
- 2 large eggs
- 1 tsp. vanilla extract
- ¾ cup buttermilk
- Frosting
- 6 oz. bittersweet or semisweet chocolate, finely chopped
- ⅓ cup heavy cream
- ½ tsp. vanilla extract
- 2 tbsps. mini chocolate chips (optional)

Direction

- For cupcakes: Set oven to 350°F to preheat. Line 12 (1/2-cup) muffin tins with paper liners.
- Whip baking powder, salt, baking soda, cocoa, whole-wheat flour and cake flour in a medium bowl.
- Whip butter (or coconut oil) and sugar in a big mixing bowl with an electric mixer on medium speed until blended. Whip in eggs, 1 at a time, until thoroughly mixed. Put in vanilla. Blend in the dry ingredients and buttermilk alternately with the mixer on low, starting and ending with dry ingredients and scraping the sides of the bowl as necessary, until just mixed. Split the batter among the lined cups. (They should be about 3/4 full.)
- Bake the cupcakes for 18 to 22 minutes until a cake tester inserted into the center exits clean. Cool for 5 minutes in the pan. Put to a wire rack and cool completely.
- In the meantime, for frosting: In a heatproof medium bowl, put chocolate. Heat vanilla and cream in a small saucepan over medium heat until simmering (don't let it boil). Add the cream on top of the chocolate and let sit for 3 minutes. Mix until smooth, then blend using an electric mixer for 1 to 2 minutes until fluffy and very slightly lightened in color.
- Smear the frosting on the cooled cupcakes and top with mini chips, if preferred.

Nutrition Information

- Calories: 295 calories;
- Total Carbohydrate: 40 g
- Cholesterol: 59 mg
- Total Fat: 15 g
- Fiber: 3 g
- Protein: 5 g
- Sodium: 204 mg
- Sugar: 23 g
- Saturated Fat: 9 g

134. Double Peanut Bars

"No-bake cream cheese dessert squares made with peanut butter and chopped peanuts."
Serving: Makes 12 servings. | Prep: 20m | Ready in: 4h20m

Ingredients

- 25 vanilla wafers, finely crushed (about 1 cup)
- 1/2 cup PLANTERS Dry Roasted Peanuts, finely chopped
- 2 Tbsp. granulated sugar
- 1/3 cup margarine or butter, melted
- 1 pkg. (8 oz.) PHILADELPHIA Cream Cheese, softened
- 3/4 cup powdered sugar
- 1/2 cup creamy peanut butter
- 1 tub (8 oz.) COOL WHIP Whipped Topping, thawed, divided

Direction

- Combine the margarine, granulated sugar, peanuts and wafer crumbs. Take out 2 tbsp of crumb mixture, then put side. Firmly press the leftover crumb mixture on the bottom of an 8 or 9-inches square pan, then put it aside.
- In a big bowl, beat the powdered sugar and cream cheese using an electric mixer on medium speed, until it becomes fluffy and light. Put in peanut butter, then stir well. Mix in 2 cups of whipped topping gently. Evenly spread on top of the crust.
- Let it chill in the fridge for 4 hours or until it becomes firm. Put the leftover whipped topping and reserved crumb mixture on top just prior to serving. Keep the remaining desert in the fridge.

Nutrition Information

- Calories: 340
- Total Carbohydrate: 24 g
- Cholesterol: 20 mg
- Total Fat: 25 g
- Fiber: 1 g
- Protein: 6 g
- Sodium: 250 mg
- Sugar: 16 g
- Saturated Fat: 10 g

135. Double-chocolate Cream Roll

"Low-fat cake roll sprinkled with creamy fudge and caramel. This cake recipe doesn't require a normal whipped cream since the non-dairy garnish makes it unique."
Serving: 12 servings. | Prep: 50m | Ready in: 50m

Ingredients

- 1-1/2 tsps. shortening
- 5 large eggs, separated
- 1 tsp. vanilla extract
- 1 cup plus 2 tsps. confectioners' sugar, divided
- 3 tbsps. baking cocoa
- 1/8 tsp. salt
- 1-1/2 cups cold fat-free milk
- 2 packages (3.3 oz. each) instant white chocolate pudding mix or 2 packages (3.4 oz.) instant vanilla pudding mix
- 1 carton (8 oz.) frozen reduced-fat whipped topping, thawed
- 3 tbsps. fat-free caramel ice cream topping, divided
- 1/2 cup chopped walnuts, divided
- 1 tbsp. fat-free hot fudge ice cream topping, warmed

Direction

- Spray some oil on a 15x10x1-in baking sheet. Grease some shortening on a paraffin paper and line it in the baking sheet then set aside. Using high speed, whisk egg yolks in a big mixing bowl until the texture becomes thick and yellowish in color. Mix in vanilla. Using another mixing bowl, mix cocoa, salt and 1 cup confectioners' sugar; add the dry mixture gradually into the egg yolk mixture. Prepare a small mixing bowl and whisk egg whites until it forms a stiff peak. Add it and mix gently into egg yolk mixture. Pour the batter into prepared baking sheet. Place it in the oven and bake the cake for 14-16 minutes at 350 degrees. Once cooked, the cake will bounce back when pressed lightly. Prepare a linen towel and dust it off with some confectioners' sugar. Flip the cake immediately in the towel. Carefully remove the paraffin paper from the cake. Jelly-roll the cake in the towel and place on a wire shelve to cool thoroughly. Prepare a small mixing bowl and pour the pudding mix and milk. Mix for 2 minutes using a low speed and gently combine in whipped topping. Scoop out 1 cup and set aside. Unroll the cooled cake and evenly spread the filling within 1/2 inside of the edges. Topped with 2 tbsps. of caramel and drizzle with 6 tbsps. of walnuts. Roll the cake up again and evenly spread the filling into the cake. Garnish with warm fudge sauce and top with caramel. Drizzle again with some walnuts. Put a cake cover and keep refrigerated for 1 hour. Serve chilled. Keep all leftovers refrigerated.

Nutrition Information

- Calories: 227 calories
- Total Carbohydrate: 33 g
- Cholesterol: 89 mg
- Total Fat: 8 g
- Fiber: 1 g
- Protein: 5 g
- Sodium: 301 mg

136. Dreamy Orange Cupcakes

"These cupcakes are blend of two great flavors: vanilla and orange."

Serving: 24 | Prep: 30m | Ready in: 1h45m

Ingredients

- 1 (18.25 oz.) package orange cake mix
- 3/4 cup creamy salad dressing (such as Miracle Whip®)
- 1 (1.3 oz.) envelope dry whipped topping mix (such as Dream Whip®)
- 3/4 cup freshly squeezed orange juice
- 3 large eggs
- 2 tbsps. grated orange zest
- 1 (13 oz.) jar marshmallow creme
- 1/2 cup unsalted butter at room temperature
- 1/2 cup vegetable shortening
- 1/2 cup unsalted butter at room temperature
- 1/2 cup vegetable shortening
- 1/4 cup freshly squeezed orange juice
- 1 tbsp. orange zest
- 1/4 tsp. vanilla extract
- 2 drops orange paste food coloring, or as desired
- 4 cups confectioners' sugar

Direction

- Preheat the oven to 175°C or 350°F. Line paper liners on 2 dozen muffin cups.
- In a big bowl, whip 2 tbsps. of orange zest, 3/4 cup of orange juice, eggs, whipped topping mix, creamy salad dressing and orange cake mix on low speed using electric mixer for a minute, till mixture moisten. Use spatula to scrape down bowl sides, then raise speed to moderate and keep whipping till thoroughly incorporated, for an additional of 2 minutes. Pour batter into prepped cupcake cups, filling it roughly 2/3 full.
- In prepped oven, bake for 15 minutes, till an inserted toothpick into the middle of cupcake gets out clean. Cool for 10 minutes in pans prior to transferring on wire rack to fully cool prior to frosting.
- Prepare cream topping: use an electric mixer to whip half cup of unsalted butter, half cup of shortening and marshmallow crème in bowl till creamy and smooth. Put half-inch thick cream topping layer on top of every cooled cupcake, with knife to smear the topping even. Let roughly half-inch orange cupcake to expose under white layer.
- Prepare orange butter cream: in bowl, whip half cup of shortening and half cup of unsalted butter till fluffy and light. Stir in food coloring, vanilla extract, zest from an orange and quarter cup orange of juice till thoroughly

blended. Slowly whip in confectioners' sugar till smooth.
- Turn frosting onto piping bag equipped with one big star tip, and pipe single layer of orange butter cream in a decorative manner, finishing in one peak, on top of cream topping on cupcakes.

Nutrition Information

- Calories: 411 calories;
- Total Carbohydrate: 53.5 g
- Cholesterol: 47 mg
- Total Fat: 21.4 g
- Protein: 2 g
- Sodium: 278 mg

137. Dutch Oven Apple Crisp

"A Dutch oven apple crisp."
Serving: 8

Ingredients

- 2 1/2 cups Macintosh apples - peeled, cored and quartered
- 2 cups rolled oats
- 2 cups packed brown sugar
- 1 cup all-purpose flour
- 3/4 cup milk

Direction

- Preheat the oven to 190 °C or 375 °F.
- In a big Dutch oven, mix brown sugar and apples.
- Allow to bake for half an hour.
- Mix oats, flour and milk. Put mixture on top of brown sugar and apples.
- Let bake for an hour. Serve.

Nutrition Information

- Calories: 374 calories;
- Total Carbohydrate: 86 g
- Cholesterol: 2 mg
- Total Fat: 2 g
- Protein: 5.2 g
- Sodium: 27 mg

138. Easy Banana Ice Cream

"A good recipe to use overripe bananas! Peel, wrap in plastic wrap then freeze them."
Serving: 2 | Prep: 5m | Ready in: 5m

Ingredients

- 2 peeled and chopped bananas, frozen
- 1/2 cup skim milk

Direction

- Blend 1/4 cup of skim milk and frozen bananas for 30 seconds in a blender. Add leftover 1/4 cup of milk; blend for 30 more seconds till smooth on high speed.

Nutrition Information

- Calories: 126 calories;
- Total Carbohydrate: 30 g
- Cholesterol: 1 mg
- Total Fat: 0.4 g
- Protein: 3.4 g
- Sodium: 27 mg

139. Easy Blueberry-lemon Parfait

""The foods in this simple recipe are powerhouses of nutrition. Why this one is great for you: Gut-protecting bacteria in Ginger is a mild anti-blood-clotting agent; High antioxidants: low saturated fat: eating 6-oz. a day of yogurt lessened hay-fever attacks and colds.""
Serving: 4

Ingredients

- 2 cups fresh or thawed frozen blueberries
- 2 (8 oz.) cartons non-fat lemon yogurt
- 10 gingersnaps, crumbled

Direction

- Layer 1/2 cup blueberries, next 1/2 cup yogurt, then crumbled gingersnaps in each of 4 tall wineglasses or parfait glasses.

Nutrition Information

- Calories: 227 calories;
- Total Carbohydrate: 45.4 g
- Cholesterol: 3 mg
- Total Fat: 2.9 g
- Protein: 6.5 g
- Sodium: 130 mg

140. Easy Chiffon Pie

"Eveyone loves this fluffy berries pie."
Serving: 8 servings. | Prep: 15m | Ready in: 15m

Ingredients

- 1 package (.3 oz.) sugar-free strawberry gelatin
- 3/4 cup boiling water
- 1-1/4 cps cold water
- 1 cup frozen reduced-fat whipped topping, thawed
- 2-1/4 cups sliced fresh strawberries, divided
- 1 reduced-fat graham cracker crust (8 inches)

Direction

- Dissolve the gelatin in a large bowl of the boiling water. Mix in the cold water. Place in the refrigerator until slightly thickened. Fold in two cups strawberries and whipped topping. Transfer into the crust. Place in the refrigerator until set, or about 3 hours. Add the remaining strawberries for garnish.

Nutrition Information

- Calories: 138 calories
- Total Carbohydrate: 21 g
- Cholesterol: 0 mg
- Total Fat: 4 g
- Fiber: 1 g
- Protein: 2 g

- Sodium: 117 mg

141. Easy Chocolate Sherbet

"Add strawberries or orange peel strips and mint leaf for garnish."
Serving: 8 | Prep: 5m | Ready in: 2h5m

Ingredients

- 1 cup sugar
- 3/4 cup unsweetened cocoa powder
- 1 1/2 cups water
- 2 tbsps. amaretto (almond flavored liqueur)

Direction

- Whisk amaretto, water, cocoa and sugar together in a medium bowl till smooth.
- Transfer the mixture into an ice cream freezer container then freeze following the manufacturer's instructions.

Nutrition Information

- Calories: 130 calories;
- Total Carbohydrate: 31.2 g
- Cholesterol: 0 mg
- Total Fat: 1.1 g
- Protein: 1.6 g
- Sodium: 3 mg

142. Easy Lemonade Icebox Pie

"Very tasty and easy to make."
Serving: 8 servings. | Prep: 10m | Ready in: 10m

Ingredients

- 1 can (12 oz.) fat-free evaporated milk
- 3/4 cup thawed pink lemonade concentrate
- 1-1/2 cups reduced-fat whipped topping
- 1 reduced-fat graham cracker crust (8 inches)
- 1 medium lemon, sliced

Direction

- Combine lemonade concentrate and milk in a bowl; fold in the whipped topping. Transfer to the crust. Place in freezer about 3 hours. Decorate with the lemon slices.

Nutrition Information

- Calories: 202 calories
- Total Carbohydrate: 34 g
- Cholesterol: 2 mg
- Total Fat: 5 g
- Fiber: 0 g
- Protein: 4 g
- Sodium: 145 mg

143. Easy Rhubarb Pie

"This rhubarb pie is very tasty."
| Prep: 30m

Ingredients

- 4 cups Chopped Rhubarb
- 1 1/3 cups Sugar
- 6 tbsps. All-Purpose Flour
- 1 tbsps. Butter
- 2 rounds Pillsbury Pie Crust 9"

Direction

- Turn the oven to 450°F (230°C) to preheat.
- Mix together flour and sugar. Sprinkle 1/4 of this mixture over the pie plate with the pastry. Heap over this mixture with rhubarb. Sprinkle flour and the leftover sugar over. Dot butter by small pieces over. Put on the top crust to cover.
- On the lowest rack in the oven, put the pie. Bake for 15 minutes. Lower the oven heat to 350°F (175°C), and keep baking for 40-45 minutes. Enjoy cold and warm.

144. Easy Vanilla Ice Cream

"So easy!"
Serving: 7 servings. | Prep: 10m | Ready in: 30m

Ingredients

- 2 cups cold fat-free milk
- 1 can (14 oz.) fat-free sweetened condensed milk
- 1 package (1 oz.) sugar-free instant vanilla pudding mix

Direction

- Whisk all the ingredients in large bowl until the mixture is thickened and blended. Place in the ice cream freezer to freeze following the manufacturer's instructions.
- Move to the freezer container. Freeze, covered, until firm, about 60 mins.

Nutrition Information

- Calories: 196 calories
- Total Carbohydrate: 41 g
- Cholesterol: 5 mg
- Total Fat: 0 g
- Fiber: 0 g
- Protein: 7 g
- Sodium: 264 mg

145. Eggnog Pudding

"Whip up this recipe instead of serving the plain old vanilla pudding."
Serving: 6 | Prep: 10m | Ready in: 2h10m

Ingredients

- 1 (5.1 oz.) package instant vanilla pudding mix
- 4 dashes ground cinnamon
- 2 dashes ground nutmeg
- 2 dashes ground cloves
- 1 pinch ground ginger

- 3 cups cold milk

Direction

- In a bowl, mix together cloves, ginger, nutmeg, cinnamon and dry pudding mix until well-combined. Whisk in milk while stirring for 2 minutes, until there are no lumps anymore.
- Transfer the pudding into serving dishes and chill until set, about 2 hours.

Nutrition Information

- Calories: 154 calories;
- Total Carbohydrate: 28.8 g
- Cholesterol: 10 mg
- Total Fat: 2.8 g
- Protein: 4.1 g
- Sodium: 394 mg

146. Elderberry Soup

""A refreshing, light and special summary soup.""
Serving: 4 | Prep: 25m | Ready in: 45m

Ingredients

- 5 oz. elderberries
- 1 quart water, divided
- 1 1/2 tsps. cornstarch
- 1/2 lb. apples - peeled, cored and diced
- 1 lemon peel
- white sugar to taste

Direction

- Boil 2 cups of water and elderberries in a pot. Turn the heat down to low; simmer for 10 minutes. Take away from the heat; puree till smooth in a blender; transfer back to the pot. Stir 1 tbsp. of the puree with cornstarch in a small bowl; mix into the pot to thicken.
- Boil the remaining water and apples in a separate pot. Add in lemon peel. Turn the heat down to low and simmer for 10 minutes. Take the peel away. Combine the elderberry mixture into the apple mixture; add in sugar to sweeten to taste.

Nutrition Information

- Calories: 64 calories;
- Total Carbohydrate: 16.6 g
- Cholesterol: 0 mg
- Total Fat: 0.3 g
- Protein: 0.4 g
- Sodium: 10 mg

147. Favorite Marbled Chocolate Cheesecake Bars

"Yummy yet low-fat bars."
Serving: about 4 dozen. | Prep: 20m | Ready in: 40m

Ingredients

- 3/4 cup water
- 1/3 cup butter
- 1-1/2 oz. unsweetened chocolate, chopped
- 2 cups all-purpose flour
- 1-1/2 cups packed brown sugar
- 1 tsp. baking soda
- 1/2 tsp. salt
- 1 large egg
- 1 large egg white
- 1/2 cup reduced-fat sour cream
- CREAM CHEESE MIXTURE:
- 1 package (8 oz.) reduced-fat cream cheese
- 1/3 cup sugar
- 1 large egg white
- 1 tbsp. vanilla extract
- 1 cup (6 oz.) miniature semisweet chocolate chips

Direction

- Mix and cook chocolate, butter and water in small saucepan on low heat till melted; mix till smooth. Cool.
- Mix salt, baking soda, brown sugar and flour in big bowl; beat sour cream, egg white and egg in on low speed till just combined. Beat

chocolate mixture in till smooth. Beat vanilla, egg white, sugar and cream cheese till smooth in another bowl; put aside.
- Spread chocolate batter in 15x10x1-in. baking pan coated in cooking spray. By tablespoonfuls, drop cream cheese mixture on batter; use knife to cut through batter to swirl. Sprinkle chocolate chips on.
- Bake for 20-25 minutes till an inserted toothpick in middle exits clean at 375°. On wire rack, cool.

Nutrition Information

- Calories: 95 calories
- Total Carbohydrate: 15 g
- Cholesterol: 10 mg
- Total Fat: 4 g
- Fiber: 0 g
- Protein: 2 g
- Sodium: 90 mg

148. Fig Filling For Pastry

"You can store leftovers in a tightly covered container in the fridge. You can double this easily."
Serving: 24 | Prep: 25m | Ready in: 30m

Ingredients

- 1 lb. dried figs
- 1 orange, zested
- 1/2 cup semisweet chocolate chips
- 1/4 cup whiskey
- 1/2 cup chopped walnuts
- 1 tsp. cinnamon
- 1/4 cup maple sugar

Direction

- Use scissors to remove fig stems. In batches, chop in food processor.
- Mix cinnamon, maple syrup, walnuts, whiskey, chocolate chips, orange zest and chopped figs in nonstick pan. Heat till chocolate melts, frequently mixing, on medium heat. Completely cool.

Nutrition Information

- Calories: 95 calories;
- Total Carbohydrate: 16.9 g
- Cholesterol: 0 mg
- Total Fat: 2.9 g
- Protein: 1.1 g
- Sodium: 3 mg

149. Finnish Berry Dessert

"A refreshing dessert recipe."
Serving: 8 servings. | Prep: 30m | Ready in: 30m

Ingredients

- 1-1/2 cups blueberries
- 1-1/2 cups fresh strawberries, quartered
- 1 cup unsweetened raspberries
- 3 tbsps. sugar, divided
- 2 tbsps. cornstarch
- 1-1/2 cups apple-raspberry juice cocktail
- Low-fat vanilla frozen yogurt, optional

Direction

- Mix together the 2 tbsp sugar and fruit in a big heatproof bowl. Mix together the juice and cornstarch in a saucepan until it becomes smooth, then boil. Let it cook and stir until it becomes thick or for 2 minutes. Take it out of the heat and allow to cool for 10 minutes. Pour on top of the fruit, then toss until coated. Sprinkle the leftover sugar on top. Put on cover and let it chill in the fridge. You may serve in individual dessert plates, then put frozen yogurt on top, if preferred.

Nutrition Information

- Calories: 78 calories
- Total Carbohydrate: 19 g
- Cholesterol: 0 mg
- Total Fat: 0 g
- Fiber: 3 g
- Protein: 0 g
- Sodium: 3 mg

150. Flax Seed Carrot Cake

"A guilt-free, delicious, and fruity version of carrot cake."
Serving: 12 | Prep: 25m | Ready in: 9h5m

Ingredients

- 3 egg whites
- 2/3 cup white sugar
- 1/4 cup nonfat milk
- 1/3 cup applesauce
- 1 tsp. vanilla extract
- 1/4 tsp. almond extract (optional)
- 1 1/3 cups whole wheat flour
- 2/3 cup all-purpose flour
- 2 tbsps. ground flax seed
- 2 tsps. ground cinnamon
- 1/2 tsp. ground nutmeg
- 1/2 tsp. ground cloves
- 1 tsp. baking soda
- 1/3 cup chopped walnuts
- 1/4 cup raisins
- 1/2 (8 oz.) can crushed pineapple, drained
- 1 cup grated carrot

Direction

- Preheat an oven to 175 °C or 350 °F. With vegetable cooking spray, slightly grease a loaf pan, 9x5 inch in size.
- In small bowl, beat the almond extract, vanilla, applesauce, milk, sugar and egg whites together; stir till well incorporated. Sift the baking soda, cloves, nutmeg, cinnamon, flax seed, whole wheat flour and flour together in big bowl. Into the flour, stir the egg; mix till well incorporated. Fold in the drained pineapple, carrot, raisins and walnuts. Into prepped pan, put the batter.
- In prepped oven, bake for 40 minutes till a toothpick pricked into the middle gets out clean, yet not exactly dry. Reserve for 10 to 20 minutes to cool prior to placing in refrigerator for overnight.

Nutrition Information

- Calories: 178 calories;
- Total Carbohydrate: 33.9 g
- Cholesterol: < 1 mg
- Total Fat: 3.5 g
- Protein: 4.8 g
- Sodium: 131 mg

151. Flourless Dark Chocolate Cake

"You can treat yourself and your partner this luscious and moist chocolate cake for this year's Valentine's day without using flour – no more guilt!"
Serving: 12 servings. | Prep: 25m | Ready in: 55m

Ingredients

- 4 large eggs, separated
- 3 tbsps. butter
- 8 oz. dark baking chocolate, chopped
- 1/3 cup plus 1/4 cup sugar, divided
- 1 container (2-1/2 oz.) prune baby food
- 1-1/2 tsps. vanilla extract
- Confectioners' sugar

Direction

- Pour egg whites into a small bowl; rest for half an hour at room temperature. Start preheating the oven to 350 degrees. Grease a 9-inch springform pan with cooking spray, then lay on a baking sheet.
- Heat chocolate and butter, stirring continuously, on low heat to melt in a small saucepan. Turn off the heat and let cool a little. Beat egg yolks for 3 minutes over high speed in a big bowl until it becomes dense a little. Slowly pour in a third cup of sugar; whisk until it reaches a thick consistency and resembles the color of a lemon. Mix in chocolate mixture, vanilla and baby food.
- Beat egg whites, using clean beater, over medium speed until it forms soft peaks. Slowly add in the rest of the sugar, 1 tbsp. each time, beating over high speed before

adding another spoon until no sugar lumps remain. Keep beating until firm and sheeny peaks form. Fold 1/4 egg whites into chocolate mixture, then the rest of the egg whites.

- Add into the greased pan. Bake until a toothpick slid into the middle comes out with moist crumbs, about 30 to 35 minutes. Place on a wire rack to cool, about 20 minutes. Detach sides from pan using a knife; take off rim from the pan. Let cake chill through. Sprinkle on confectioners' sugar, then serve.

Nutrition Information

- Calories: 188 calories
- Total Carbohydrate: 22 g
- Cholesterol: 78 mg
- Total Fat: 11 g
- Fiber: 2 g
- Protein: 4 g
- Sodium: 50 mg

152. Fluffy Cherry Frosting

"Creamy frosting with a touch of cherry flavor."
Serving: 8 cups. | Prep: 25m | Ready in: 25m

Ingredients

- 1-1/2 cups sugar
- 4 egg whites
- 1/4 cup water
- 1/4 cup maraschino cherry juice
- 1/2 tsp. cream of tartar
- 1 tsp. vanilla extract
- 1/2 tsp. cherry extract or 1/4 tsp. almond extract

Direction

- Mix together the cream of tartar, cherry juice, water, egg whites and sugar in a heavy saucepan. Beat it for 1 minute on low speed using a portable mixer. Keep on beating on low atop low heat for about 10 minutes, until the frosting reads 160 degrees using a candy thermometer.
- Pour it into a bowl of a heavy-duty stand mixer; put in the extracts. Beat it for about 7 minutes on high, until it forms stiff peaks.

Nutrition Information

- Calories: 107 calories
- Total Carbohydrate: 26 g
- Cholesterol: 0 mg
- Total Fat: 0 g
- Fiber: 0 g
- Protein: 1 g
- Sodium: 19 mg

153. Fluffy Orange Gelatin Pie

"This citrus recipe is so wonderful."
Serving: 8 servings. | Prep: 15m | Ready in: 15m

Ingredients

- 1 can (15 oz.) mandarin oranges
- 1 package (3 oz.) orange gelatin
- 1 can (5 oz.) evaporated milk, chilled
- 1 reduced-fat graham cracker crust (8 inches)
- 1 medium navel orange, sliced

Direction

- Drain the liquid from the oranges to measuring cup. Put enough water to measure one cup; put the oranges aside. Add liquid to the saucepan; boil. Whisk in gelatin till dissolved.
- Move into big bowl; add the mixer beaters into the bowl. Keep covered and refrigerated till the mixture is syrupy.
- Put in the milk. Beat on high speed till almost doubled. Fold in the mandarin oranges. Add to the crust. Keep in the refrigerator till becoming set, 2 to 3 hours. Use the slices of the orange to decorate.

Nutrition Information

- Calories: 202 calories
- Total Carbohydrate: 37 g

- Cholesterol: 6 mg
- Total Fat: 4 g
- Fiber: 1 g
- Protein: 4 g
- Sodium: 140 mg

154. Fresh Cranberry Salad

"Use whipped cream, bananas, pineapple and marshmallows to make heavenly-flavored salad."
Serving: 6 | Prep: 15m | Ready in: 13h35m

Ingredients

- 1 lb. cranberries
- 8 oz. miniature marshmallows
- 2 cups white sugar
- 1 (20 oz.) can crushed pineapple with juice
- 1 banana, sliced
- 1 cup unsweetened whipped cream

Direction

- Place cranberries in a blender or a food processor and coarsely grind. Transfer the ground cranberries to a large bowl then add pineapple, sugar and marshmallows and stir. Refrigerate the mixture overnight. Add whipped cream and sliced banana, and stir just before serving.

Nutrition Information

- Calories: 505 calories;
- Total Carbohydrate: 127.4 g
- Cholesterol: 10 mg
- Total Fat: 2.3 g
- Protein: 1.6 g
- Sodium: 33 mg

155. Fresh Fruit Compote

"Let round a meal with this fruit dessert, a colorful medley of pears, strawberries, peaches and apples."
Serving: 7 servings. | Prep: 10m | Ready in: 40m

Ingredients

- 1/2 medium lemon
- 1/2 cup water
- 1/4 cup honey
- 2 cups sliced peeled apples
- 2 cups sliced peeled peaches
- 1 cup sliced peeled pears
- 1/3 cup apricot spreadable fruit
- 2 cups sliced strawberries
- 1 cup seedless red grapes
- 7 tbsps. vanilla yogurt

Direction

- Cut from lemon peel with 2 strips with the length of 1 inch then squeeze juice from lemon. Mix together lemon peel strips, lemon juice, honey and water in a big saucepan. Put in pears, peaches and apples then bring the mixture to a boil. Lower heat then cook without a cover until fruit is tender, about 15 to 20 minutes.
- Take away from the heat and get rid of lemon peel. Turn fruit to a big bowl with a slotted spoon and get rid of poaching liquid. Stir in grapes, strawberries and spreadable fruit. Cover and chill for 4 hours to overnight. Serve together with a slotted spoon and put yogurt on top of each serving.

Nutrition Information

- Calories: 166 calories
- Total Carbohydrate: 41 g
- Cholesterol: 1 mg
- Total Fat: 1 g
- Fiber: 4 g
- Protein: 2 g
- Sodium: 14 mg

156. Fresh No-bake Fruit Pie

"This is a great summer treat. A no-bake fresh berry fruit pie. Serve your favorite whipped cream."
Serving: 8 | Prep: 15m | Ready in: 1h40m

Ingredients

- 1 (16 oz.) package fresh strawberries, hulled and large berries cut in half
- 1 pint fresh blueberries
- 1 (6 oz.) container fresh raspberries
- 1 (6 oz.) container fresh blackberries
- 1 cup water
- 1/2 cup white sugar
- 3 tbsps. cornstarch
- 1/4 cup water
- 1 (9 inch) prepared shortbread pie crust (such as Keebler®)

Direction

- In a bowl, mix blackberries, raspberries, blueberries, and strawberries thoroughly. Spoon out 3/4 cup of mixed berries and put into a saucepan with sugar and a cup water; put remaining berries aside. Boil the mixture and turn heat down to medium-low.
- In a bowl, whip 1/4 cup water and cornstarch until smooth and mix the cornstarch mixture into the hot fruit syrup; mix about 2 minutes until the mixture thickens. Let cool completely, mixing sometimes for about 20 minutes.
- Put the thick berry mixture into fresh berries until well-combined; put sauce and berries into shortbread pie shell. Put into refrigerator at least 1 hour until chilled.

Nutrition Information

- Calories: 232 calories;
- Total Carbohydrate: 44.2 g
- Cholesterol: 0 mg
- Total Fat: 5.6 g
- Protein: 2.2 g
- Sodium: 104 mg

157. Fresh Strawberry Granita

"This frozen iced dessert can be made anytime, best served during summer."
Serving: 8 | Prep: 10m | Ready in: 2h25m

Ingredients

- 2 lbs. ripe strawberries, hulled and halved
- 1/3 cup white sugar, or to taste
- 1 cup water
- 1/2 tsp. lemon juice (optional)
- 1/4 tsp. balsamic vinegar (optional)
- 1 tiny pinch salt

Direction

- With cold water, rinse strawberries; let it drain. Put berries into a blender; add salt, balsamic vinegar, lemon juice, water and sugar.
- Pulse the mixture several times to get it moving then, blend for about 1 minute until smooth. Transfer to a large baking dish. Puree should be only about 3/8 inch deep in the dish.
- Put the dish without a cover in the freezer for about 45 minutes until the mixture barely starts to freeze around the edges. Its center will be slushy.
- Stir the crystals lightly with a fork from the edge of the granita mixture into the center; mix thoroughly. Close the freezer; chill for 30-40 minutes more until granita becomes nearly frozen. Using a fork, mix lightly as before, scraping the crystals loose. Freeze again and stir 3-4 times with a fork until the granita becomes light, looks fluffy and dry, and crystals are separate.
- Divide granita into small serving bowls; serve.

Nutrition Information

- Calories: 69 calories;
- Total Carbohydrate: 17.1 g
- Cholesterol: 0 mg
- Total Fat: 0.3 g
- Protein: 0.8 g

- Sodium: 26 mg

158. Frosty Cantaloupe Sherbet

"A great way to use up overripe cantaloupe."
Serving: 6 servings. | Prep: 20m | Ready in: 20m

Ingredients

- 1 small ripe cantaloupe
- 2 cups cold fat-free milk, divided
- 1/3 cup sugar
- 1 envelope unflavored gelatin
- 1/4 cup light corn syrup
- 1/4 tsp. salt

Direction

- Slice the cantaloupe in half; throw away the seeds. Scoop the pulp out (makes 4 cups of melon). Add the cantaloupe and 1 cup milk into a food processor or blender; cover and process till smooth.
- Mix together the sugar and remaining milk in a large saucepan. Sprinkle gelatin on top; let it sit for 1 minute. Heat on low heat, stir till the gelatin is dissolved thoroughly.
- Stir the corn syrup, salt and pureed cantaloupe into the mix. Transfer into a 13-in. x 9-in. pan. Freeze, covered, till partially frozen for about 3 hours, stir frequently.
- Add the cantaloupe mixture into a blender; process, covered, till smooth. Pour the mixture back into the pan. Freeze, covered, till almost frozen for about 1 hour.

Nutrition Information

- Calories: 152 calories
- Total Carbohydrate: 35 g
- Cholesterol: 2 mg
- Total Fat: 0 g
- Fiber: 1 g
- Protein: 5 g
- Sodium: 170 mg

159. Frosty Peach Pie Supreme

"An outstanding dessert made with only 4 ingredients."
Serving: 8 servings. | Prep: 10m | Ready in: 10m

Ingredients

- 1 cup sliced fresh or frozen peaches, divided
- 2 cups (16 oz.) fat-free reduced-sugar peach yogurt
- 1 carton (8 oz.) frozen reduced-fat whipped topping, thawed
- 1 reduced-fat graham cracker crust (8 inches)

Direction

- Chop 1/2 of the peaches finely, then put it in a bowl. Mix in yogurt. Fold in the whipped topping, then scoop into the crust.
- Put on cover and let it freeze for 4 hours or until it becomes firm. Prior to slicing, let it chill in the fridge for 45 minutes, then put the leftover peaches on top.

Nutrition Information

- Calories: 202 calories
- Total Carbohydrate: 30 g
- Cholesterol: 1 mg
- Total Fat: 6 g
- Fiber: 0 g
- Protein: 3 g
- Sodium: 127 mg

160. Frozen Fruit Salad

""Invigorating and yummy recipe! Flavorful and tart!""
Serving: 6 | Prep: 15m | Ready in: 1h15m

Ingredients

- 1/2 cup white sugar
- 2 cups water
- 1 (6 oz.) can frozen orange juice concentrate, thawed
- 1 (6 oz.) can frozen lemonade concentrate, thawed

- 4 bananas, sliced
- 1 (20 oz.) can crushed pineapple with juice
- 1 (10 oz.) package frozen strawberries, thawed

Direction

- Melt sugar in water. Mix in the strawberries, crushed pineapple with juice, bananas, lemonade and orange juice. Place into a glass pan that is 9x13 inch. Place inside the freezer until firm. Once ready to present, before trying to slice, let it sit out for about 5 minutes.

Nutrition Information

- Calories: 350 calories;
- Total Carbohydrate: 89.9 g
- Cholesterol: 0 mg
- Total Fat: 0.5 g
- Protein: 2.5 g
- Sodium: 5 mg

161. Frozen Pistachio Dessert With Raspberry Sauce

"Raspberry sauce brightens the flavor of this dish."
Serving: 12 servings. | Prep: 25m | Ready in: 35m

Ingredients

- 1-1/2 cups crushed vanilla wafers (about 45 wafers)
- 1/4 cup finely chopped pistachios
- 1/4 cup reduced-fat butter, melted
- 1-1/4 cups fat-free milk
- 1 package (1 oz.) sugar-free instant pistachio pudding mix
- 6 oz. reduced-fat cream cheese
- 1 carton (8 oz.) frozen fat-free whipped topping, thawed, divided
- 1 package (12 oz.) frozen unsweetened raspberries, thawed
- 2 tbsps. sugar
- 2 tbsps. orange liqueur or orange juice
- 2 tbsps. chopped pistachios

Direction

- Combine butter, wafers and finely chopped pistachios in a small bowl. Press onto bottom a 9-in. springform pan coated with the cooking spray. Put the pan on baking sheet. Bake for 10 mins at 350°, until lightly browned. Place on a wire rack to cool.
- In the meantime, whisk pudding mix and milk in a small bowl for 2 mins. Allow to stand until soft-set, about 2 mins. Beat the cream cheese in large bowl until smooth. Then beat in pudding.
- For garnish, put aside 3/4 cup of the whipped topping. Fold the remaining whipped topping into the cream cheese mixture. Add the filling over the crust. Put in freezer 5 hours or up to overnight. Place the remaining whipped topping in refrigerator, covered.
- To make sauce: in a food processor, put liqueur, sugar and raspberries. Cover, process until smooth, about 1 to 2 mins. Strain and remove the pulp and seeds. Place in the refrigerator until serving.
- Discard the dessert from freezer 15 mins before using. Discard the sides of the pan. Add the remaining whipped topping and chopped pistachios for garnish. Enjoy with sauce.

Nutrition Information

- Calories: 214 calories
- Total Carbohydrate: 28 g
- Cholesterol: 18 mg
- Total Fat: 9 g
- Fiber: 2 g
- Protein: 4 g
- Sodium: 268 mg

162. Frozen Strawberry Torte

"The special dessert!"
Serving: 10 servings. | Prep: 40m | Ready in: 40m

Ingredients

- 2 cups fresh strawberries, divided
- 1/4 cup sugar
- 1/2 cup fat-free milk
- 3 drops red food coloring, optional
- 1 package (1 oz.) sugar-free instant vanilla pudding mix
- 2 cups reduced-fat whipped topping
- 1 loaf (13.6 oz.) reduced-fat lb. cake

Direction

- Mash one cup of the strawberries with sugar in a bowl; allow to stand for half an hour. If desired, put in food coloring and milk. Scatter with the pudding mix, then stir until they are well blended. Fold in the whipped topping. Split the cake into 3 horizontal layers. Arrange the bottom layer on a serving plate, then spread with half a cup of the strawberry mixture. Repeat the layers. Place the third cake layer on top; spread over the sides and top of the cake with the remaining strawberry mixture.
- Freeze, covered, at least 60 mins or overnight. Discard from freezer. After 15 mins, slice. Add the remaining strawberries for garnish.

Nutrition Information

- Calories: 175 calories
- Total Carbohydrate: 37 g
- Cholesterol: 1 mg
- Total Fat: 1 g
- Fiber: 1 g
- Protein: 2 g
- Sodium: 301 mg

163. Fruit-filled Angel Food Torte

"A refreshing torte recipe."
Serving: 12 servings. | Prep: 15m | Ready in: 15m

Ingredients

- 1 carton (12 oz.) frozen reduced-fat whipped topping, thawed, divided
- 1 can (15 oz.) reduced-sugar fruit cocktail, drained
- 1 prepared angel food cake (8 to 10 oz.)
- 1 can (11 oz.) mandarin oranges, drained
- 1 large navel orange, sliced, optional
- Fresh mint, optional

Direction

- Fold 1 1/2 cups of whipped topping into fruit cocktail till just blended; horizontally, split cake to 3 layers. Put 1 layer on a serving plate; spread 1/2 fruit mixture then repeat layers. Put leftover cake layer on top.
- Frost sides and top with leftover whipped topping; put mandarin oranges over top. Refrigerate till serving; if desired, serve with mint and orange slices.

Nutrition Information

- Calories: 0g sugar total.

164. Fruit-packed Gelatin Salad

"This fruity gelatin becomes more attractive thanks to the cream cheese frosting. Combined with banana, pineapple, and berry, it is sure to be a star in dining tables."
Serving: 15 servings. | Prep: 20m | Ready in: 20m

Ingredients

- 2 packages (.3 oz. each) sugar-free strawberry gelatin
- 2 cups boiling water
- 2 packages (12 oz. each) frozen unsweetened strawberries, thawed and cut in half
- 1 can (20 oz.) unsweetened crushed pineapple

- 3 medium firm bananas, sliced
- 1 package (8 oz.) reduced-fat cream cheese
- 1 cup (8 oz.) fat-free sour cream
- 1/2 cup chopped walnuts, toasted

Direction

- Melt gelatin with boiling water in a large bowl. Add bananas, pineapple, and strawberries, mix. Pour into a 13x9-in. dish covered with cooking spray. Chill while covered until partly firm for about 1 hour.
- Combine sour cream and cream cheese in a small bowl till blended. Pour over gelatin mixture and spread carefully. Cover and chill until set. Garnish with some walnuts before serving.

Nutrition Information

- Calories: 142 calories
- Total Carbohydrate: 19 g
- Cholesterol: 13 mg
- Total Fat: 6 g
- Fiber: 2 g
- Protein: 5 g
- Sodium: 105 mg

165. Fruity Sherbet Dessert

"Refreshing and simple."
Serving: 2-1/2 quarts (20 servings). | Prep: 10m | Ready in: 10m

Ingredients

- 1/2 gallon pineapple sherbet, softened
- 2 packages (8 oz. each) frozen unsweetened raspberries, partially thawed
- 2 medium firm bananas, diced
- 1/2 tsp. almond extract

Direction

- In a big bowl, put sherbet; fold in leftover ingredients. Cover; freeze till firm or for 3 hours minimum.

Nutrition Information

- Calories: 133 calories
- Total Carbohydrate: 30 g
- Cholesterol: 5 mg
- Total Fat: 2 g
- Fiber: 2 g
- Protein: 1 g
- Sodium: 37 mg

166. Fudgy Peanut Butter Brownies

"This is a low-fat option when you crave those rich and fudgy brownies. Not less flavorful than any of your favorite chocolate brownie."
Serving: 20 brownies. | Prep: 20m | Ready in: 45m

Ingredients

- 2 cups sugar
- 1-1/2 cups all-purpose flour
- 3/4 cup baking cocoa
- 1/2 tsp. salt
- 2/3 cup unsweetened applesauce
- 3/4 cup egg substitute
- 2 tsps. vanilla extract
- FILLING:
- 3 oz. reduced-fat cream cheese, softened
- 1/3 cup reduced-fat peanut butter
- 1/4 cup sugar
- 1/4 cup egg substitute
- 1 tsp. vanilla extract
- FROSTING:
- 1 cup confectioners' sugar
- 3 tbsps. baking cocoa
- 2 tbsps. 2% milk
- 1 tsp. vanilla extract
- 1 tsp. water

Direction

- Mix together salt, cocoa, flour and sugar in a big bowl. Whisk in vanilla, egg substitute and applesauce. Spray a 13x9-inch baking pan with cooking spray and put in 1/2 batter.

- Whisk ingredients for the filling in a small bowl until smooth. Scoop the filling by tablespoonfuls and place on top of the batter. Put the remaining batter on top; swirl peanut butter mixture by cutting through the batter with a knife.
- Bake in 325-degree oven until the center is nearly set and edges are firm, about 25 to 30 minutes. Place a on a wire rack to cool.
- Whisk together ingredients for frosting in a small bowl until smooth. Frost the brownies.

Nutrition Information

- Calories: 201 calories
- Total Carbohydrate: 40 g
- Cholesterol: 3 mg
- Total Fat: 3 g
- Fiber: 2 g
- Protein: 5 g
- Sodium: 119 mg

167. Fudgy White Chocolate Pudding Pie

"A gooey and rich pie that will be very much loved. People don't seem to realize this is made with no sugar pudding mixes."
Serving: 8 servings. | Prep: 20m | Ready in: 20m

Ingredients

- 2 cups cold-fat-free milk, divided
- 1 package (1.4 oz.) sugar-free instant chocolate fudge pudding mix
- 1 carton (8 oz.) frozen reduced-fat whipped topping, thawed, divided
- 1 reduced-fat graham cracker crust (8 inches)
- 1 package (1 oz.) sugar-free instant white chocolate or vanilla pudding mix
- 1/2 oz. semisweet chocolate, shaved

Direction

- Beat chocolate fudge pudding mix and one cup milk in a small bowl until they become a little thicker, 2 minutes. Fold 1/2 whipped topping into the mixture. Spread onto crust.
- In a separate bowl, beat white chocolate pudding mix and remaining milk until they become a little thicker, 2 minutes. Fold the rest of whipped topping into mixture; lather on top of the fudge pudding layer. Chill in the refrigerator to set for 4 hours. Sprinkle shaved chocolate on top to decorate.

Nutrition Information

- Calories: 208 calories
- Total Carbohydrate: 28 g
- Cholesterol: 1 mg
- Total Fat: 7 g
- Fiber: 1 g
- Protein: 4 g
- Sodium: 154 mg

168. Ginger Thins

"Spiced dish with a dollop of lemon sherbet."
Serving: 3-1/2 dozen. | Prep: 15m | Ready in: 25m

Ingredients

- 6 tbsps. butter, softened
- 1/2 cup plus 2 tbsps. sugar, divided
- 2 tbsps. molasses
- 1 tbsp. cold strong brewed coffee
- 1-1/4 cups all-purpose flour
- 3/4 tsp. ground ginger
- 1/2 tsp. baking soda
- 1/2 tsp. ground cinnamon
- 1/4 tsp. ground cloves
- 1/8 tsp. salt
- Melted semisweet chocolate and chopped crystallized ginger, optional

Direction

- Cream half a cup of sugar and butter in a big bowl, until it becomes fluffy and light, then put the leftover sugar aside. Beat in the coffee and molasses into the creamed mixture. Mix

together the leftover ingredients, then add it into the creamed mixture until blended well (the dough will get soft).
- Put on cover and let it freeze for 15 minutes. Form the dough to 7-inch roll and flatten it to an inch thick. Use plastic to wrap it and let it freeze for 8 hours to overnight.
- Take off the wrap from the dough and slice it into 1/8-inch pieces. Put it on the baking trays lined with parchment and place it two inches apart. Sprinkle the reserved sugar on top. Let it bake for 8 to 10 minutes at 350 degrees or until it becomes firm. Take it out of the pans, then transfer to wire racks to let it cool. Dunk the cookies in melted chocolate and sprinkle ginger on top, if preferred.

Nutrition Information

- Calories: 81 calories
- Total Carbohydrate: 12 g
- Cholesterol: 8 mg
- Total Fat: 3 g
- Fiber: 1 g
- Protein: 1 g
- Sodium: 75 mg

169. Gingerbread Cookies

"These cookies will bring the merriness of your Christmas dinner!"
Serving: 30

Ingredients

- 1 1/2 cups dark molasses
- 1 cup packed brown sugar
- 2/3 cup cold water
- 1/3 cup shortening
- 7 cups all-purpose flour
- 2 tsps. baking soda
- 1 tsp. salt
- 1 tsp. ground allspice
- 2 tsps. ground ginger
- 1 tsp. ground cloves
- 1 tsp. ground cinnamon

- 1 (16 oz.) package chocolate frosting

Direction

- Heat the oven to 350°F (175°C). Grease lightly the one piece of the cookie sheet.
- Combine the water, molasses, shortening, and water.
- Sieve the baking soda, cinnamon, ginger, flour, cloves, allspice, and salt together. Mix into the sugar mixture, stirring well until combined. Keep in the refrigerator, 2 hours.
- Roll the dough out into 1/4-in. the thickness on a floured board. Using the floured gingerbread cutter, cut out cookies from the dough. Put on the cookies sheet, 2 inches apart. For 10 to 12 minutes, bake and allow cooling before decorating using frosting.

Nutrition Information

- Calories: 264 calories;
- Total Carbohydrate: 51.7 g
- Cholesterol: 0 mg
- Total Fat: 5.3 g
- Protein: 3.2 g
- Sodium: 199 mg

170. Graham Cracker Banana Split Dessert

"Even the diabetic can eat this."
Serving: 15 servings. | Prep: 25m | Ready in: 25m

Ingredients

- 2 cups reduced-fat graham cracker crumbs (about 10 whole crackers)
- 5 tbsps. reduced-fat margarine, melted
- 1 can (12 oz.) cold reduced-fat evaporated milk
- 3/4 cup cold fat-free milk
- 2 packages (1 oz. each) sugar-free instant vanilla pudding mix
- 2 medium firm bananas, sliced
- 1 can (20 oz.) unsweetened crushed pineapple, drained

- 1 carton (8 oz.) frozen reduced-fat whipped topping, thawed
- 3 tbsps. chopped walnuts
- 2 tbsps. chocolate syrup
- 5 maraschino cherries, quartered

Direction

- Mix together margarine and cracker crumbs; pat into a 13-in. x 9-in. dish sprayed with cooking spray.
- Whisk together the evaporated milk, fat-free milk and pudding mixes in a large bowl for 2 minutes (mixture will thicken).
- Evenly spread the pudding over the crust. Layer in the bananas, then pineapple and whipped topping. Sprinkle nuts on top and drizzle the top with chocolate syrup. Place cherries on top. Chill in refrigerator for no less than 1 hour before cutting.

Nutrition Information

- Calories: 194 calories
- Total Carbohydrate: 33 g
- Cholesterol: 4 mg
- Total Fat: 6 g
- Fiber: 1 g
- Protein: 3 g
- Sodium: 312 mg

171. Graham Cracker Crust

"Use softened butter in lieu of melted butter in this no-back recipe. This creates a better consistency for the crust."
Serving: 8 | Prep: 5m | Ready in: 1h5m

Ingredients

- 1 1/2 cups graham cracker crumbs
- 6 tbsps. butter, softened
- 1/3 cup white sugar

Direction

- In a bowl, combine sugar, butter and crumbs. Press the mixture into a 9-inch pie plate. Press the crumbs up the side of the plate with a spoon and press the crumbs down on the top using the side of your hand.
- Put in refrigerate for at least an hour before adding the filling.

Nutrition Information

- Calories: 175 calories;
- Total Carbohydrate: 20.4 g
- Cholesterol: 23 mg
- Total Fat: 10.2 g
- Protein: 1.2 g
- Sodium: 157 mg

172. Grandma Moyer's Rhubarb And Strawberry Coffee Cake

"I got this recipe from my grandmother. Since no less than the mid 80's, it has been lost. After my mom passed away, I found it in the middle of an old book I obtained. This delicious coffee cake is something that the family has been trying to recreate for years. It is very flavorful and moist. I prefer it to be a bit sweeter so I added the strawberries. People don't often use rhubarb anymore, but those who do always want to find new methods to spread the love."
Serving: 15 | Prep: 15m | Ready in: 1h

Ingredients

- 2 cups white sugar
- 2 eggs
- 1 cup cold coffee
- 3 cups all-purpose flour
- 2 tsps. baking soda
- 2 tsps. ground cinnamon
- 1/2 tsp. salt
- 3 cups chopped rhubarb
- 1 1/2 cups sliced strawberries
- 1/2 cup brown sugar
- 1/2 cup chopped pecans (optional)

Direction

- Set oven to preheat at 175°C (350°F). Grease and flour a baking pan 9x13-inch in size.

- Beat together eggs and white sugar in a large bowl until smooth; mix in the coffee. Whisk salt, cinnamon, baking soda, and flour in a separate bowl. To the moist ingredients, beat in the dry ingredients until just incorporated; mix strawberries and rhubarb into the batter. Transfer batter into the prepared cake pan and sprinkle pecans and brown sugar on top.
- In the preheated oven, bake until the cake is light brown and a toothpick comes out clean when inserted into the middle, for 45 to 50 minutes.

Nutrition Information

- Calories: 270 calories;
- Total Carbohydrate: 56 g
- Cholesterol: 25 mg
- Total Fat: 3.9 g
- Protein: 4.1 g
- Sodium: 259 mg

173. Granola Blondies

""Add a little fun to your fudgy blondies with the crunchy texture of granola. The dried fruit sweetened the treat so naturally.""

Serving: 1 dozen. | Prep: 15m | Ready in: 40m

Ingredients

- 1 egg
- 1 egg white
- 1-1/4 cups packed brown sugar
- 1/4 cup canola oil
- 1 cup all-purpose flour
- 1 tsp. baking powder
- 1/2 tsp. salt
- 2 cups reduced-fat granola with raisins
- 1 cup dried cranberries or cherries

Direction

- Beat oil, brown sugar, egg white and egg in a big bowl until incorporated. Mix together salt, baking powder and flour; slowly whisk into the wet mixture just until incorporated. Mix in cranberries and granola (batter's consistency will be thick).
- Spray a square baking pan (9 inches) with cooking spray and spread with batter. Bake in 350-degree oven until the cake is set and turns golden brown, about 25 to 30 minutes. Place on a wire rack to cool. Slice into bars.

Nutrition Information

- Calories: 256 calories
- Total Carbohydrate: 49 g
- Cholesterol: 18 mg
- Total Fat: 6 g
- Fiber: 2 g
- Protein: 3 g
- Sodium: 173 mg

174. Granola Cereal Bars

""This recipe is perfect for dessert, breakfast or anytime as an instant snack. You can out raisins in place of chocolate chips if wished.""

Serving: 1 dozen. | Prep: 15m | Ready in: 15m

Ingredients

- 1/2 cup packed brown sugar
- 1/2 cup creamy peanut butter
- 1/4 cup light corn syrup
- 1 tsp. vanilla extract
- 2 cups old-fashioned oats
- 1-1/2 cups crisp rice cereal
- 1/4 cup miniature chocolate chips

Direction

- Mix in a microwave-safe bowl the corn syrup, peanut butter and brown sugar; then cover and put in a microwave on high for 2 minutes or until mixture comes to a boil, whisking once. Mix in the vanilla; put in cereal and oats. Add in chocolate chips and fold. Then press into a 9-inch square pan coated with cooking spray. Let it cool and slice into bars.

Nutrition Information

- Calories: 199 calories
- Total Carbohydrate: 31 g
- Cholesterol: 0 mg
- Total Fat: 7 g
- Fiber: 2 g
- Protein: 5 g
- Sodium: 88 mg

175. Granola Fruit Bars

"A healthy and delicious bar for snack time or breakfast."
Serving: 8 servings. | Prep: 10m | Ready in: 10m

Ingredients

- 1/2 cup chopped dried apples
- 1/3 cup honey
- 1/4 cup raisins
- 1 tbsp. brown sugar
- 1/3 cup reduced-fat peanut butter
- 1/4 cup apple butter
- 1/2 tsp. ground cinnamon
- 1/2 cup old-fashioned oats
- 1/3 cup honey crunch or toasted wheat germ
- 1/4 cup chopped pecans
- 2-1/2 cups cornflakes

Direction

- In a large saucepan, combine brown sugar, raisins, honey and apples. Heat until boiling over medium heat, stir frequently. Cook and stir for 1 more minute. Take away from the heat; mix in peanut butter until it melts.
- Add cinnamon and apple butter. Mix in the pecans, wheat germ and oats. Fold in the cornflakes. Pat firmly into an 8-in. square pan sprayed with cooking spray. Refrigerate until set, about 1 hour. Slice into bars. Refrigerate in an airtight container to store.

Nutrition Information

- Calories: 239 calories
- Total Carbohydrate: 42 g
- Cholesterol: 0 mg
- Total Fat: 7 g
- Fiber: 3 g
- Protein: 6 g
- Sodium: 160 mg

176. Green Apple Sorbet With Pistachios

"Light and tasty!"
Serving: 4 | Prep: 15m | Ready in: 25m

Ingredients

- Sorbet:
- 2 large green apples, chopped
- 1/2 cup water
- 1/4 cup white sugar
- 1 tbsp. fresh lemon juice
- Toppings:
- 1 green apple, sliced
- 1/2 cup pistachios, or to taste
- 1 tbsp. confectioners' sugar

Direction

- Combine water, white sugar, lemon juice and 2 chopped apples in the food processor and process until mixture is smooth.
- Transfer blended apple puree to an ice cream machine and follow manufacturer's directions to make frozen sorbet, 10-15 minutes.
- To serve, garnish with pistachios, sliced green apple and confectioners' sugar.

Nutrition Information

- Calories: 217 calories;
- Total Carbohydrate: 38.2 g
- Cholesterol: 0 mg
- Total Fat: 7.3 g
- Protein: 3.6 g
- Sodium: 68 mg

177. Green Tomato Mincemeat

"A wonderful recipe to use green tomatoes."
Serving: 120 | Prep: 45m | Ready in: 4h45m

Ingredients

- 8 quarts green tomatoes, minced
- 8 quarts minced, cored apples
- 1/2 lb. beef suet
- 6 lbs. brown sugar
- 1 cup distilled white vinegar
- 2 tbsps. salt
- 2 tbsps. ground cinnamon
- 2 tbsps. ground cloves
- 2 tbsps. ground allspice
- 2 lbs. raisins
- 32 oz. candied mixed citrus peel (optional)
- 7 large orange, peeled, sectioned, and cut into bite-size
- 2 lemons, finely chopped

Direction

- Mix candied peel, raisins, chopped lemons, chopped oranges, vinegar, brown sugar, suet or oil, apples, and green tomatoes in a very large stockpot. Flavor with allspice, cloves, cinnamon, and salt. Put a cover on and cook for 3 hours on low heat.
- Following the manufacturer's directions, sterilize 30 canning jars (a pint) and lids.
- Fill the sterilized jars with the filling, leaving a 1/2 inch head space. Use a clean, damp cloth to wipe the jar. Put lids on jars to cover and screw on the jar rings.
- In a hot water canner, heat the water. Arrange the jars in the rack and lower the jars into the canner slowly. Cover the jars completely with water, and the water should be hot yet not boiling. Boil the water and pulse for 10 minutes.

Nutrition Information

- Calories: 179 calories;
- Total Carbohydrate: 42.1 g
- Cholesterol: 1 mg
- Total Fat: 2 g
- Protein: 0.9 g
- Sodium: 126 mg

178. Guava Preserves

"Moist and very sweet Venezuelan dessert recipe."
Serving: 30 | Prep: 30m | Ready in: 1h15m

Ingredients

- 24 guavas, peeled
- 2 quarts water
- 4 cups white sugar
- 1 cup fresh orange juice
- 1 cup white sugar, or as needed
- plantain leaves for wrapping (optional)

Direction

- In a big pot, put the guavas and pour water approximately 2 quarts enough to cover the guavas, then boil. Let it simmer for around half an hour on medium heat. Let the fruit drain and pass it through a food mill or strainer so it will be turned into pulp.
- In a copper or stainless-steel pot, put the pulp and mix in orange juice and 4 cups of sugar. Let it cook on medium heat and use a wooden spoon to mix it continuously, until the mixture becomes thick enough to peel off the pan's bottom.
- Cover approximately 1/2 of the leftover sugar on the surface of a 10x15-inch jelly roll pan, then pour in the hot guava mixture and sprinkle the leftover sugar on top. Allow to cool to room temperature. Once it is cooled, slice it into squares and use dried plantain leaves to wrap it if you want. You may opt to wrap it in cellophane or waxed paper if dried plantain leaves are unavailable.

Nutrition Information

- Calories: 182 calories;
- Total Carbohydrate: 44.5 g
- Cholesterol: 0 mg

- Total Fat: 0.7 g
- Protein: 1.9 g
- Sodium: 3 mg

179. Guilt-free Chocolate Cake

""This delicious cake turns out a wonderful dessert.""
Serving: 12 servings. | Prep: 10m | Ready in: 45m

Ingredients

- 1 package devil's food cake mix (regular size)
- 1-1/3 cups water
- 1 cup reduced-fat plain yogurt
- 1/2 cup baking cocoa
- 2 egg whites
- 1 egg
- 1-1/2 tsps. confectioners' sugar

Direction

- Mix together egg, egg whites, cocoa, yogurt, water and cake mix in a large bowl; beat for 30 seconds on low. Beat for 2 minutes on medium.
- Transfer into a 10-in. fluted tube pan sprayed with cooking spray. Bake at 350° till a toothpick turns out clean when inserted into the center, about 35-40 minutes. Allow to cool for 10 minutes; take away from the pan and allow to cool completely on a wire rack. Dust with confectioners' sugar.

Nutrition Information

- Calories: 191 calories
- Total Carbohydrate: 40 g
- Cholesterol: 19 mg
- Total Fat: 3 g
- Fiber: 2 g
- Protein: 5 g
- Sodium: 399 mg

180. Harvest Snack Cake

""This moist cake recipe calls for just simple ingredients.""
Serving: 15 servings. | Prep: 15m | Ready in: 45m

Ingredients

- 2 cups whole wheat flour
- 1-1/4 cups packed brown sugar
- 2 tsps. baking soda
- 3/4 tsp. ground cinnamon
- 1/2 tsp. ground nutmeg
- 1/8 to 1/4 tsp. ground ginger
- 2 eggs
- 1/2 cup unsweetened applesauce
- 1 tsp. vanilla extract
- 1-1/2 cups shredded carrots
- 1 cup raisins

Direction

- In a large bowl, mix together ginger, nutmeg, cinnamon, baking soda, brown sugar and flour. Mix vanilla, applesauce and eggs; combine into the dry ingredients just till moisten. Fold in raisins and carrots. (The batter should be thick.).
- Scatter evenly on a 13 x 9-inch baking pan greased using cooking spray. Bake at 350° till a toothpick comes out clean when inserted into the center, 30-35 minutes. Place on a wire rack to cool.

Nutrition Information

- Calories: 170 calories
- Total Carbohydrate: 39 g
- Cholesterol: 28 mg
- Total Fat: 1 g
- Fiber: 3 g
- Protein: 3 g
- Sodium: 191 mg

181. Healthier (but Still) The Best Rolled Sugar Cookies

"A guilt-free and amazing sugar cookies recipe made with sugar-like sweetener."
Serving: 60 | Prep: 20m | Ready in: 1h28m

Ingredients

- 1 1/2 cups butter, softened
- 1 cup granular sucralose sweetener (such as Splenda®)
- 1/3 cup white sugar
- 4 eggs
- 1 tsp. vanilla extract
- 5 cups all-purpose flour
- 2 tsps. baking powder

Direction

- In a big bowl, cream together the sugar, sweetener and butter until smooth. Beat in vanilla extract and eggs, then stir in baking powder and flour. Put cover on and chill the dough for a minimum of 1 hour or overnight.
- Set an oven to preheat to 200°C (400°F).
- On a floured surface, roll out the dough to 1/4- to 1/2-inch thick. Use any cookie cutter to cut it into shapes. On ungreased baking trays, put the cookies 1 inch apart.
- Bake for about 6-8 minutes in the preheated oven until they turn golden. Allow to completely cool.

Nutrition Information

- Calories: 88 calories;
- Total Carbohydrate: 9.3 g
- Cholesterol: 25 mg
- Total Fat: 5 g
- Protein: 1.5 g
- Sodium: 54 mg

182. Healthier Apple Crisp II

"A healthy dessert made with walnuts, white whole wheat flour, unpeeled apples and less sugar."
Serving: 12 | Prep: 30m | Ready in: 1h15m

Ingredients

- 10 cups unpeeled, cored, and sliced apples
- 1/2 cup white sugar
- 1 tbsp. white whole wheat flour
- 1 tsp. ground cinnamon
- 1/2 cup water
- 1 cup quick cooking oats
- 1 cup white whole wheat flour
- 1/2 cup packed brown sugar
- 1/2 cup chopped walnuts
- 1/4 tsp. baking powder
- 1/4 tsp. baking soda
- 1/2 cup butter, melted

Direction

- Set an oven to preheat to 175°C (350°F).
- In a 9x13-inch pan put the sliced apples. Combine the ground cinnamon, 1 tbsp flour and white sugar, then sprinkle it on top of the apples. Evenly pour the water all over.
- Mix together the melted butter, walnuts, baking soda, baking powder, brown sugar, 1 cup of flour and oats, then evenly crumble on top of the apple mixture.
- Let it bake for around 45 minutes at 175°C (350°F).

Nutrition Information

- Calories: 280 calories;
- Total Carbohydrate: 43.9 g
- Cholesterol: 20 mg
- Total Fat: 11.6 g
- Protein: 3.4 g
- Sodium: 95 mg

183. Healthier Apple Pie By Grandma Ople

"A better version of an apple pie recipe made with less butter and no sugar."
Serving: 8 | Prep: 30m | Ready in: 1h30m

Ingredients

- 1 recipe pastry for a 9 inch double crust pie
- 1/4 cup unsalted butter
- 3 tbsps. all-purpose flour
- 1/4 cup water
- 1/2 cup packed brown sugar
- 8 Granny Smith apples - peeled, cored and sliced

Direction

- Set an oven to preheat to 220°C (425°F). In a saucepan, melt the butter. Mix in flour to form a paste, then add brown sugar and water, then boil. Lower the temperature and allow it to simmer.
- Put the bottom crust in the pan and fill it with apples, mounded a bit. Put a latticework of crust to cover. Pour the butter liquid and sugar gently on top of the crust. Slowly pour to avoid running off.
- Let it bake in the preheated oven for 15 minutes. Lower the temperature to 175°C (350°F). Keep on baking for 35 to 45 minutes until the apples become soft.

Nutrition Information

- Calories: 413 calories;
- Total Carbohydrate: 55.3 g
- Cholesterol: 15 mg
- Total Fat: 21 g
- Protein: 3.5 g
- Sodium: 240 mg

184. Healthier Award Winning Soft Chocolate Chip Cookies

"An altered dish made with raisins and applesauce that has 1/2 less the fat."
Serving: 72 | Prep: 15m | Ready in: 1h30m

Ingredients

- 4 1/2 cups all-purpose flour
- 2 tsps. baking soda
- 1 cup butter, softened
- 1/2 cup unsweetened applesauce
- 1 1/2 cups packed brown sugar
- 1/2 cup white sugar
- 2 (3.4 oz.) packages instant vanilla pudding mix
- 4 eggs
- 2 tsps. vanilla extract
- 2 cups semisweet chocolate chips
- 1 cup raisins
- 2 cups chopped walnuts (optional)

Direction

- Set an oven to preheat to 175°C (350°F). Sift together the baking soda and flour.
- In a big bowl, beat the white sugar, brown sugar, applesauce and butter using an electric mixer until smooth. Stir in instant pudding until well combined. Mix in eggs, one at a time, letting each egg combine into the butter mixture prior to adding the next one. Beat in vanilla extract. Blend the flour mixture into the butter mixture until just combined. Fold in walnuts, raisins and chocolate chips, then mix just enough to evenly blend. On the ungreased baking trays, drop spoonfuls of the dough 2 inches apart.
- Let bake in the preheated oven for 10-12 minutes until the edges of the cookies turn golden brown. Allow to cool on wire racks.

Nutrition Information

- Calories: 138 calories;
- Total Carbohydrate: 19.5 g
- Cholesterol: 17 mg

- Total Fat: 6.5 g
- Protein: 1.9 g
- Sodium: 97 mg

185. Healthier Best Big, Fat, Chewy Chocolate Chip Cookie

"Healthy yet yummy and chewy treat."
Serving: 18 | Prep: 10m | Ready in: 1h25m

Ingredients

- 2 cups all-purpose flour
- 1/2 tsp. baking soda
- 1/2 cup unsalted butter, melted
- 1/4 cup non-fat plain yogurt
- 1 cup packed brown sugar
- 1/2 cup white sugar
- 1 tbsp. vanilla extract
- 1 egg
- 1 egg yolk
- 1 cup semisweet chocolate chips
- 1/2 cup blueberries
- 1/2 cup dried cranberries

Direction

- Set the oven to 165°C or 325°F to preheat. Use parchment paper to line baking sheets or coat them with grease.
- In a small bowl, sift baking soda and flour together, then put aside.
- In a bowl, beat together white sugar, brown sugar, yogurt and melted butter until combined. Beat in egg yolk, egg and vanilla extract until the mixture is creamy and light, then mix in flour mixture just until combined. Mix in cranberries, blueberries and chocolate chips by hand with a wooden spoon, then drop 1/4 cup of cookie dough onto prepped baking sheets, 3 in. apart.
- In the preheated oven, bake for 15-17 minutes, until edges are toasted slightly. Allow to cool on baking sheets for 5 minutes prior to removing to wire racks to cool thoroughly.

Nutrition Information

- Calories: 232 calories;
- Total Carbohydrate: 38 g
- Cholesterol: 35 mg
- Total Fat: 8.7 g
- Protein: 2.6 g
- Sodium: 47 mg

186. Healthier Best Brownies

"A healthier version of a brownie recipe that has chocolatey flavor and frosting."
Serving: 16 | Prep: 25m | Ready in: 1h20m

Ingredients

- 1/4 cup butter
- 1/2 cup white sugar
- 2 eggs
- 1/3 cup applesauce
- 1 tsp. vanilla extract
- 1/3 cup unsweetened cocoa powder
- 1/3 cup white whole wheat flour
- 1/4 tsp. salt
- 1/4 tsp. baking powder
- 3 tbsps. butter, softened
- 3 tbsps. unsweetened cocoa powder
- 1 tbsp. honey
- 1 tsp. vanilla extract
- 1/2 cup confectioners' sugar

Direction

- Set an oven to preheat to 350 degrees F or 175 degree C, then grease and flour an 8-inch square pan.
- In a big saucepan, melt 1/4 cup of the butter on low heat. Take it out of the heat and stir in 1 tsp vanilla extract, applesauce, eggs and white sugar. Beat in baking powder, salt, flour and 1/3 cup of cocoa powder, then spread it into the prepped pan.
- Let it bake in the preheated oven for 20-25 minutes until the brownies are just set in the middle.

- In a bowl, mix together the confectioner's sugar, 1 tsp vanilla extract, honey, 2 tbsp. cocoa powder and 3 tbsp. butter and beat it until it has a smooth consistency. While they are still warm, frost the brownies.

Nutrition Information

- Calories: 115 calories;
- Total Carbohydrate: 15.1 g
- Cholesterol: 37 mg
- Total Fat: 6.1 g
- Protein: 1.7 g
- Sodium: 89 mg

187. Healthier Best Chocolate Chip Cookies

"A lighter version of the cookie recipe made with sweet potato puree and juice from orange."
Serving: 24 | Prep: 20m | Ready in: 1h

Ingredients

- 1/2 cup butter, softened
- 1/4 cup sweet potato puree
- 1/2 cup white sugar
- 1 cup packed brown sugar
- 1/2 cup orange juice
- 4 egg whites
- 2 tsps. vanilla extract
- 1 tsp. baking soda
- 2 tsps. hot water
- 3 cups all-purpose flour
- 2 cups semisweet chocolate chips
- 1 cup chopped walnuts

Direction

- Set an oven to preheat to 175°C (350°F).
- In a big bowl, beat the orange juice, brown sugar, white sugar, sweet potato and butter using an electric mixer until smooth. Add the egg whites, one at a time, letting each egg combine into the butter mixture prior to adding the next. Beat in vanilla extract. In a small bowl, dissolve the baking soda in hot water, then add it to the sweet potato batter. Stir in walnuts, chocolate chips and flour. Roll the dough into walnut-sized balls and put two inches apart onto the ungreased baking trays.
- Let it bake in the preheated oven for around 10 minutes until the edges turn brown nicely.

Nutrition Information

- Calories: 249 calories;
- Total Carbohydrate: 35.8 g
- Cholesterol: 10 mg
- Total Fat: 11.4 g
- Protein: 3.7 g
- Sodium: 96 mg

188. Healthier Beth's Spicy Oatmeal Raisin Cookies

"Spicy and chewy oatmeal raisin cookies made with less sugar and more white whole wheat flour."
Serving: 36 | Prep: 15m | Ready in: 27m

Ingredients

- 3/4 cup all-purpose flour
- 3/4 cup white whole wheat flour
- 1 tsp. baking soda
- 1 tsp. ground cinnamon
- 1/2 tsp. ground cloves
- 1/2 tsp. salt
- 1 cup butter, softened
- 1/2 cup packed light brown sugar
- 1/4 cup white sugar
- 2 eggs
- 1 tsp. vanilla extract
- 3 cups rolled oats
- 1 cup raisins

Direction

- Set an oven to preheat to 175°C (350°F). In a bowl, mix together the salt, cloves, cinnamon, baking soda, whole wheat flour and all-purpose flour.

- In a big bowl, beat the white sugar, brown sugar and butter using an electric mixer until it has a smooth texture. Add eggs, one at a time, letting each egg combine into the butter mixture prior to adding the next. Beat in vanilla extract with the last egg. Stir in flour mixture until just combined. Fold in raisins and rolled oats, then mix just enough to blend evenly. Roll the dough into walnut-sized balls and put two inches apart onto the ungreased baking trays.
- Let bake in the preheated oven for 10-12 minutes until golden and light. Allow them to cool for 2 minutes prior to cooling fully on a wire rack, then store in an airtight container.

Nutrition Information

- Calories: 123 calories;
- Total Carbohydrate: 16.2 g
- Cholesterol: 24 mg
- Total Fat: 5.9 g
- Protein: 2 g
- Sodium: 109 mg

189. Healthier Big Soft Ginger Cookies

"Taste the delicious flavor of this cookie with one big bite!"
Serving: 24 | Prep: 15m | Ready in: 40m

Ingredients

- 1 1/4 cups all-purpose flour
- 1 cup white whole wheat flour
- 2 tsps. ground ginger
- 1 tsp. baking soda
- 3/4 tsp. ground cinnamon
- 1/2 tsp. ground cloves
- 1/4 tsp. salt
- 3/4 cup unsalted butter
- 3/4 cup white sugar
- 1 egg
- 1 tbsp. water
- 1/4 cup molasses
- 3 tbsps. natural (raw) sugar

Direction

- Heat the oven to 350°F (175°C). Sieve the whole-wheat flour and all-purpose flour, salt, cinnamon, ginger, baking soda, and cloves together.
- Using an electric mixer, whisk the 3/4 cups of sugar and butter into a big bowl until smooth. Stir in the egg. Beat in the molasses and water. Slowly mix in the flour mixture just until combined. Roll out the dough to balls that are walnut-sized. Put into the unprepared baking pans, 2 inches apart and slightly flatten.
- Place in the heated oven and bake until cookies turn golden brown for 8 to 10 minutes. Let cookies cool on the baking pans, 5 minutes. Transfer on wire racks to completely cool. Keep on a tightly sealed container.

Nutrition Information

- Calories: 135 calories;
- Total Carbohydrate: 19.1 g
- Cholesterol: 23 mg
- Total Fat: 6.1 g
- Protein: 1.7 g
- Sodium: 83 mg

190. Healthier Cake Balls

"A super addicting recipe that's healthy because it uses organic cake mix. Shortening and bittersweet chocolate instead of chocolate confectioners coating make it healthier too.""
Serving: 36 | Prep: 40m | Ready in: 1h35m

Ingredients

- 1 (18.25 oz.) package natural cake mix
- 2 large eggs
- 1 cup low-fat milk
- 1 tsp. vanilla extract
- 1 (16 oz.) package chocolate frosting
- 3 oz. chopped semisweet chocolate
- 1 tbsp. natural shortening

Direction

- Set oven to preheat at 350°F (175°C). Grease 2 round 8-inch cake tins lightly or one 9x13-in. cake pan. Flour the tins.
- Pour cake mix in a bowl. Add milk, eggs, and vanilla extract. Beat with an electric mixer for a minute in low speed. Turn speed up to medium-high and beat for two more minutes. Scrape the sides of the bowl. Pour batter to the cake tin.
- Bake in the oven for 40-50 minutes, if you are using a 9x13-inch tin, and 25-35 minutes if you are using an 8-inch cake tin, until the inserted toothpick comes out clean. Let it rest for 10 minutes.
- While it is still warm, crumble the cake into a bowl. Mix in the frosting well.
- Melt shortening and chopped chocolate in a bowl over medium heat in the microwave, for 1 minute. (You can also melt the shortening and chopped chocolate in a metal bowl placed on top of a pot of simmering water, mix occasionally until it's smooth.)
- Mold into chocolate cake balls, using a scoop or melon baller. Dip them in the warmed chocolate mix using a fork or toothpick. Cool down on waxed paper.

Nutrition Information

- Calories: 135 calories;
- Total Carbohydrate: 21 g
- Cholesterol: 11 mg
- Total Fat: 5.4 g
- Protein: 1.5 g
- Sodium: 125 mg

191. Healthier Chantal's New York Cheesecake

""An easy hassle-free cake that turns out delightfully yummy. I made sure to slash some fat content to make it healthier, and it still tastes rich for a dessert.""
Serving: 12 | Prep: 30m | Ready in: 2h30m

Ingredients

- 15 graham crackers, crushed
- 2 tbsps. butter, melted
- 4 (8 oz.) packages Neufchatel cheese
- 1 1/2 cups white sugar
- 3/4 cup low-fat (1%) milk
- 4 eggs
- 1 cup reduced-fat sour cream
- 1 tbsp. vanilla extract
- 1/4 cup all-purpose flour

Direction

- Prepare an oven by heating it to 175 degrees C or 350 degrees F. Take a 9-inch springform pan and grease it.
- In a bowl, combine melted butter and graham cracker crumbs. Press them onto the surface of the springform pan.
- Mix together the sugar and Neufchatel cheese to a smooth texture. Pour in the milk, and mix it well with one egg at a time, stirring well to blend. Add in the sour cream, vanilla extract, and flour until blended well and smooth. Take the cream cheese and pour into the prepared crust.
- Let it bake in the preheated oven for an hour until the center sets. Switch off the oven, then leave the cake in the oven for another 5 to 6 hours and let it cool to avoid cracking. Place in the fridge, then serve.

Nutrition Information

- Calories: 452 calories;
- Total Carbohydrate: 44.5 g
- Cholesterol: 132 mg
- Total Fat: 25.4 g
- Protein: 12.1 g

- Sodium: 456 mg

192. Healthier Creamy Rice Pudding

"A healthier rice pudding recipe made with brown rice."
Serving: 4 | Prep: 45m | Ready in: 1h5m

Ingredients

- 1 1/2 cups water
- 3/4 cup uncooked brown rice
- 1 1/2 cups low-fat milk
- 1/3 cup white sugar
- 1/4 tsp. salt
- 1/2 cup low-fat milk
- 1 egg, beaten
- 2/3 cup raisins
- 1 tbsp. butter
- 1/2 tsp. vanilla extract

Direction

- In a saucepan, mix together the rice and water on high heat, then boil. Lower the heat to medium-low, put cover and let it simmer for around 45 minutes until it becomes tender.
- In a clean saucepan, mix together the salt, sugar, 1 1/2 cups milk and cooked rice. Let it cook for 15 to 20 minutes on medium heat until it becomes creamy and thick. Stir in raisins, beaten egg and leftover 1/2 cup of milk. Let it cook for additional 2 minutes, mixing continuously. Take it out of the heat and stir in vanilla extract and butter. Serve it warm.

Nutrition Information

- Calories: 363 calories;
- Total Carbohydrate: 69.2 g
- Cholesterol: 59 mg
- Total Fat: 6.4 g
- Protein: 9.2 g
- Sodium: 252 mg

193. Healthier No Bake Cookies I

"This cookies recipe is so healthy and amazing."
Serving: 36 | Prep: 10m | Ready in: 45m

Ingredients

- 1 1/4 cups white sugar
- 1/2 cup low-fat (1%) milk
- 1/2 cup butter
- 4 tbsps. unsweetened cocoa powder
- 1/2 cup crunchy peanut butter
- 3 cups quick-cooking oats
- 1/2 cup unsweetened coconut
- 1 tsp. vanilla extract

Direction

- Mix the cocoa, butter, milk, and sugar in the saucepan. Boil and cook for roughly 1 1/2 minutes till the sugar is dissolved. Take out of the heat and stir in the vanilla extract, coconut, oats and peanut butter. Roll the dough into walnut-sized balls and position onto the waxed paper. Allow it to cool down till hardened.

Nutrition Information

- Calories: 108 calories;
- Total Carbohydrate: 13.1 g
- Cholesterol: 7 mg
- Total Fat: 5.7 g
- Protein: 2.1 g
- Sodium: 38 mg

194. Healthier Southern Peach Cobbler

"A healthy version of the recipe made with peaches."
Serving: 4 | Prep: 20m | Ready in: 1h

Ingredients

- 8 fresh peaches - peeled, pitted, and sliced into thin wedges
- 2 tbsps. brown sugar
- 1/4 tsp. ground cinnamon
- 1/8 tsp. ground nutmeg
- 1 tsp. fresh lemon juice
- 2 tsps. cornstarch
- 1 cup whole wheat pastry flour
- 1/4 cup white sugar
- 1/4 cup brown sugar
- 1 tsp. baking powder
- 1/2 tsp. salt
- 6 tbsps. unsalted butter, chilled and cut into small pieces
- 1/4 cup boiling water
- 2 tbsps. brown sugar
- 1 tsp. ground cinnamon

Direction

- Set an oven to preheat to 220°C (425°F).
- In a big bowl, mix together the cornstarch, lemon juice, nutmeg, 1/4 tsp cinnamon, 2 tbsp. brown sugar and peaches, then toss until evenly coated; pour into a 2-quart baking dish.
- Let it bake for 10 minutes in the preheated oven.
- In the meantime, in a big bowl, mix together the salt, baking powder, 1/4 cup brown sugar, white sugar and flour. Use a pastry blender or your fingertips to blend in the butter until the mixture looks like coarse meal. Mix in water until just blended.
- Take out the peaches from the oven and drop spoonfuls of the flour mixture on top of them.
- Combine 1 tsp ground cinnamon and 2 tbsp. brown sugar. Sprinkle cinnamon-sugar mixture over the entire cobbler. Let it bake for about 30 minutes until the topping turns golden.

Nutrition Information

- Calories: 446 calories;
- Total Carbohydrate: 71 g
- Cholesterol: 46 mg
- Total Fat: 17.7 g
- Protein: 3.3 g
- Sodium: 431 mg

195. Healthy And Tasty Strawberry Sherbet

"A tasty, simple and quick strawberry sherbet."
Serving: 4 | Prep: 5m | Ready in: 1h5m

Ingredients

- 2 cups frozen strawberries
- 2 tbsps. white sugar
- 1 tsp. lemon juice

Direction

- In a food processor, put strawberries and beat about 30 seconds until smooth. Beat in lemon juice and sugar, about 10 seconds more.
- Put sherbet in the freezer for about 1 hour until solid.

Nutrition Information

- Calories: 63 calories;
- Total Carbohydrate: 16.5 g
- Cholesterol: 0 mg
- Total Fat: 0.1 g
- Protein: 0.5 g
- Sodium: 2 mg

196. Healthy Apple Cobbler

"The scent of cinnamon and apples in this dish always reminds me of fall."
Serving: 8 servings. | Prep: 20m | Ready in: 50m

Ingredients

- 1/3 cup sugar
- 1 tbsp. cornstarch
- 1/2 tsp. ground cinnamon
- 1/4 tsp. ground nutmeg
- 4 cups sliced peeled tart apples (about 4 large)
- 1/3 cup orange juice
- TOPPING:
- 1 cup all-purpose flour
- 1/3 cup plus 2 tsps. sugar, divided
- 1-1/2 tsps. baking powder
- 1/4 tsp. salt
- 1/4 cup cold butter, cubed
- 1/2 cup fat-free milk

Direction

- Mix the nutmeg, cinnamon, cornstarch and sugar in a big bowl. Put in apples and orange juice; mix to coat. Add to an 11x7-inch baking pan greased with cooking spray.
- To make topping, mix salt, baking powder, 1/3 cup sugar and flour. Stir in butter until the mixture looks much like coarse crumbs. Mix in milk just until moisten. Put 8 mounds onto the apple mix. Dust with leftover sugar. Bake for 30-35 minutes at 375° or until a toothpick inserted into the topping exists clean. Serve warm (optional).

Nutrition Information

- Calories: 253 calories
- Total Carbohydrate: 49 g
- Cholesterol: 16 mg
- Total Fat: 6 g
- Fiber: 3 g
- Protein: 2 g
- Sodium: 184 mg

197. Healthy Banana Cookies

"These cookies are both tasty and nutritious."
Serving: 36 | Prep: 15m | Ready in: 50m

Ingredients

- 3 ripe bananas
- 2 cups rolled oats
- 1 cup dates, pitted and chopped
- 1/3 cup vegetable oil
- 1 tsp. vanilla extract

Direction

- Set oven at 175°C (350°F) and start preheating.
- Smash bananas in a big bowl. Mix in vanilla, oil, dates and oats. Blend well, let rest for 15 minutes. Drop them by teaspoonfuls on an uncoated cookie tray.
- Put them in the preheated oven and bake until they turn light brown, or for 20 minutes.

Nutrition Information

- Calories: 56 calories;
- Total Carbohydrate: 8.4 g
- Cholesterol: 0 mg
- Total Fat: 2.4 g
- Protein: 0.8 g
- Sodium: < 1 mg

198. Healthy Blackberry Cobbler

"This treat is so healthy and delicious."
Serving: 10 servings. | Prep: 15m | Ready in: 60m

Ingredients

- 1/2 cup sugar
- 4-1/2 tsps. quick-cooking tapioca
- 1/4 tsp. ground allspice
- 5 cups fresh or frozen blackberries, thawed
- 2 tbsps. orange juice
- DOUGH:
- 1 cup all-purpose flour
- 1/3 cup plus 1 tbsp. sugar, divided

- 1/4 tsp. baking soda
- 1/4 tsp. salt
- 1/3 cup vanilla yogurt
- 1/3 cup fat-free milk
- 3 tbsps. butter, melted

Direction

- In the big bowl, mix allspice, tapioca, and sugar. Put in the orange juice and blackberries; coat by tossing. Allow it to rest for 15 minutes. Scoop to the 2-quart baking plate that is coated using the cooking spray.
- In the big bowl, mix salt, baking soda, a third cup of the sugar and flour. Mix butter, milk and yogurt; whisk to the dry ingredients till becoming smooth. Spread on berry mixture.
- Bake at 350 degrees for 20 minutes. Drizzle with the rest of the sugar. Bake till turning golden-brown or for 25 to 30 minutes more. Serve while warm.

Nutrition Information

- Calories: 199 calories
- Total Carbohydrate: 40 g
- Cholesterol: 10 mg
- Total Fat: 4 g
- Fiber: 4 g
- Protein: 3 g
- Sodium: 135 mg

199. Holiday Baked Apples

"Baked red apples with a sweet and strong flavor and a buttery cinnamon filling with the taste of coconut. It is delicious on its own or it can go well with vanilla ice cream."
Serving: 1 | Prep: 10m | Ready in: 40m

Ingredients

- 1 large Red Delicious apple
- 2 tbsps. brown sugar
- 1 tbsp. butter, softened
- 1 tbsp. finely shredded coconut
- 1 tsp. ground cinnamon
- 1 pinch brown sugar, or to taste (optional)
- 1 pinch ground cinnamon, or to taste (optional)

Direction

- Set oven to 350 0 F (175 0 C) and preheat.
- Cut out the core and seeds from apple, leaving about a 1/2 in the bottom, creating a well-like hole. In a bowl, combine 1 tsp. cinnamon, coconut, butter and 2 tbsps. brown sugar; fill brown sugar mixture into the well in the apple. Put stuffed apple onto a baking dish.
- Put in the prepared oven and bake for about 30 minutes until apple is tender. Move baked apple to a serving bowl and drizzle over apple with the rest of juices from baking dish; add 1 pinch brown sugar and cinnamon to scatter on top.

Nutrition Information

- Calories: 348 calories;
- Total Carbohydrate: 62 g
- Cholesterol: 31 mg
- Total Fat: 13.2 g
- Protein: 1 g
- Sodium: 105 mg

200. Homemade Lemon Cheese Pie

"A lighter version of a scrumptious pie."
Serving: 10 servings. | Prep: 30m | Ready in: 45m

Ingredients

- 1 sheet refrigerated pie pastry
- 1 cup sugar
- 1/4 cup plus 2 tsps. cornstarch
- 1/2 tsp. salt
- 1 cup water
- 2 tbsps. butter
- 2 tsps. grated lemon peel
- 3 to 4 drops yellow food coloring, optional
- 1/2 cup plus 1 tsp. lemon juice, divided
- 1 package (8 oz.) fat-free cream cheese

- 1/2 cup confectioners' sugar
- 1 cup reduced-fat whipped topping

Direction

- Roll out the pastry gently in a 12- inch round, then move to a 9-inch pie plate. Cut the pastry to half an inch far off the edge of the plate and set aside the scraps for the garnish, then flute the edges. Use a double thickness of heavy-duty foil to line the unpricked pastry shell and let it bake for 8 minutes at 450 degrees. Take off the foil and let it bake for another 5 minutes. Allow to cool on a wire rack.
- Roll out the scraps of pastry into 1/8-inch thick. Use 1 1/2-inch cookie cutters to cut out star shapes, then put it on a baking tray. Let it bake for 8 minutes at 450 degrees or until it turns golden brown. Let it cool on a wire rack.
- Mix together the salt, cornstarch and sugar in a big saucepan until combined, mix in water to blend then boil. Let it cook and stir for 2 minutes or until it becomes very thick. Take it out of the heat, then mix in food coloring if preferred, lemon peel and butter. Mix in half a cup of lemon juice gently. Allow to cool for about an hour to room temperature.
- Beat the confectioner's sugar and cream cheese in a big bowl, until it becomes smooth. Fold in the leftover lemon juice and whipped topping. Spread it on the crust, then put the lemon filling on top. Let it chill in the fridge for 6 hours or until the top becomes set. Put pastry stars on top as a garnish.

Nutrition Information

- Calories: 341 calories
- Total Carbohydrate: 55 g
- Cholesterol: 15 mg
- Total Fat: 11 g
- Fiber: 0 g
- Protein: 5 g
- Sodium: 431 mg

201. Homemade Strawberry Rhubarb Sauce

"You will want to serve your pancakes with this strawberry and rhubarb sauce repeatedly."
Serving: 1-3/4 cups. | Prep: 10m | Ready in: 15m

Ingredients

- 2 cups halved fresh strawberries
- 1 cup sliced fresh or frozen rhubarb
- 2/3 cup sugar
- 1 tbsp. cornstarch
- 2 tbsps. cold water

Direction

- Combine sugar, rhubarb, and strawberries in a small saucepan; heat over medium heat, stirring to dissolve sugar, until mixture comes to a boil. Stir water and cornstarch together in a small bowl until smooth; mix into fruit mixture. Cook, stirring, for 1 to 2 minutes, until mixture is thickened. Serve warm; or cover and chill until cold before serving.

202. Honey Baked Apples

"Baked apples with cranberries filling and glazed with brown sugar and honey."
Serving: 6 | Prep: 15m | Ready in: 1h15m

Ingredients

- 6 green apples
- 1 1/2 cups fresh cranberries
- 2 1/4 cups water
- 3/4 cup packed brown sugar
- 3 tbsps. honey
- 6 scoops vanilla ice cream

Direction

- Set an oven to preheat to 175°C (350°F).
- Take off the peel from the top third of each apple, then core. In a baking dish, put the

apples and put as many cranberries as you can fit to fill the core holes.
- In the meantime, in a small saucepan, mix together the honey, brown sugar and water, then boil and mix from time to time, until the honey and sugar dissolves, if needed. When it boils, pour the mixture on top of the apples.
- Let it bake in the preheated oven for an hour and baste it using the juices every 15-20 minutes. Serve together with vanilla ice cream.

Nutrition Information

- Calories: 252 calories;
- Total Carbohydrate: 61 g
- Cholesterol: 9 mg
- Total Fat: 2.3 g
- Protein: 1.3 g
- Sodium: 27 mg

203. Honey Bun Cake

"This moist, fluffy cake is absolutely brilliant."
Serving: 20 servings. | Prep: 20m | Ready in: 55m

Ingredients

- 1 package yellow or white cake mix (regular size)
- 4 egg whites
- 1 cup (8 oz.) sour cream
- 2/3 cup unsweetened applesauce
- 1/2 cup packed brown sugar
- 2 tsps. ground cinnamon
- 1-1/2 cups confectioners' sugar
- 2 tbsps. milk
- 1 tsp. vanilla extract

Direction

- Mix together applesauce, sour cream, egg whites and dry cake mix in a big bowl, then beat on low speed until moisten. Beat again on medium speed for another 2 minutes.
- Transfer half into a 13-inch x9-inch baking pan coated with grease. Mix cinnamon and brown sugar, then sprinkle on top of batter. Use leftover batter to cover, use a knife to cut through to swirl. Bake at 325 degrees until a toothpick exits clean, about 35 to 40 minutes. Allow to cool on a wire rack.
- To make glaze, mix together vanilla, milk and confectioners' sugar until smooth, then sprinkle over warm cake to serve.

Nutrition Information

- Calories: 185 calories
- Total Carbohydrate: 36 g
- Cholesterol: 5 mg
- Total Fat: 4 g
- Fiber: 1 g
- Protein: 2 g
- Sodium: 198 mg

204. Honey Lemon Cookies

"Delicious cookies with lemon peel flavor coated with wheat germ."
Serving: about 4 dozen. | Prep: 20m | Ready in: 35m

Ingredients

- 1/3 cup butter, softened
- 1/2 cup sugar
- 1/2 cup honey
- 1 egg
- 1 tsp. grated lemon peel
- 2-1/4 cups all-purpose flour
- 1/2 cup toasted wheat germ, divided
- 1 tsp. baking powder
- 1/4 tsp. salt

Direction

- Cream the sugar and butter in a bowl. Beat in the lemon peel, egg and honey. Mix together the salt, baking powder, a quarter cup of wheat germ and flour, then slowly add into the creamed mixture. Put on cover and let it chill in the fridge for an hour or until it is easy to be handled.
- Roll the dough into 1-inch balls, then roll it in the leftover wheat germ. Put it on the cooking

spray coated baking trays and place it 2 inches apart. Let it bake for 11 to 12 minutes at 350 degrees or until it turns light brown in color. Transfer to wire racks to let it cool. Keep it in a plastic bag that's resealable.

Nutrition Information

- Calories: 172 calories
- Total Carbohydrate: 30 g
- Cholesterol: 24 mg
- Total Fat: 5 g
- Fiber: 1 g
- Protein: 3 g
- Sodium: 95 mg

205. Honey Spice Snack Cake

"This scrumptious spice cake is very extraordinary with the addition of ground cloves, applesauce and honey."
Serving: 12 servings. | Prep: 15m | Ready in: 30m

Ingredients

- 2 cups all-purpose flour
- Sugar substitute equivalent to 3/4 cup sugar
- 2-1/2 tsps. baking powder
- 1-1/2 tsps. ground cinnamon
- 1/2 tsp. baking soda
- 1/4 tsp. ground nutmeg
- 1/4 tsp. ground cloves
- 1/8 tsp. salt
- 2 eggs
- 3/4 cup unsweetened applesauce
- 1/4 cup canola oil
- 1/4 cup honey
- 1/4 cup finely chopped walnuts, toasted
- 1/2 tsp. confectioners' sugar

Direction

- Mix the first 8 ingredients together in a big bowl. Whisk together honey, oil, applesauce and egg, then stir into the dry mixture just until moisten. Fold in walnuts.
- Transfer into a square baking pan of 9-inch sprayed with cooking spray. Bake at 350 degrees until a toothpick pricked in the center exits clean, about 15 to 20 minutes. Allow to cool on a wire rack and sprinkle confectioners' sugar on top.

Nutrition Information

- Calories: 181 calories
- Total Carbohydrate: 26 g
- Cholesterol: 35 mg
- Total Fat: 7 g
- Fiber: 1 g
- Protein: 4 g
- Sodium: 172 mg

206. Honeydew Blueberry Soup

"It's a tasty cold soup made of blueberries and honey dew."
Serving: 6 | Prep: 10m | Ready in: 45m

Ingredients

- 1 honeydew melon
- 1 pint blueberries
- 6 oatmeal cookies

Direction

- Cut melon into chunks, from the rind. In a blender or food processor, puree melon chunks until smooth. Transfer in a big bowl and stir into pureed melon with blueberries. Refrigerate until quite chilled.
- To serve, scoop soup into individual bowls and crumble over each serving with an oatmeal cookie.

Nutrition Information

- Calories: 176 calories;
- Total Carbohydrate: 37.7 g
- Cholesterol: 0 mg
- Total Fat: 3.2 g
- Protein: 2.5 g
- Sodium: 96 mg

207. Hot Cinnamon Candy Covered Apples

"You should have a candy thermometer to use. This recipe is for hot cinnamon candy covered the apple."
Serving: 6 | Prep: 20m | Ready in: 3h20m

Ingredients

- 1/2 cup confectioners' sugar
- 6 apples
- 2 cups water
- 2 cups white sugar
- 2 cups light corn syrup
- 1 tbsp. red food coloring
- 1 tsp. cinnamon oil

Direction

- Line aluminum foil on a cookie sheet and dust it with confectioners' sugar.
- Discard stems from apples and wash them thoroughly. Use a rounded wooden craft stick to spear each apple through the bottom. Dry thoroughly and put aside.
- Heat corn syrup, sugar, and water to a boil in a large saucepan. Lower the heat to medium-high. Keep heating to boil, stirring to avoid burning, until the mixture achieves 300°F (150°C). Take away from heat, and while stirring, put in cinnamon oil and food coloring.
- Working quickly, plunge each apple into the candy mixture, coating well. Arrange apples on the prepared cookie sheet to cool. Chill in the refrigerator for 2 hours.

Nutrition Information

- Calories: 696 calories;
- Total Carbohydrate: 183.6 g
- Cholesterol: 0 mg
- Total Fat: 0.5 g
- Protein: 0.3 g
- Sodium: 68 mg

208. Huckleberry Buckle II

"Cobbler recipe made with berries."
Serving: 8 | Prep: 10m | Ready in: 1h

Ingredients

- 1/4 cup butter
- 1/2 cup white sugar
- 1 cup all-purpose flour
- 1 tsp. baking powder
- 1/4 tsp. salt
- 1/2 cup milk
- 2 1/2 cups huckleberries
- 3/4 cup white sugar
- 1/2 cup boiling water
- 1 tbsp. butter

Direction

- Set an oven to preheat to 190°C (375°F), then grease the base of a 9-inch square pan.
- Cream half a cup of sugar and a quarter cup of butter in a big bowl. Mix together the salt, baking powder and flour in another small bowl, then mix it into the butter mixture. Mix in milk (the mixture will get lumpy and thick). Spread the batter to the prepped pan.
- Mix together the half a cup of boiling water, 3/4 cup sugar and berries in a big bowl, then pour on top of the batter in the pan. Dot the leftover 1 tbsp of butter on top.
- Let it bake for 45-50 minutes in the preheated oven.

Nutrition Information

- Calories: 276 calories;
- Total Carbohydrate: 50.7 g
- Cholesterol: 20 mg
- Total Fat: 7.8 g
- Protein: 2.5 g
- Sodium: 179 mg

209. Jo-ann's Power Bars

"Nutritious, filling and delicious power bars made with dried fruits and nuts."
Serving: 12 | Prep: 10m | Ready in: 40m

Ingredients

- 1 cup quick-cooking rolled oats
- 1/2 cup whole wheat flour
- 1/2 cup wheat and barley nugget cereal (e.g. Grape-Nuts™)
- 1/2 tsp. ground cinnamon
- 1 beaten egg
- 1/4 cup applesauce
- 1/4 cup honey
- 3 tbsps. brown sugar
- 2 tbsps. vegetable oil
- 1/4 cup unsalted sunflower seeds
- 1/4 cup chopped walnuts
- 1 (7 oz.) bag chopped dried mixed fruit

Direction

- Set an oven to preheat to 165°C (325°F). Use aluminum foil to line a 9-inch square baking pan. Use cooking spray to spritz the foil.
- Mix together the cinnamon, cereal, flour and oats in a big bowl. Add the oil, brown sugar, honey, applesauce and egg, then stir well. Mix in the dried fruit, walnuts and sunflower seeds. Evenly spread the mixture in the prepped pan.
- Let it bake until it turns light brown around the edges and becomes firm or for half an hour. Allow to cool. Lift it from the pan using the foil, then slice it into squares or bars and keep it in the fridge.

Nutrition Information

- Calories: 197 calories;
- Total Carbohydrate: 33.4 g
- Cholesterol: 16 mg
- Total Fat: 6.6 g
- Protein: 4.1 g
- Sodium: 40 mg

210. Kiwi Lime Gelatin

"Green dessert with lime, oranges and kiwifruit."
Serving: 8 servings. | Prep: 15m | Ready in: 15m

Ingredients

- 6 kiwifruit, peeled, sliced and quartered
- 1 cup dry white wine or diet lemon-lime soda
- 2 packages (3 oz. each) lime gelatin
- 3 cups diet lemon-lime soda, chilled
- 2 tbsps. orange juice
- 1 can (11 oz.) mandarin oranges, drained

Direction

- Heat up kiwi with wine or soda to a boil in a saucepan. Cook over medium heat, mixing sometimes, for 5 minutes. Put in gelatin; mix until dissolved. Mix in orange juice and chilled soda. Chill until set partially.
- Fold in oranges. Add to a six-cup mold sprayed with cooking spray. Chill 8 hours or overnight until set.

Nutrition Information

- Calories: 81 calories
- Total Carbohydrate: 16 g
- Cholesterol: 0 mg
- Total Fat: 0 g
- Fiber: 2 g
- Protein: 1 g
- Sodium: 31 mg

211. Lemon Blueberry Cheesecake

"Upgrade from traditional cheesecake, this recipe will bring you a new and delicious cake to serve dessert."
Serving: 12 servings. | Prep: 30m | Ready in: 30m

Ingredients

- 1 package (3 oz.) lemon gelatin
- 1 cup boiling water

- 1 cup graham cracker crumbs
- 2 tbsps. butter, melted
- 1 tbsp. canola oil
- 3 cups (24 oz.) fat-free cottage cheese
- 1/4 cup sugar
- TOPPING:
- 2 tbsps. sugar
- 1-1/2 tsps. cornstarch
- 1/4 cup water
- 1-1/3 cups fresh or frozen blueberries, divided
- 1 tsp. lemon juice

Direction

- Dissolve gelatin in boiling water in a large bowl. Let cool. In a small bowl, mix oil, butter, and crumbs. Press onto the bottom of a 9-inch springform pan. Let chill.
- In a blender, blend, covered, sugar and cottage cheese until smooth. While blending, slowly put in cooled gelatin. Transfer into crust; cover and leave in the refrigerator overnight.
- To make the topping, in a small saucepan, mix cornstarch and sugar; slowly whisk in water until smooth. Put in 1 cup of blueberries. Heat to a boil; cook and stir for 2 minutes, until thick. Blend in lemon juice; let cool slightly.
- Place on a blender; blend, covered, until smooth. Leave in the refrigerator until chilled.
- Carefully use a knife to run around the edge of pan to loosen the cheesecake; remove the sides of the pan. Spread over the top with the blueberry mixture. Scatter with remaining blueberries. Leave the leftover in the refrigerator.

Nutrition Information

- Calories: 171 calories
- Total Carbohydrate: 27 g
- Cholesterol: 8 mg
- Total Fat: 4 g
- Fiber: 1 g
- Protein: 8 g
- Sodium: 352 mg

212. Lemon Chiffon Dessert

"A fluffy and light dessert."
Serving: 6 servings. | Prep: 20m | Ready in: 20m

Ingredients

- 2 envelopes unflavored gelatin
- 1-1/4 cups cold water, divided
- 1-1/3 cups nonfat dry milk powder
- 2-1/2 tsps. Crystal Light lemonade drink mix
- 3 to 4 drops yellow food coloring, optional
- 1/8 tsp. salt
- 3/4 cup 1% cottage cheese
- 1 cup reduced-fat whipped topping
- 1 tbsp. graham cracker crumbs

Direction

- Scatter gelatin on top of half cup cold water in a small saucepan; let sit for a minute. Cook and mix over low heat until dissolved completely; put aside.
- Mix the food coloring (optional), drink mix, milk and salt in a bowl; whip on high speed until combined. In a blender or food processor, put the cottage cheese and leftover water; cover and blend until smooth. Put in gelatin and milk mixture; cover and blend until thickened.
- Scoop into 6 6-oz. custard cups. Cover and chill for an hour. Spread whipped topping over; garnish with cracker crumbs.

Nutrition Information

- Calories: 81 calories
- Total Carbohydrate: 7 g
- Cholesterol: 2 mg
- Total Fat: 2 g
- Fiber: 0 g
- Protein: 7 g
- Sodium: 202 mg

213. Lemon Cooler Cookies

"Lemony and crisp goodies that are similar to shortbread."
Serving: 3-1/2 dozen. | Prep: 20m | Ready in: 30m

Ingredients

- 1/4 cup butter, softened
- 2 tbsps. canola oil
- 3/4 cup sugar
- 1 egg
- 1 egg white
- 1/4 cup thawed lemonade concentrate
- 2 tsps. grated lemon peel
- 2 cups all-purpose flour
- 1/2 tsp. baking powder
- 1/4 tsp. salt
- 1/8 tsp. baking soda
- 1 tbsp. yellow decorating sugar

Direction

- Beat the sugar, oil and butter in a big bowl. Beat in the lemon peel, lemonade concentrate, egg white and egg. Mix together the baking soda, salt, baking powder and flour, then slowly add into the egg mixture.
- Press the dough on the baking trays that were ungreased using a cookie press fitted with your preferred disk and place it 2 inches apart. Sprinkle yellow sugar on top. Let it bake for 8 to 10 minutes at 350 degrees or until it turns light brown on the edges. Allow to cool on wire racks.

Nutrition Information

- Calories: 116 calories
- Total Carbohydrate: 18 g
- Cholesterol: 26 mg
- Total Fat: 4 g
- Fiber: 0 g
- Protein: 2 g
- Sodium: 73 mg

214. Lemon Custard Ice Cream

"This ice cream is still taste good the next day."
Serving: 2 quarts. | Prep: 15m | Ready in: 35m

Ingredients

- 2 cups sugar
- 1/4 cup all-purpose flour
- 1/4 tsp. salt
- 4 cups milk
- 4 eggs, lightly beaten
- 3 cups heavy whipping cream
- 1 cup lemon juice

Direction

- Combine salt, flour and sugar in large saucepan. Pour in milk gradually. Boil over medium heat, then cook while stirring until thickened, about 2 mins. Take away from heat; let cool slightly.
- Stir a small amount of the hot milk mixture into eggs. Put all back into pan, whisking constantly. Cook while stirring the mixture until coating back of the metal spoon and reaching 160°.
- Take away from heat; mix in lemon juice and cream. Place the pan into a bowl of the ice water to cool quickly; stir for 2 mins. Press the waxed paper onto the custard surface. Place in the refrigerator for several hours up to overnight.
- Fill 2/3 full cylinder of the ice cream freezer; freeze following the manufacturer's instructions. Place the remaining mixture in refrigerator until it is ready to freeze. Place the ice cream in freezer container once it is frozen; freeze for 2 to 4 hours. Then serve.

Nutrition Information

- Calories: 318 calories
- Total Carbohydrate: 32 g
- Cholesterol: 123 mg
- Total Fat: 20 g
- Fiber: 0 g
- Protein: 5 g

- Sodium: 100 mg

215. Lemon Delight Cake

"Moist cake made with 4 different recipes with creamy filling and a topping that's buttery."
Serving: 18 servings. | Prep: 35m | Ready in: 01h15m

Ingredients

- 1 package lemon cake mix (regular size)
- 1-1/3 cups water
- 3/4 cup egg substitute
- 1/3 cup unsweetened applesauce
- 3 tbsps. poppy seeds
- FILLING:
- 1 package (8 oz.) reduced-fat cream cheese
- 1/2 cup confectioners' sugar
- 1 can (15-3/4 oz.) lemon pie filling
- TOPPING:
- 1/3 cup packed brown sugar
- 1/4 cup chopped pecans
- 3 tbsps. all-purpose flour
- 4-1/2 tsps. butter, melted
- 1/2 tsp. ground cinnamon
- 1/8 tsp. vanilla extract
- GLAZE:
- 1/2 cup confectioners' sugar
- 4 tsps. lemon juice

Direction

- Mix together the initial 5 ingredients in a big bowl, then beat it for half a minute on low speed. Beat it for 2 minutes on medium. Use cooking spray to coat a 13x9-inch baking pan and dust it using flour. Spread 1/2 of the batter into the pan.
- Beat the confectioner's sugar and cream cheese in a big bowl, until it becomes smooth. Mix in the pie filling. Drop it by teaspoonfuls and spread it on top of the batter gently. Put the leftover batter on top.
- Mix together the topping ingredients and sprinkle it on top of the batter. Let it bake for 40 to 45 minutes at 350 degrees or until an inserted toothpick in the middle exits clean. Allow to cool on a wire rack.
- Mix together the glaze ingredients, then drizzle on top of the cake. Put the leftovers in the fridge.

Nutrition Information

- Calories: 314 calories
- Total Carbohydrate: 54 g
- Cholesterol: 44 mg
- Total Fat: 9 g
- Fiber: 1 g
- Protein: 5 g
- Sodium: 288 mg

216. Lemon Meringue Angel Cake

"I have heard about this dessert which tastes just like a lemon meringue pie. I think it's lovely to serve and every piece is virtually fat free."
Serving: 14 servings. | Prep: 40m | Ready in: 01h15m

Ingredients

- 12 egg whites
- 1-1/2 cups sugar, divided
- 1 cup cake flour
- 2 tsps. cream of tartar
- 1-1/2 tsps. vanilla extract
- 1/4 tsp. salt
- 1 jar (10 oz.) lemon curd
- MERINGUE TOPPING:
- 4 egg whites
- 3/4 tsp. cream of tartar
- 1/2 cup sugar

Direction

- Put the egg whites into a large bowl and leave to stand for 30 minutes at room temperature. Sift together flour and 1/2 cup of sugar twice and reserve.
- Add salt, vanilla, and cream of tartar to the egg whites, then beat on medium speed until the mixture is foamy. Slowly beat in the remaining sugar on high, two tbsps. at a time,

until sugar is dissolved and stiff glossy peaks form. Slowly fold in the flour mixture, approximately half cup at a time.
- Gently scoop the batter into a 10-inch tube pan that is not greased. Use a knife to cut through the batter to get rid of air pockets. Bake for 35 to 40 minutes on lowest oven rack at 350° or until the entire top appears dry and turned golden brown. Invert the pan immediately and then cool completely for about an hour.
- Move a knife around the side and middle tube of the pan. Take out the cake, separate into 2 horizontal layers. Put the cake bottom onto a baking sheet lined with parchment paper. Spread with the lemon curd and return the cake top.
- For the meringue, beat cream of tartar and egg whites on medium in a small bowl until soft peaks are formed. Slowly beat in the sugar on high, one tbsp. at a time, until the sugar is dissolved, and stiff glossy peaks are formed. Spread all over the top and sides of the cake.
- Bake for 15 to 18 minutes at 350° or until it turned golden brown. Place onto a serving plate. Chill the leftovers.

Nutrition Information

- Calories: 238 calories
- Total Carbohydrate: 51 g
- Cholesterol: 15 mg
- Total Fat: 1 g
- Fiber: 0 g
- Protein: 5 g
- Sodium: 121 mg

217. Lemon Raspberry-filled Cake

"Light and appealing layer cake recipe."
Serving: 12 servings. | Prep: 15m | Ready in: 35m

Ingredients

- 1 package lemon cake mix (regular size)
- 2 large eggs
- 1 large egg white
- 1-1/4 cups water
- 1/4 cup unsweetened applesauce
- FROSTING:
- 2 cups confectioners' sugar
- 2 tbsps. butter, softened
- 1 tsp. vanilla extract
- 1/8 tsp. salt
- 2 to 3 tbsps. fat-free milk
- 1/2 cup 100% raspberry spreadable fruit

Direction

- Mix together the applesauce, water, egg white, eggs and cake mix in a big bowl and beat it for half a minute on low speed. Beat it for 2 minutes on medium, then pour it in 2 cooking spray coated 9-inch round baking pans.
- Let it bake for 20 to 30 minutes at 350 degrees or until an inserted toothpick in the middle exits clean. Allow to cool for 10 minutes on wire racks, then take it out of the pans to let it cool.
- To make the frosting, beat the initial 4 frosting ingredients in a big bowl, until it becomes smooth. To reach your preferred consistency, beat in enough milk.
- On a serving platter, put 1 layer of cake, then spread it with spreadable fruit. Put the 2nd layer of cake on top, then frost it.

Nutrition Information

- Calories: 313 calories
- Total Carbohydrate: 62 g
- Cholesterol: 41 mg
- Total Fat: 6 g
- Fiber: 1 g
- Protein: 3 g
- Sodium: 334 mg

218. Lemon Snack Cake

"Moist lemon cake topped with a dollop of whipped topping."
Serving: 15 servings. | Prep: 15m | Ready in: 35m

Ingredients

- 1/3 cup butter, softened
- 3/4 cup sugar
- 2 eggs
- 2 tsps. grated lemon peel
- 1-1/2 tsps. lemon extract
- 1 tsp. vanilla extract
- 2-1/2 cups all-purpose flour
- 1 tsp. baking soda
- 1/2 tsp. baking powder
- 1/4 tsp. salt
- 1 cup (8 oz.) fat-free lemon yogurt
- Reduced-fat whipped topping, optional
- Additional lemon peel, optional

Direction

- Cream the sugar and butter in a big bowl, until it becomes fluffy and light. Put in eggs, one by one, and beat it well after every addition. Beat in extracts and lemon peel. Mix together the dry ingredients, then slowly add into the creamed mixture alternating with yogurt; beat it well after every addition (the batter will get thick).
- Spread it into a cooking spray coated 13x9-inch baking pan. Let it bake for 20 to 25 minutes at 350 degrees or until an inserted toothpick in the middle exits clean. Allow to cool on a wire rack. Top it with lemon peel and whipped topping as a garnish, if preferred.

Nutrition Information

- Calories: 185 calories
- Total Carbohydrate: 30 g
- Cholesterol: 40 mg
- Total Fat: 5 g
- Fiber: 1 g
- Protein: 4 g
- Sodium: 207 mg

219. Lemon Yogurt Cream Pie

"A tempting dessert made with grated lemon peel and creamy lemon yogurt."
Serving: 8 servings. | Prep: 15m | Ready in: 15m

Ingredients

- 1 envelope unflavored gelatin
- 1/4 cup cold water
- Sugar substitute equivalent to 1/3 cup sugar
- 1/3 cup lemon juice
- 1 1/2 cups (12 oz.) fat-free lemon yogurt
- 1 tsp. grated lemon peel
- 1 carton (8 oz.) frozen reduced-fat whipped topping, thawed
- 1 reduced-fat graham cracker crust (8 inches)
- Lemon slice and mint, optional

Direction

- Sprinkle the gelatin on top of cold water in a microwavable bowl, then allow to stand for a minute. Let it microwave for 20 seconds on high without cover; mix in the lemon juice and sugar substitute. Put in lemon peel and yogurt, then stir well. Fold in the whipped topping, then scoop into the crust.
- Put on cover and let it chill in the fridge for 8 hours to overnight. If preferred, put mint and slices of lemon on top as a garnish.

Nutrition Information

- Calories: 226 calories
- Total Carbohydrate: 33 g
- Cholesterol: 1 mg
- Total Fat: 6 g
- Fiber: 1 g
- Protein: 7 g
- Sodium: 130 mg

220. Light Chocolate Cheesecake

""This low-fat chocolate cheesecake is unbelievably light your craving for sweets will be fulfilled with just a small portion.""
Serving: 10 servings. | Prep: 15m | Ready in: 40m

Ingredients

- 2 whole chocolate graham crackers, crushed
- 1/4 cup fat-free half-and-half
- 12 oz. reduced-fat cream cheese
- 1 cup (8 oz.) fat-free cottage cheese
- 1 cup sugar
- 6 tbsps. baking cocoa
- 1/4 cup all-purpose flour
- 1 tsp. vanilla extract
- 1/4 cup egg substitute
- 1/4 cup miniature semisweet chocolate chips
- 1/2 oz. white baking chocolate, shaved
- 1/2 oz. semisweet chocolate, shaved

Direction

- Using a cooking spray, grease the springform pan, 9-inch in size. Dust the pan with bread crumbs; reserve. In a food processor, put in half-and-half, cottage cheese, cream cheese, vanilla, flour, cocoa, and sugar. Process with the cover on until the consistency is smooth. In a large bowl, put inside the processed mixture and beat in egg substitute. Add in chocolate chips and lightly mix by folding. Put mixture into the pan and lay on a baking sheet.
- Put inside the oven and bake for 25-30 minutes at 325°F or until it is nearly set. Transfer to a wire rack and let cool for 10 minutes. Loosen the cake by running a knife cautiously around the pan and cool for another 1 hour or longer. Put inside the refrigerator for the night. Add shaved chocolate all over the top of the cake. Store leftovers the refrigerator.

Nutrition Information

- Calories: 243 calories
- Total Carbohydrate: 35 g
- Cholesterol: 20 mg
- Total Fat: 9 g
- Fiber: 2 g
- Protein: 9 g
- Sodium: 238 mg

221. Light Lemon Cheesecake

"My family cherishes cheesecake."
Serving: 12 servings. | Prep: 20m | Ready in: 01h30m

Ingredients

- 3/4 cup reduced-fat cinnamon graham cracker crumbs (about 4 whole crackers)
- 3 packages (8 oz. each) fat-free cream cheese
- 2 packages (8 oz. each) reduced-fat cream cheese
- 1-2/3 cups sugar
- 1/8 tsp. salt
- 9 egg whites
- 1/4 cup lemon juice
- 1-1/2 tsps. vanilla extract
- 1 tsp. grated lemon peel
- 8 strawberries, sliced
- 2 medium kiwifruit, peeled and sliced

Direction

- Dust the graham cracker crumbs over the bottom and up the sides of a well-greased 9-inch springform pan; put aside.
- Beat the salt, sugar and cream cheese in a big bowl until smooth. Put in the egg whites; beat at low speed until mixed. Mix in lemon peel, vanilla, and lemon juice.
- Pour into the prepared pan. Bake at 325 ° for 70 to 80 minutes, until the middle is nearly set. Cool for 10 minutes on a wire rack. Run a knife carefully around the pan edge to loosen; cool for another 1 hour. Refrigerate overnight. Top with kiwi and strawberries.

Nutrition Information

- Calories: 300 calories
- Total Carbohydrate: 42 g

- Cholesterol: 26 mg
- Total Fat: 8 g
- Fiber: 1 g
- Protein: 15 g
- Sodium: 522 mg

222. Light Strawberry Gelatin Pie

""This refreshing dessert has a plenty of sweet berry flavor.""
Serving: 8 servings. | Prep: 20m | Ready in: 20m

Ingredients

- 2 pints fresh strawberries, hulled
- 2 tbsps. cornstarch
- 1-1/2 cups cold water
- 1 package (.3 oz.) sugar-free strawberry gelatin
- 3 tbsps. sugar
- 1 reduced-fat graham cracker crust (8 inches)
- 2 cups reduced-fat whipped topping

Direction

- Set the four whole berries aside for garnish. Cut the remaining strawberries; set aside. Mix water and cornstarch together in a large saucepan, till smooth. Boil the mixture; cook while stirring till thickened, 2 minutes.
- Take away from the heat; mix in sugar and gelatin till dissolved. Mix in the sliced strawberries. Transfer into the crust. Refrigerate with a cover till firm, 2 hours.
- Cut the reserved strawberries in half. Use a berry half and whipped topping for garnish each serving.

Nutrition Information

- Calories: 197 calories
- Total Carbohydrate: 33 g
- Cholesterol: 0 mg
- Total Fat: 5 g
- Fiber: 2 g
- Protein: 2 g
- Sodium: 125 mg

223. Light Sweet Potato Pie

"A lightened-up version of a Southern dessert with a touch of pumpkin spice."
Serving: 8 servings. | Prep: 01h20m | Ready in: 02h05m

Ingredients

- 2 lbs. sweet potatoes (about 3 medium)
- 3/4 cup packed brown sugar
- 1/4 cup all-purpose flour
- 2 tsp. grated orange zest
- 1 tsp. pumpkin pie spice
- 1 tsp. vanilla extract
- 1/8 tsp. salt
- 1 cup fat-free milk
- 1/2 cup egg substitute
- 1 unbaked pastry shell (9 inches)
- 1/2 cup reduced-fat whipped topping

Direction

- Let the sweet potatoes bake for an hour at 350 degrees or until it becomes very soft. Let it cool a bit. Slice the potatoes in 1/2, then scoop out the pulp and get rid of the shells. In a blender or food processor, put the pulp, put on cover and process until it becomes smooth.
- Mix together the salt, vanilla, pumpkin pie spice, orange zest, flour, brown sugar and pulp in a big bowl. Mix in the egg substitute and milk until well combined, then pour it into the pastry shell.
- Let it bake for 45 to 50 minutes at 375 degrees or until an inserted knife in the middle exits clean. Allow to cool for two hours on a wire rack. Put whipped topping on as a garnish. Put the leftovers in the fridge.

Nutrition Information

- Calories: 0g sugar total.

224. Lime And Tequila Infused Strawberries

"A recipe for adults only that can be served as it is or made into strawberry shortcakes by layering on a cake with whipped cream on top."
Serving: 6 | Prep: 15m | Ready in: 1h15m

Ingredients

- 6 tbsps. triple sec
- 1/3 cup white sugar
- 1/3 cup fresh lime juice
- 3 1/2 tbsps. tequila
- 2 tbsps. grated lime zest
- 2 lbs. fresh strawberries, hulled and sliced

Direction

- In a bowl, combine lime zest, tequila, lime juice, sugar and triple sec; dissolve sugar by stirring. Put on top of the strawberries in a large bowl. Let sit and stir frequently until it creates juice, about 1 hour.

Nutrition Information

- Calories: 172 calories;
- Total Carbohydrate: 31.3 g
- Cholesterol: 0 mg
- Total Fat: 0.5 g
- Protein: 1.1 g
- Sodium: 3 mg

225. Lime Frozen Yogurt

"Delightful dessert made with frozen yogurt and frilled pineapple."
Serving: 6 servings. | Prep: 15m | Ready in: 35m

Ingredients

- 4 cups fat-free plain yogurt
- 1-1/2 cups sugar
- 2/3 cup lime juice
- 2 tbsp. grated lime zest
- 1/4 tsp. salt
- 1 large fresh pineapple, peeled and cut into 3/4-inch wedges
- Fresh mint, optional

Direction

- Mix together the salt, lime zest, lime juice, sugar and yogurt in a big bowl, then mix until the sugar dissolves. Let it freeze in an ice cream freezer following the manufacturer's directions. Let it ripen in the ice cream freezer or let it firm up for 2 to 4 hours in the refrigerator freezer prior to serving.
- Use cooking oil to moisten a paper towel using long-handled tongs and coat the grill rack lightly. Let the pineapple grill for 1 to 2 minutes per side on medium heat without cover or until it becomes heated through. Serve together with lime frozen yogurt. Put mint on top as a garnish, if preferred.

Nutrition Information

- Calories: 307 calories
- Total Carbohydrate: 75 g
- Cholesterol: 3 mg
- Total Fat: 0 g
- Fiber: 1 g
- Protein: 7 g
- Sodium: 189 mg

226. Lime Honeydew Sorbet

"With each bite of this frosty dessert, you'll taste a hint of honeydew with a surge of lime. This great flavor combo makes for a refreshing end to a summer or spring meal. An ice cream maker is required."
Serving: 4 servings. | Prep: 5m | Ready in: 25m

Ingredients

- 3 cups cubed honeydew melon
- 1/2 cup sugar
- 1/2 cup lime juice
- 1 tbsp. sweet white wine or water
- 2 tsps. grated lime zest
- 2 to 3 drops green food coloring, optional

Direction

- Mix sugar and honeydew into a blender or food processor and cover it up. Process the mixture until the sugar dissolves then add in the remaining ingredients. Cover it up and process until everything is blended together. Following the manufacturer's instructions, freeze it in an ice cream freezer. Transfer the mixture by spooning it into a freezer-safe container then cover it up. Before serving, leave it to freeze in the refrigerator freezer for 2 to 4 hours.

Nutrition Information

- Calories: 154 calories
- Total Carbohydrate: 40 g
- Cholesterol: 0 mg
- Total Fat: 1 g
- Fiber: 1 g
- Protein: 1 g
- Sodium: 14 mg

227. Lime Parfaits

""No need to quit yummy treats just because you are eating lighter! This invigorating four-ingredient dessert is simple to make and so beautiful to present. Layers of creamy ice-cold sherbet substitute with a crunchy mix of chopped nuts and cookie crumbs in the warm-weather treat.""
Serving: 6 servings. | Prep: 15m | Ready in: 15m

Ingredients

- 1/2 cup plus 2 tbsps. chocolate wafer cookie crumbs, divided
- 1/4 cup finely chopped macadamia nuts, toasted
- 3 cups lime sherbet, softened
- 1 tbsp. grated lime zest

Direction

- Mix nuts and 1/2 cup cookie crumbs in a bowl. Mix lime zest and sherbet in a separate bowl. Into six parfait glasses, put 1 tbsp. cookie mixture; then add 1/4 cup sherbet mixture on top. Continue layers. Dust with the rest of cookie crumbs. Store in the freezer, covered, until firm.

Nutrition Information

- Calories: 193 calories
- Total Carbohydrate: 32 g
- Cholesterol: 5 mg
- Total Fat: 7 g
- Fiber: 0 g
- Protein: 2 g
- Sodium: 102 mg

228. Low Fat Breakfast Cookies

"Delicious cookies for breakfast."
Serving: 8 | Prep: 10m | Ready in: 22m

Ingredients

- 1 1/2 cups rolled oats
- 1/2 cup whole wheat flour
- 1/2 cup all-purpose flour
- 1/2 cup light brown sugar
- 1 1/2 tsps. wheat germ
- 1/2 tsp. baking powder
- 1/2 tsp. baking soda
- 1/4 tsp. salt
- 1 ripe banana, mashed
- 1/4 cup unsweetened applesauce
- 2 egg whites
- 1 tsp. vanilla extract
- 1/2 cup chocolate chips
- 1/2 cup dried cranberries

Direction

- Preheat the oven to 175°C or 350°Fahrenheit. Place a silicone mat or parchment paper on a baking sheet.
- In a big bowl, mix salt, oats, baking soda, whole wheat flour, baking powder, all-purpose flour, wheat germ, and brown sugar

together. Stir in vanilla extract, banana, egg whites, and applesauce. Softly incorporate cranberries and chocolate chips into the batter. Scoop a tbsp. of batter at a time in the baking sheet.
- Bake for 12 mins in the 350°Fahrenheit oven until golden.

Nutrition Information

- Calories: 260 calories;
- Total Carbohydrate: 52.7 g
- Cholesterol: 0 mg
- Total Fat: 4.5 g
- Protein: 5.5 g
- Sodium: 203 mg

229. Low-fat Chocolate Cookies

"Besides being low-fat, these soft cookies still taste so chocolatey and rich."
Serving: about 3-1/2 dozen. | Prep: 15m | Ready in: 25m

Ingredients

- 1/2 cup unsweetened applesauce
- 1/3 cup canola oil
- 3 large egg whites
- 3/4 cup sugar
- 3/4 cup packed brown sugar
- 2 tsps. vanilla extract
- 2-2/3 cups all-purpose flour
- 1/2 cup baking cocoa
- 1 tsp. baking soda
- 1/2 tsp. salt
- 1/4 cup miniature semisweet chocolate chips

Direction

- Mix together egg whites, oil and applesauce in a big bowl. Beat in vanilla and sugars. Mix together salt, baking soda, cocoa and flour; pour little by little into the applesauce mixture and beat thoroughly. Chill while covered until slightly firm, about 2 hours.
- Scoop by rounded teaspoonfuls of dough, place 2 inches apart onto cookie sheets greased with cooking spray. Sprinkle chocolate chips on top. Bake in 350-degree oven until set, about 8 to 10 minutes. Transfer to wire racks.

Nutrition Information

- Calories: 78 calories
- Total Carbohydrate: 14 g
- Cholesterol: 0 mg
- Total Fat: 2 g
- Fiber: 1 g
- Protein: 1 g
- Sodium: 63 mg

230. Mahogany Devil's Food Cake

"A delicious most-requested dessert recipe."
Serving: 12 servings. | Prep: 20m | Ready in: 40m

Ingredients

- 2 tbsps. butter, softened
- 2 cups sugar
- 2 eggs
- 1 tsp. vanilla extract
- 2-1/2 cups all-purpose flour
- 1/2 cup baking cocoa
- 2 tsps. baking soda
- 1/2 tsp. salt
- 1 cup buttermilk
- 1 cup hot water
- FROSTING:
- 1-1/4 cups sugar
- 3 egg whites
- 1/4 cup water
- 2 tbsps. light corn syrup
- 1/2 tsp. cream of tartar
- 1 tsp. vanilla extract
- 1/2 tsp. almond extract

Direction

- Use cooking spray to coat the three 9-inch round baking pans and sprinkle flour on top, then put aside. Beat the sugar and butter in a bowl for around 2 minutes, until it becomes crumbly. Put in eggs, one by one, and beat it well after every addition, then beat in vanilla. Mix together the salt, baking soda, cocoa and flour, then add it to the creamed mixture, alternating with the buttermilk. Pour in water, then stir well. Pour it into the prepped pans, then let it bake for 20 to 25 minutes at 350 degrees or until an inserted toothpick exits clean. Allow to cool for 10 minutes, then take it out of the pans and transfer to wire racks to let it fully cool.

- To make the frosting, mix together the cream of tartar, corn syrup, water, egg whites and sugar in a heavy saucepan. Beat it for 1 minute on low speed using a portable mixer, then keep on beating on low atop low heat for about 5 minutes, until it reads 160 degrees on a candy thermometer. Pour in the bowl of a heavy-duty stand mixer, then add the extract. Beat it for about 7 minutes on high, until it forms stiff peaks. Spread the frosting on the sides and tops and in between layers of the cake.

Nutrition Information

- Calories: 368 calories
- Total Carbohydrate: 80 g
- Cholesterol: 42 mg
- Total Fat: 4 g
- Fiber: 1 g
- Protein: 6 g
- Sodium: 378 mg

231. Make-ahead Lemon Bombe

"A refreshing dessert made with plenty of whipped cream and sugar."
Serving: 14 servings. | Prep: 30m | Ready in: 30m

Ingredients

- 1 package (16 oz.) angel food cake mix
- 2 envelopes unflavored gelatin
- 1/4 cup cold water
- 1 cup boiling water
- 1 can (12 oz.) frozen orange juice concentrate, thawed
- Sugar substitute equivalent to 1 cup sugar
- 2 tbsps. lemon juice
- 1/4 tsp. grated lemon peel
- 1/8 tsp. salt
- 3 cartons (8 oz. each) frozen reduced-fat whipped topping, thawed, divided
- 1/2 cup sweetened shredded coconut, toasted
- Mint leaves, maraschino cherries, lemon and orange slices, optional

Direction

- Prepare and let the cake bake following the package instructions using a 10-inch tube pan that's ungreased. Slice the cooled cake to 1 1/2-inch cubes, then put aside.
- Sprinkle gelatin on top of cold water in a big bowl, then allow to stand for a minute. Pour in boiling water, then mix until the gelatin dissolves. Add salt, lemon peel, lemon juice, sugar substitute and orange juice concentrate. Let it chill in the fridge for half an hour or until it becomes partly set. Fold in the two cartons of whipped topping.
- Use 2 overlapping pieces of plastic wrap to line a 5 1/2-quart bowl and let the plastic wrap hang atop the bowl's edge. Mix together the whipped topping mixture and cake cubes gently in a separate big bowl. Scoop into the prepped bowl, then push it against the side gently to avoid holes. Put on cover and let it chill in the fridge for a minimum of 24 hours.
- Just prior to serving, take off the cover from the bombe, then turn it upside down on a serving plate. Take off the plastic wrap and bowl, then frost it using the leftover whipped topping and sprinkle coconut on top. If preferred, put slices of orange, lemon, cherries and mint on top as a garnish.

Nutrition Information

- Calories: 301 calories
- Total Carbohydrate: 52 g
- Cholesterol: 0 mg
- Total Fat: 7 g

- Fiber: 1 g
- Protein: 4 g
- Sodium: 225 mg

232. Makeover Chocolate Zucchini Cake

"A rich and moist chocolate flavored cake with less sugar, fat and calories."
Serving: 14 servings. | Prep: 15m | Ready in: 01h10m

Ingredients

- 2 eggs
- 2 egg whites
- 1-1/2 cups sugar
- 1/2 cup packed brown sugar
- 1/2 cup unsweetened applesauce
- 1/2 cup canola oil
- 1/4 cup corn syrup
- 3 oz. unsweetened chocolate, melted and cooled
- 3 cups all-purpose flour
- 1-1/2 tsps. baking powder
- 1 tsp. baking soda
- 1 tsp. salt
- 3 cups shredded zucchini, squeezed dry
- 1/2 cup finely chopped nuts
- 1 tsp. confectioners' sugar

Direction

- Beat the initial 8 ingredients in a big bowl until it becomes smooth. Mix together the salt, baking soda, baking powder and flour, then slowly add it to the egg mixture and stir just until blended. Fold in the nuts and zucchini.
- Pour it into a cooking spray and flour coated 10-inch fluted tube pan. Let it bake for 55 to 65 minutes at 350 degrees or until an inserted toothpick in the middle exits clean. Allow it to cool for 10 minutes prior to taking it out from the pan to fully cool on a wire rack. Dust confectioner's sugar on top.

Nutrition Information

- Calories: 373 calories
- Total Carbohydrate: 59 g
- Cholesterol: 30 mg
- Total Fat: 14 g
- Fiber: 2 g
- Protein: 6 g
- Sodium: 311 mg

233. Makeover Coconut Cookies

"A lighter version of the coconutty cookies that has 1/4 of the saturated fat, 1/2 of the fat and 2/3 of the calories."
Serving: 3-1/2 dozen. | Prep: 15m | Ready in: 25m

Ingredients

- 1/4 cup butter, softened
- 1/4 cup canola oil
- 1/2 cup packed brown sugar
- 1/4 cup sugar
- 1 egg
- 3 egg whites
- 3 tsps. vanilla extract
- 2 tsps. coconut extract
- 1-3/4 cups all-purpose flour
- 3 tsps. baking powder
- 1/2 tsp. salt
- 4 cups cornflakes

Direction

- Mix together the sugars, oil and butter in a big bowl, then beat in extracts, egg whites and egg. Mix together the salt, baking powder and flour. Slowly add it to the egg mixture. Mix in corn flakes.
- Drop by tablespoonfuls onto cooking trays coated baking spray and place it 2 inches apart. Let it bake for 10 to 12 minutes at 375 degrees or until it turns light brown. Take it out and transfer to wire racks.

Nutrition Information

- Calories: 69 calories

- Total Carbohydrate: 10 g
- Cholesterol: 8 mg
- Total Fat: 3 g
- Fiber: 0 g
- Protein: 1 g
- Sodium: 94 mg

234. Makeover Crispy Oat Cookies

"A trimmed-down version of the cookie recipe with 1/2 less the fat and saturated fat and 40% less calories than the original recipe."
Serving: 5 dozen. | Prep: 20m | Ready in: 30m

Ingredients

- 1/4 cup butter, softened
- 1/4 cup canola oil
- 1 cup sugar, divided
- 1 tbsp. water
- 1 egg
- 1 tsp. vanilla extract
- 3/4 cup all-purpose flour
- 1/4 cup cornstarch
- 1 tsp. baking soda
- 1 tsp. cream of tartar
- 1/2 tsp. salt
- 1-1/2 cups crisp rice cereal
- 1 cup quick-cooking oats
- 1/3 cup sweetened shredded coconut
- 1/4 cup chopped walnuts

Direction

- Beat the water, 3/4 cup sugar, oil and butter in a bowl. Beat in vanilla and egg. Mix together the salt, cream of tartar, baking soda, cornstarch and flour, then slowly add it to the butter mixture. Stir in the nuts, coconut, oats and cereal (the dough will get sticky).
- Form it into 1-inch balls, then roll some of it on the leftover sugar. On the baking trays that were coated with cooking spray, put the dough and place it 2 inches apart. Use a glass dipped in the leftover sugar to flatten it. Let it bake for 10 to 12 minutes at 350 degrees or until it turns light brown. Transfer to wire racks to cool.

Nutrition Information

- Calories: 50 calories
- Total Carbohydrate: 7 g
- Cholesterol: 6 mg
- Total Fat: 2 g
- Fiber: 0 g
- Protein: 1 g
- Sodium: 58 mg

235. Makeover Meringue Coconut Brownies

"This snack have a flavorful, rich chocolate taste."
Serving: 2 dozen. | Prep: 30m | Ready in: 60m

Ingredients

- 1/3 cup butter, softened
- 1/3 cup plus 3/4 cup packed brown sugar, divided
- 1/3 cup sugar
- 1 tsp. vanilla extract
- 2 cups all-purpose flour
- 1/2 tsp. baking soda
- 1/4 tsp. salt
- 1/3 cup fat-free milk
- 1 cup (6 oz.) semisweet chocolate chips
- 1 cup sweetened shredded coconut
- 1/2 cup chopped walnuts
- 3 egg whites
- 1/4 tsp. cream of tartar

Direction

- In a small bowl, melt the butter, a third cup of brown sugar and sugar until fluffy and light. Add in vanilla and beat well. Combine the baking soda, salt and flour; add it to the creamed mixture alternating with the milk, beat well after each addition. Coat a 13 inchx9inch baking tray with cooking spray.

Press the mixture into the tray and drizzle with coconut, walnuts, and chocolate chips.
- In a big bowl, whisk cream of tartar and egg whites until soft peaks form. Slowly whisk in the remaining brown sugar, 1 tbsp. at a time. Whisk until stiff peaks form. Pour over the top.
- Let it bake for 30-35 minutes at 350° (do not overbake). Check with a toothpick by inserting in the center, if it comes out clean, it's done.
- Let it cool on a wire rack. Slice into bars. Keep it in the refrigerator to store.

Nutrition Information

- Calories: 181 calories
- Total Carbohydrate: 27 g
- Cholesterol: 7 mg
- Total Fat: 8 g
- Fiber: 1 g
- Protein: 2 g
- Sodium: 92 mg

236. Makeover Peanut Butter Pie

"A trimmed sown version of a delicious pie recipe made with fat-free frozen whipped topping, skim milk, reduced-fat peanut butter and fat-free cream cheese."
Serving: 8 slices. | Prep: 20m | Ready in: 20m

Ingredients

- 3 oz. fat-free cream cheese, softened
- 1/3 cup reduced-fat peanut butter
- 1/2 cup confectioners' sugar
- 1/4 cup fat-free milk
- 1 carton (8 oz.) frozen fat-free whipped topping, thawed
- 1 chocolate crumb crust (9 inches)

Direction

- Beat the cream cheese in a bowl until it becomes fluffy. Stir in the sugar and peanut butter. Slowly add the milk and stir well. Fold in the whipped topping gently, then scoop into the crust. Let it chill in the fridge overnight.

Nutrition Information

- Calories: 280 calories
- Total Carbohydrate: 35 g
- Cholesterol: 2 mg
- Total Fat: 12 g
- Fiber: 1 g
- Protein: 6 g
- Sodium: 325 mg

237. Makeover Pear Cheesecake

"A lighter version of the original recipe made with fat-free milk, reduced-fat cream cheese, less butter in the crust and reduced-fat graham cracker crumbs."
Serving: 12 servings. | Prep: 20m | Ready in: 01h05m

Ingredients

- 1-1/4 cups reduced-fat graham cracker crumbs (about 7 whole crackers)
- 3 tbsps. plus 3/4 cup sugar, divided
- 3 tbsps. butter, melted
- 2 medium ripe pears, peeled and sliced
- FILLING:
- 3 packages (8 oz. each) reduced-fat cream cheese
- 3 tbsps. all-purpose flour
- 1 egg
- 1/4 cup egg substitute
- 1/2 cup fat-free milk
- 2 tbsps. lemon juice
- 1-1/2 tsps. grated lemon peel

Direction

- Mix together the butter, 3 tbsp. sugar and cracker crumbs in a small bowl, then press it onto the bottom and 1 1/4-inch up the sides of a cooking spray coated 9-inch springform pan. Let it chill in the fridge for 30 minutes. Lay out the pear slices on top of the crust.
- Beat the flour, leftover sugar and cream cheese in a big bowl until it becomes smooth, then

add the egg substitute and egg and beat it on low speed just until blended. Stir in the lemon peel and juice and milk, then pour it on top of the pears.
- Let it bake for 45 to 50 minutes at 350 degrees or until the middle becomes set. Allow it to cool for 10 minutes on a wire rack. Run a knife carefully around the edge of the pan to loosen and let it cool for an additional hour. Let it chill overnight. Chill the leftovers in the fridge.

Nutrition Information

- Calories: 272 calories
- Total Carbohydrate: 29 g
- Cholesterol: 57 mg
- Total Fat: 14 g
- Fiber: 1 g
- Protein: 8 g
- Sodium: 258 mg

238. Makeover Red Velvet Cake

"A lighter makeover version of a cake recipe that has been a favorite for over 45 years."
Serving: 16 servings. | Prep: 20m | Ready in: 35m

Ingredients

- 1/4 cup butter, softened
- 1 cup sugar
- 2 large eggs
- 1/4 cup unsweetened applesauce
- 1 bottle (1 oz.) red food coloring
- 1 tsp. white vinegar
- 1 tsp. vanilla extract
- 2-1/4 cups cake flour
- 2 tsps. baking cocoa
- 1 tsp. baking soda
- 1 tsp. salt
- 1 cup buttermilk
- FROSTING:
- 4-1/2 tsps. all-purpose flour
- 1/2 cup fat-free milk
- 1/2 cup butter, softened
- 1/2 cup sugar
- 1/2 tsp. vanilla extract

Direction

- Line parchment paper in the two 9-inch round baking pans and use cooking spray to coat the paper and sprinkle it with flour, then put aside. Beat the sugar and butter in a big bowl until well combined, then add eggs, one at a time and beat it well after every addition. Beat in vanilla, vinegar, food coloring and applesauce.
- Mix together the salt, baking soda, cocoa and flour, then add it to the butter mixture alternately with the buttermilk. Pour it into the prepped pans and let it bake for 14 to 18 minutes at 350 degrees or until an inserted toothpick in the middle exits clean. Allow it to cool for 10 minutes prior to taking it out from the pans to fully cool on wire racks.
- To make the frosting, whisk the milk and flour in a small saucepan until it becomes smooth, then boil. Let it cook and stir for 2 minutes. Allow it to cool to room temperature. Cream the sugar and butter in a small bowl until it becomes fluffy and light. Beat in vanilla and flour mixture, then spread it on top of the cake and between the layers.

Nutrition Information

- Calories: 241 calories
- Total Carbohydrate: 36 g
- Cholesterol: 50 mg
- Total Fat: 9 g
- Fiber: 0 g
- Protein: 3 g
- Sodium: 315 mg

239. Makeover Rocky Road Fudge Brownies

"A satisfying makeover recipe with less fat and fewer calories."
Serving: 2 dozen. | Prep: 20m | Ready in: 45m

Ingredients

- 1 package reduced-fat fudge brownie mix (13-inch x 9-inch pan size)
- 1/2 cup chopped pecans
- 2 cups miniature marshmallows
- 1 cup marshmallow creme
- 1/4 cup fat-free milk
- 3 tbsps. butter
- 3 tbsps. baking cocoa
- 1 oz. unsweetened chocolate
- 1 cup confectioners' sugar
- 1/2 tsp. vanilla extract

Direction

- Prepare the brownie mix following the package instructions, then mix in pecans. Spread the batter into a cooking spray coated 13x9-inch baking pan. Let it bake for 25 to 30 minutes at 350 degrees until an inserted toothpick in the middle exits clean. Sprinkle marshmallows on top. Let it cool on a wire rack.
- Mix together the chocolate, cocoa, butter, milk and marshmallow creme in a big saucepan. Cook and stir on low heat until smooth and melted.
- Move to a big bowl, then beat in vanilla and confectioners' sugar until it becomes smooth. Drizzle it on top of marshmallows.

Nutrition Information

- Calories: 180 calories
- Total Carbohydrate: 32 g
- Cholesterol: 4 mg
- Total Fat: 6 g
- Fiber: 1 g
- Protein: 2 g
- Sodium: 109 mg

240. Makeover Spice Crumb Cake

"This cake recipe made with apple sauce, butter and small amount of oil is low in cholesterol, fat and calories."
Serving: 18 servings. | Prep: 15m | Ready in: 50m

Ingredients

- 1 egg
- 2 egg whites
- 2 cups buttermilk
- 1/4 cup canola oil
- 1/3 cup unsweetened applesauce
- 2 tbsps. molasses
- 2-1/2 cups all-purpose flour
- 1-1/2 cups packed brown sugar
- 1-1/4 tsps. baking soda
- 1-3/4 tsps. each ground cinnamon, nutmeg and cloves
- 1/2 tsp. baking powder
- 1/2 tsp. salt
- TOPPING:
- 1/3 cup packed brown sugar
- 3/4 cup all-purpose flour
- 1/4 tsp. each ground cinnamon, nutmeg and cloves
- 1/4 cup cold butter, cubed

Direction

- Beat the molasses, applesauce, oil, buttermilk, egg whites and egg in a big bowl. Mix together the salt, baking powder, spices, baking soda, brown sugar and flour, then add to the egg mixture and stir well. Pour it into a cooking spray coated 13x9-inch baking pan.
- To make topping, in a bowl, mix together the spices, flour and brown sugar, then slice in the butter until the mixture looks like coarse crumbs. Sprinkle it on top of the batter. Let it bake for 35 to 40 minutes at 350 degrees until an inserted toothpick in the middle exits clean. Allow it to cool on a wire rack.

Nutrition Information

- Calories: 249 calories
- Total Carbohydrate: 42 g
- Cholesterol: 20 mg
- Total Fat: 8 g
- Fiber: 1 g
- Protein: 4 g
- Sodium: 241 mg

241. Makeover Sweet Potato Pecan Pie

"A richer and healthier made-over pie recipe made with more spices."
Serving: 8 servings. | Prep: 25m | Ready in: 01h10m

Ingredients

- 1 sheet refrigerated pie pastry
- 1-1/2 cups mashed sweet potatoes
- 1/3 cup 2% milk
- 1/4 cup packed dark brown sugar
- 1 tbsp. reduced-fat butter, melted
- 1/2 tsp. vanilla extract
- 1/4 tsp. salt
- 1/2 tsp. ground cinnamon
- 1/4 tsp. ground allspice
- 1/4 tsp. ground nutmeg
- PECAN LAYER:
- 1 large egg
- 1/3 cup packed dark brown sugar
- 1/3 cup corn syrup
- 1 tbsp. reduced-fat butter, melted
- 1/4 tsp. vanilla extract
- 2/3 cup chopped pecans

Direction

- Unroll the pastry on a lightly floured surface, then move to a 9-inch pie plate. Cut the pastry to 1/2-inch beyond the edge of the plate and flute the edges.
- Mix together the spices, salt, vanilla, butter, brown sugar, milk and sweet potatoes in a small bowl, then spread it into the pastry shell evenly.
- To make the pecan layer, whisk the brown sugar and egg in a separate small bowl until combined. Add vanilla, butter and corn syrup, then stir well. Mix in pecans. Pour it on top of the sweet potato mixture.
- Let it bake for 45 to 55 minutes at 350 degrees or until an inserted knife in the middle exits clean. Allow it to fully cool on a wire rack. Let it chill in the fridge for a minimum of 3 hours prior to serving.

Nutrition Information

- Calories: 363 calories
- Total Carbohydrate: 53 g
- Cholesterol: 36 mg
- Total Fat: 17 g
- Fiber: 3 g
- Protein: 4 g
- Sodium: 255 mg

242. Makeover White Fruitcake

"A brighter and lighter version of a fruitcake recipe."
Serving: 20 servings. | Prep: 20m | Ready in: 01h50m

Ingredients

- 3/4 cup red candied cherries
- 3/4 cup green candied cherries
- 1-1/4 cups brandy, divided
- 6 large eggs, separated
- 2 large egg whites
- 1/2 cup butter, softened
- 1-1/2 cups sugar
- 4 cups all-purpose flour
- 1/2 cup unsweetened applesauce
- 1-1/2 cups sliced almonds
- 1-1/2 cups golden raisins
- 3/4 cup sweetened shredded coconut

Direction

- Mix together 1/4 cup of brandy and cherries in a small bowl, then allow it to stand overnight. In a big bowl, put 8 egg whites and allow it to stand for 30 minutes at room temperature.
- Cream the sugar and butter in a big bowl until well combined, then add egg yolks, one at a time and beat it well after every addition. Beat in the leftover brandy. Slowly add the flour to the creamed mixture alternately with applesauce.
- Beat the egg whites using clean beaters until it forms stiff peaks, then fold it into the batter. Fold in coconut, raisins, almonds and cherry mixture. Spoon gently into a cooking spray coated 10-inch tube pan with removable bottom. Let it bake for 1 1/2 to 1 3/4 hours at 300 degrees or until an inserted toothpick in the middle exits clean.
- Allow it to cool for 10 minutes prior to taking it out from the pan to fully cool on a wire rack.

Nutrition Information

- Calories: 352 calories
- Total Carbohydrate: 56 g
- Cholesterol: 75 mg
- Total Fat: 11 g
- Fiber: 2 g
- Protein: 7 g
- Sodium: 80 mg

243. Makeover White Layer Cake

"A pared-down dessert that is low in fat, cholesterol and calories."
Serving: 14 servings. | Prep: 20m | Ready in: 40m

Ingredients

- 1/4 cup shortening
- 1-1/2 cups sugar
- 4 large egg whites
- 1/4 cup unsweetened applesauce
- 1-1/2 tsps. vanilla extract
- 2-1/4 cups cake flour, sifted
- 1 tsp. baking powder
- 1/2 tsp. baking soda
- 1/2 tsp. salt
- 1 cup buttermilk
- FROSTING:
- 3 cups confectioners' sugar
- 1/4 cup butter, softened
- 1 tbsp. light corn syrup
- 2 tsps. vanilla extract
- 1/8 tsp. salt
- 2 to 3 tbsps. 1% milk

Direction

- Use cooking spray to coat two 9-inch round baking pans and dust them with flour; put aside. Cream the sugar and shortening in a bowl for about 2 minutes or until crumbly. Slowly add the egg whites and beat well. Beat in vanilla and applesauce. Mix together the salt, baking soda, baking powder and flour, then add to the batter alternately with buttermilk until blended.
- Pour it into the prepped pans. Let bake for 20 to 25 minutes at 350 degrees or until an inserted toothpick in the middle exits clean. Allow them to cool for 10 minutes prior to taking out from the pans to the wire racks to fully cool.
- To make frosting, beat the salt, vanilla, corn syrup, butter and confectioners' sugar in a bowl. Beat in enough milk until the frosting reaches the spreading consistency. Spread it between layers and on top and sides of the cake.

Nutrition Information

- Calories: 330 calories
- Total Carbohydrate: 65 g
- Cholesterol: 10 mg
- Total Fat: 7 g
- Fiber: 1 g
- Protein: 3 g
- Sodium: 256 mg

244. Maple Banana Ice Cream

"Creamy dessert that's dairy-free and made with Almond Breeze Almond-Cashew Blend."
Serving: 4 | Prep: 10m | Ready in: 20m

Ingredients

- 4 ripe bananas
- 1/2 cup Almond Breeze Original OR any Almond Breeze Almond-Cashew Blend
- 2 tbsps. maple syrup
- 1 tbsp. honey
- 1 tsp. vanilla extract
- 1 vanilla bean
- 1 pinch salt

Direction

- In a blender, mix together all the ingredients and prior to blending, cut the vanilla bean lengthwise, then scrape the knife down the interior of the bean to extract the seeds. Put these with the other ingredients in a blender and blend until it becomes smooth. Move the ingredients to an ice cream maker and it's done. This is an easy recipe and going to the grocery store to buy the ingredients for the recipe is the hardest part. Keep the ice cream in the freezer prior to serving because this dessert melts quickly.
- If an ice cream maker is unavailable, you can cut the bananas to thin pieces and put it on the baking trays lined with parchment and let it freeze ideally overnight. Put these and the remaining ingredients into the blender and blend it until it becomes smooth, then serve right away. The texture of this dessert is similar to soft serve yet is still very delicious.

Nutrition Information

- Calories: 171 calories;
- Total Carbohydrate: 42.6 g
- Cholesterol: 0 mg
- Total Fat: 0.7 g
- Protein: 1.4 g
- Sodium: 57 mg

245. Meringue Candy Canes

"Minty, cute and easy to make red-and-white striped treats that melt in your mouth."
Serving: 4 dozen. | Prep: 20m | Ready in: 01h10m

Ingredients

- 3 large egg whites
- 1/2 tsp. cream of tartar
- 3/4 cup sugar
- 1/4 tsp. peppermint extract
- Red paste food coloring

Direction

- Beat the egg whites in a big bowl until it becomes foamy. Put in cream of tartar and beat it on medium speed, until it forms soft peaks. Slowly add sugar, a tbsp. at a time, and beat it for about 6 minutes on high, until the sugar dissolves and it forms stiff peaks. Beat in the peppermint extract.
- Trim off a small hole from the pastry bag's corner, then insert star tip number 21. Brush the 3 equally spaced quarter inch strips of red food coloring on the bag's interior from the tip to 3/4 of the way up the bag's top using a new paintbrush. Fill the bag carefully with meringue.
- Pipe 3-inch candy canes on the baking trays lined with parchment. Let it bake for 25 minutes at 225 degrees. Rotate the baking trays to a separate oven rack. Let it bake for another 25 minutes or until it becomes firm to touch. Turn off the oven and leave the cookies in the oven with the door slightly open for a minimum of an hour or until it cools down.

Nutrition Information

- Calories: 13 calories
- Total Carbohydrate: 3 g
- Cholesterol: 0 mg

- Total Fat: 0 g
- Fiber: 0 g
- Protein: 0 g
- Sodium: 3 mg

246. Microwave Hot Fudge Sundae Cake

"A low-fat and quick recipe."
Serving: 10 servings. | Prep: 20m | Ready in: 20m

Ingredients

- 1 cup all-purpose flour
- 3/4 cup sugar
- 2 tbsps. plus 1/4 cup baking cocoa, divided
- 2 tsps. baking powder
- 1/4 tsp. salt
- 1/2 cup fat-free milk
- 2 tbsps. canola oil
- 1 tsp. vanilla extract
- 1/2 cup chopped pecans
- 1 cup packed brown sugar
- 1-3/4 cups boiling water
- 10 tbsps. reduced-fat whipped topping

Direction

- In an ungreased 2-1/2-quart microwave-safe dish, mix together the salt, sugar, 2 tbsps. cocoa, baking powder and flour. Stir milk, oil and vanilla into the mix until incorporated. Fold nuts into the mixture. Mix together the brown sugar and remaining cocoa; sprinkle on top of the batter.
- Add boiling water on top of the batter (do not stir). Microwave on high, with no cover, until cake's top springs back once touched lightly, for about 7-8 minutes. Serve with whipped topping.

Nutrition Information

- Calories: 274 calories
- Total Carbohydrate: 50 g
- Cholesterol: 0 mg

- Total Fat: 8 g
- Fiber: 2 g
- Protein: 3 g
- Sodium: 121 mg

247. Mile-high Lime Pie

"Fluffy and light pie with creamy and sweet lime filling that you can make ahead made with convenient items."
Serving: 8 servings. | Prep: 10m | Ready in: 10m

Ingredients

- 1 can (14 oz.) fat-free sweetened condensed milk
- 1 cup (8 oz.) reduced-fat sour cream
- 1/3 cup plus 2 tbsps. lime juice
- 5 drops green food coloring, optional
- 1 carton (8 oz.) frozen reduced-fat whipped topping, thawed
- 1 reduced-fat graham cracker crust (8 inches)

Direction

- Mix together the food coloring if preferred, lime juice, sour cream and milk in a big bowl, then fold in the whipped topping. Pour it into the crust and let it chill in the fridge for a minimum of 12 hours.

Nutrition Information

- Calories: 355 calories
- Total Carbohydrate: 57 g
- Cholesterol: 12 mg
- Total Fat: 9 g
- Fiber: 1 g
- Protein: 7 g
- Sodium: 171 mg

248. Mixed Berry Pizza

"Tempting appetizer with fresh fruit."
Serving: 20 servings. | Prep: 10m | Ready in: 20m

Ingredients

- 1 tube (8 oz.) refrigerated reduced-fat crescent rolls
- 11 oz. reduced-fat cream cheese
- 1/2 cup apricot preserves
- 2 tbsps. confectioners' sugar
- 2 cups sliced fresh strawberries
- 1 cup fresh blueberries
- 1 cup fresh raspberries

Direction

- Unroll crescent roll dough. Put on a 15x10x1-in. baking pan that's been sprayed with cooking spray. Press 1in. up the sides and bottom of a pan to make a crust. Seal perforations and seams. Bake for 8-10 minutes or until golden at 375°. Completely cool.
- Beat cream cheese in a big bowl until smooth. Beat confectioners' sugar and preserves in. Spread on crust. Refrigerate, covered, for 1-2 hours.
- Prior to serving, top with berries. Slice to 20 pieces.

Nutrition Information

- Calories: 110 calories
- Total Carbohydrate: 15 g
- Cholesterol: 9 mg
- Total Fat: 5 g
- Fiber: 1 g
- Protein: 3 g
- Sodium: 143 mg

249. Mixed Berry Shortcake

"A fun summer dessert."
Serving: 8 servings. | Prep: 25m | Ready in: 40m

Ingredients

- 1/2 cup plus 1/3 cup sugar, divided
- 3 tbsps. cornstarch
- 2-3/4 cups fat-free milk
- 2 egg yolks, lightly beaten
- 1 tsp. vanilla extract
- 2 cups all-purpose flour
- 1 tsp. baking powder
- 1/4 tsp. baking soda
- 1/4 tsp. salt
- 6 tbsps. cold butter
- 2/3 cup buttermilk
- 4 cups sliced fresh strawberries
- 4 cups fresh blueberries
- 8 whole strawberries, halved
- 1/2 cup reduced-fat whipped topping

Direction

- Mix cornstarch and 1/2 cup sugar in heavy saucepan. Mix milk in till blended; boil on medium low heat. Mix and cook till thick for 1-2 minutes; take off heat. Mix small amount into egg yolks; put all in pan, constantly mixing. Take off heat; mix vanilla in. Put in bowl; press plastic wrap piece over custard. Refrigerate.
- Mix leftover sugar, salt, baking soda, baking powder and flour in bowl. Cut butter in till it looks like coarse crumbs. Mix buttermilk in till you make a soft dough. Gently pat to 9-in. square baking pan that's coated in cooking spray. Bake for 15-20 minutes till lightly browned at 400°. Cool on wire rack.
- Slice shortcake to 3/4-in. cubes. Alternate layers of blueberries, sliced strawberries, custard and shortcake in parfait glasses. Garnish with dollop of whipped topping and halved strawberries.

Nutrition Information

- Calories: 382 calories
- Total Carbohydrate: 66 g
- Cholesterol: 77 mg
- Total Fat: 12 g
- Fiber: 5 g
- Protein: 6 g
- Sodium: 290 mg

250. Mock Ice Cream Sandwiches

"Ice cream treat with less fat."
Serving: 8 sandwiches. | Prep: 15m | Ready in: 15m

Ingredients

- 2 cups fat-free whipped topping
- 1/2 cup miniature semisweet chocolate chips
- 8 whole chocolate graham crackers

Direction

- Mix together the chocolate chips and whipped topping in a bowl. Cut or break the graham crackers in 1/2. Spread the whipped topping mixture on top of the 1/2 of crackers and put the leftover crackers on top. Use plastic to wrap it and let it freeze for a minimum of 1 hour.

Nutrition Information

- Calories: 180 calories
- Total Carbohydrate: 28 g
- Cholesterol: 0 mg
- Total Fat: 7 g
- Fiber: 1 g
- Protein: 2 g
- Sodium: 88 mg

251. Mock Strawberry Cheesecake Tart

"The beautiful and astounding strawberry dessert!"
Serving: 1 serving. | Prep: 5m | Ready in: 5m

Ingredients

- 3 tbsps. fat-free whipped topping
- 2 tbsps. reduced-fat cream cheese
- Sugar substitute equivalent to 2 tsps. sugar
- 1/4 cup chopped fresh strawberries
- 1/2 whole graham cracker, crumbled

Direction

- Combine sugar substitute, cream cheese and whipped topping in the small dessert dish until smooth. Mix in the strawberries and top with a sprinkle of the cracker crumbs.

Nutrition Information

- Calories: 137 calories
- Total Carbohydrate: 16 g
- Cholesterol: 17 mg
- Total Fat: 6 g
- Fiber: 1 g
- Protein: 4 g
- Sodium: 139 mg

252. Mom's Pumpkin Pie

"A rich pie with spices."
Serving: 8 | Prep: 30m | Ready in: 1h30m

Ingredients

- 1 recipe pastry for a 9 inch single crust pie
- 3 eggs
- 1 egg yolk
- 1/2 cup white sugar
- 1/2 cup packed brown sugar
- 1 tsp. salt
- 1/2 tsp. ground cinnamon
- 1/2 tsp. ground nutmeg
- 1/2 tsp. ground ginger

- 1/4 tsp. ground cloves
- 1 1/2 cups milk
- 1/2 cup heavy whipping cream
- 2 cups pumpkin puree

Direction

- Preheat an oven to 220°C/425°F.
- Mix brown sugar, white sugar, egg yolk and eggs in big bowl. Add cloves, ginger, nutmeg, cinnamon and salt; mix in cream and milk slowly. Mix pumpkin in; put filling in pie shell.
- In preheated oven, bake for 10 minutes. Lower heat to 175°C/350°F; bake for another 40-45 minutes till filling is set.

Nutrition Information

- Calories: 345 calories;
- Total Carbohydrate: 44.3 g
- Cholesterol: 119 mg
- Total Fat: 16.5 g
- Protein: 6.6 g
- Sodium: 611 mg

253. Momma Lamb's Famous Fruit Salad

"Delectable fruit salad from pineapple, maraschino cherries and mandarin oranges. Enjoy!"
Serving: 6 | Prep: 5m | Ready in: 35m

Ingredients

- 1 (20 oz.) can pineapple chunks
- 1 (5 oz.) package instant vanilla pudding mix
- 1 (15 oz.) can mandarin oranges, drained
- 1 (10 oz.) jar maraschino cherries, drained
- 3 bananas

Direction

- In a large bowl, drain all of the juice from pineapple. Put pineapple chunks aside.
- Add vanilla pudding mix to the pineapple juice and stir well until smooth. Mix in maraschino cherries, mandarin oranges and pineapple chunks. Stir well. Keep in the fridge for at least half an hour.
- Just before serving, cut bananas in slices into the bowl and fold in.

Nutrition Information

- Calories: 274 calories;
- Total Carbohydrate: 70.2 g
- Cholesterol: 0 mg
- Total Fat: 0.5 g
- Protein: 1.6 g
- Sodium: 342 mg

254. No-bake Almond Bites

"No bake treats that are chewy, easy and quick to prepare."
Serving: 1-1/2 dozen. | Prep: 10m | Ready in: 10m

Ingredients

- 1 cup crushed reduced-fat vanilla wafers (about 30 wafers)
- 1 cup confectioners' sugar, divided
- 1/2 cup chopped almonds
- 2 tbsps. baking cocoa
- 2 tbsps. apple juice
- 2 tbsps. corn syrup
- 1/4 tsp. almond extract

Direction

- Mix together the cocoa, almonds, half a cup of confectioner's sugar and wafer crumbs in a big bowl. Mix together the extract, corn syrup and apple juice, then mix it into the crumb mixture until combined.
- Form it into 1-inch balls, then roll it in the leftover confectioners' sugar. Keep it in an airtight container.

Nutrition Information

- Calories: 81 calories
- Total Carbohydrate: 15 g
- Cholesterol: 0 mg

- Total Fat: 2 g
- Fiber: 1 g
- Protein: 1 g
- Sodium: 25 mg

255. No-bake Chocolate Oat Cookies

"These excellent coconut oat cookies require no baking at all!"
Serving: 3 dozen. | Prep: 10m | Ready in: 20m

Ingredients

- 2 cups sugar
- 1/2 cup fat-free milk
- 1/2 cup butter, cubed
- 3 cups quick-cooking oats
- 1 cup sweetened shredded coconut
- 6 tbsps. baking cocoa
- 1/2 tsp. vanilla extract

Direction

- Mix butter, milk and sugar together in a large saucepan; boil and stir continuously. Boil for 2 minutes. Take off from the heat.
- Stir in vanilla, cocoa, coconut and oats.
- Quickly dollop rounded tablespoonfuls of batter onto waxed paper. Allow to stand for about 60 minutes until set.

Nutrition Information

- Calories: 108 calories
- Total Carbohydrate: 18 g
- Cholesterol: 7 mg
- Total Fat: 4 g
- Fiber: 1 g
- Protein: 1 g
- Sodium: 35 mg

256. No-bake Lemon Cheesecake

"Attempt our No-Bake Lemon Cheesecake with a light and marvelous surface and tart lemon enhance."
Serving: 8 servings | Prep: 15m | Ready in: 4h15m

Ingredients

- 1 pkg. (3.4 oz.) JELL-O Lemon Flavor Instant Pudding
- 1-1/4 cups cold milk
- 2 pkg. (8 oz. each) PHILADELPHIA Cream Cheese, softened
- 2 Tbsp. sugar
- 1 tsp. lemon juice
- 1 cup thawed COOL WHIP Whipped Topping
- 1 ready-to-use shortbread pie crust (6 oz.)

Direction

- 1. In medium bowl, beat the milk and pudding mix using whisk for 2 minutes.
- 2. In a large bowl with mixer, beat the lemon juice, sugar and cream cheese until mixed. Put in the pudding gradually, beating well after every addition. Mix in the COOL WHIP gently. Spoon into the crust.
- 3. Refrigerate for 4 hours.

Nutrition Information

- Calories: 400
- Total Carbohydrate: 35 g
- Cholesterol: 80 mg
- Total Fat: 26 g
- Fiber: 0 g
- Protein: 6 g
- Sodium: 480 mg
- Sugar: 23 g
- Saturated Fat: 17 g

257. No-fuss Rice Pudding

"A quick recipe."
Serving: 2 servings. | Prep: 20m | Ready in: 20m

Ingredients

- 1 cup cooked rice
- 1 egg white
- 1 cup fat-free milk
- 1/4 cup sugar
- 1/4 cup golden raisins
- Dash ground cinnamon
- Dash ground nutmeg

Direction

- Mix egg white and rice in small microwave-safe bowl; mix in raisins, sugar and milk. Microwave on high, uncovered, for 1 1/2 minutes; mix. Microwave at 50% power, mixing every 2 minutes, for 7 minutes. Sprinkle nutmeg and cinnamon. Cover; stand for 15 minutes.

Nutrition Information

- Calories: 306 calories
- Total Carbohydrate: 68 g
- Cholesterol: 3 mg
- Total Fat: 0 g
- Fiber: 2 g
- Protein: 9 g
- Sodium: 99 mg

258. No-oat Apple Crisp

"Crispy crust on surface and sweet apples on the bottom."
Serving: 12

Ingredients

- 8 apples
- 1 cup all-purpose flour
- 1 cup white sugar
- 1 tbsp. baking powder
- 1 egg
- 1 1/2 tbsps. ground cinnamon
- 1/4 cup white sugar
- 1 tbsp. butter, melted

Direction

- Combine egg, baking powder, 1 cup sugar and flour together. Mixture will resemble cornmeal.
- Peel the apples, remove core, and cut. Combine with half tbsp. of the cinnamon. In an oiled 8-in. square pan, add apples. On top of the apples, scatter the flour mixture. Combine a quarter cup of sugar and a tbsp. of cinnamon together; scatter over crisp surface. Pour margarine or butter over.
- Bake for an hour at 150°C (or 300°F). Serve while warm.

Nutrition Information

- Calories: 184 calories;
- Total Carbohydrate: 42.5 g
- Cholesterol: 18 mg
- Total Fat: 1.6 g
- Protein: 1.9 g
- Sodium: 136 mg

259. Oatmeal Fruit Cookie Mix In A Jar

"This cookie recipe is so amazing."
Serving: 12

Ingredients

- 1/2 cup packed brown sugar
- 1/4 cup white sugar
- 3/4 cup wheat germ
- 1 cup quick cooking oats
- 1/2 cup dried cherries
- 1/2 cup golden raisins
- 2/3 cup flaked coconut
- 1 cup all-purpose flour
- 1/2 tsp. baking soda
- 1/2 tsp. salt

Direction

- Combine the baking soda, salt and flour.
- Begin with brown sugar, layer ingredients in 1-liter-sized glass jar in given order. End with flour mixture.
- Attach a card with following instructions: For the Oatmeal Fruit Cookies 1. Preheat oven to 175 degrees C (350 degrees F). Use parchment paper to line 1 baking sheet. 2. Empty contents of jar to the big bowl. With the wooden spoon, blend mixture till well-mixed. 3. Use hands to work in half cup of the softened butter/margarine till mixture looks like coarse crumbs. 4. Beat 1 egg along with a quarter cup of milk and 1 tsp. of vanilla. Still use your hands/the wooden spoon, blend egg mixture to dough till well-mixed. 5. Drop the tsp.-sized mounds with 2-in. apart to prepped baking sheet. Bake at 175 degrees C (350 degrees F) till edges turn light brown or for 10-14 minutes. Put the cookies onto the rack to finish the cooling. Makes roughly 2 dozen cookies.

Nutrition Information

- Calories: 197 calories;
- Total Carbohydrate: 40.7 g
- Cholesterol: 0 mg
- Total Fat: 2.4 g
- Protein: 4.3 g
- Sodium: 167 mg

260. Oatmeal Peanut Butter Cookies

"A nice variation of original peanut butter cookie"
Serving: 48 | Prep: 15m | Ready in: 1h

Ingredients

- 1/2 cup shortening
- 1/2 cup margarine, softened
- 1 cup packed brown sugar
- 3/4 cup white sugar
- 1 cup peanut butter
- 2 eggs
- 1 1/2 cups all-purpose flour
- 2 tsps. baking soda
- 1 tsp. salt
- 1 cup quick-cooking oats

Direction

- Preheat the oven to 350°F (175°C).
- Cream together the peanut butter, white sugar, brown sugar, margarine and shortening in a large bowl until mixture is smooth. Beat in one egg at a time until well combined.
- Mix together the salt, baking soda and flour; stir into the creamed mixture. Stir in oats until just mixed. Drop onto ungreased cookie sheets by teaspoonfuls.
- Bake in the preheated oven for 10 to 15 minutes or until cookies are just light browned. Remember not to over bake. Allow to cool and then keep in an airtight container to store.

Nutrition Information

- Calories: 120 calories;
- Total Carbohydrate: 12.8 g
- Cholesterol: 8 mg
- Total Fat: 7.1 g
- Protein: 2.3 g
- Sodium: 152 mg

261. Old-fashioned Fruit Soup

""I got this recipe from a high-school friend many years ago.""
Serving: 6 | Prep: 15m | Ready in: 1h30m

Ingredients

- 3/4 cup chopped dried apricots
- 3/4 cup chopped prunes
- 6 cups cold water
- 1 cinnamon stick
- 2 slices lemon
- 3 tbsps. instant tapioca

- 1 cup white sugar
- 2 tbsps. raisins
- 1 tbsp. dried currants
- 1 tart apple - peeled, cored and chopped

Direction

- Combine water, prunes and apricots together in a large pot; allow to rest for 30 minutes.
- Mix in sugar, tapioca, lemon slices and cinnamon stick; boil over medium-high heat. Turn the heat down; simmer with a cover for 10 minutes. Mix in apple, currants and raisins; simmer till the apples become tender, 5 minutes longer. Take away from the heat; allow to cool completely. Take the cinnamon stick away; place in the refrigerator till cold.

Nutrition Information

- Calories: 236 calories;
- Total Carbohydrate: 61.3 g
- Cholesterol: 0 mg
- Total Fat: 0.2 g
- Protein: 1 g
- Sodium: 3 mg

262. One-ingredient Sorbet

"Use banana, strawberry, or a combination of both to make a good, no-added-sugar sorbet. You can make this ingenious recipe in minutes. Be creative and use other frozen fruits as well."
Serving: 6 | Prep: 10m | Ready in: 2h10m

Ingredients

- 12 fresh strawberries, hulled and chopped
- 5 bananas, peeled and chopped

Direction

- Keep the bananas and strawberries in separate resealable plastic bags or containers. Let it freeze for at least 2 hours or overnight.
- Process the strawberries in a food processor or blender until smooth.
- Process also the bananas in a food processor or blender until smooth.

Nutrition Information

- Calories: 99 calories;
- Total Carbohydrate: 25.2 g
- Cholesterol: 0 mg
- Total Fat: 0.4 g
- Protein: 1.3 g
- Sodium: 1 mg

263. Orange Baked Alaska

"A refreshing treat."
Serving: 6 | Prep: 20m | Ready in: 4h23m

Ingredients

- 1 pint orange sherbet
- 3 oranges
- 3 egg whites
- 6 tbsps. white sugar
- 1/4 tsp. cream of tartar

Direction

- Scoop orange sherbet to 6 balls; put onto plate. Freeze for a minimum of 4 hours till very firm.
- Across the center, slice oranges in half; use a small knife to cut around edges. Remove membrane and fruit; reserve peel shells and fruit. Chop orange sections; put them into bottom of the shells.
- Preheat an oven to 220°C/450°F. Whip egg whites using an electric mixer till foamy in a clean metal or glass bowl; stir in cream of tartar. Beat in sugar slowly while whipping till glossy and stiff.
- Put orange shells onto baking sheet; into each one, add a sherbet ball. Use meringue to cover sherbet, sealing to the edges of orange peel.
- In preheated oven, bake till browned for 5 minutes. Remove; immediately serve.

Nutrition Information

- Calories: 96 calories;
- Total Carbohydrate: 22.6 g
- Cholesterol: 0 mg
- Total Fat: 0.1 g
- Protein: 2.6 g
- Sodium: 28 mg

264. Orange Cashew Bars

"Cashews and oranges make a fantastic combination for a holiday bar."
Serving: 2-1/2 dozen. | Prep: 25m | Ready in: 40m

Ingredients

- 4 oz. reduced-fat cream cheese
- 1/2 cup confectioners' sugar
- 1/4 cup packed brown sugar
- 1 large egg yolk
- 2 tsps. vanilla extract
- 1-1/2 cups all-purpose flour
- FILLING:
- 1 cup packed brown sugar
- 3 large egg whites
- 1 large egg
- 3 tbsps. all-purpose flour
- 2 tsps. vanilla extract
- 1/2 tsp. orange extract
- 1/4 tsp. salt
- 1-1/2 cups salted cashews, coarsely chopped
- ICING:
- 3/4 cup confectioners' sugar
- 4 tsps. orange juice
- 1 tsp. grated orange zest

Direction

- Preheat the oven to 350°. Whisk sugars and cream cheese in a big bowl till smooth. Whisk in vanilla and egg yolk. Slowly mix in flour.
- Force dough 1/4 in. up sides and onto bottom of a sprayed with cooking spray 13x9-inch baking pan. Bake till edges are light brown, about 15 to 20 minutes. Allow to cool on a wire rack for 10 minutes.
- For filling, whisk salt, extracts, flour, egg, egg whites, and brown sugar in a big bowl till smooth. Mix in cashews. Put into crust. Bake till set, about 15 to 20 minutes more.
- Allow to cool fully in pan on a wire rack. Combine icing ingredients in a small bowl; sprinkle on top. Slice into bars.

Nutrition Information

- Calories: 145 calories
- Total Carbohydrate: 21 g
- Cholesterol: 17 mg
- Total Fat: 5 g
- Fiber: 0 g
- Protein: 3 g
- Sodium: 98 mg

265. Orange Cream Pops

"A fun swirled orange pop."
Serving: 8 | Prep: 15m | Ready in: 8h20m

Ingredients

- 2 cups Almond Breeze Vanilla almondmilk
- 1/4 cup sugar
- 2 tbsps. cornstarch + 2 tsps. cornstarch
- 2 tbsps. coconut oil
- 1 tsp. vanilla extract
- 1/4 cup orange juice concentrate, thawed

Direction

- Whisk extract, coconut oil, cornstarch, sugar and Almond Breeze in a small saucepan; simmer, frequently whisking. Cook for 5 minutes on low heat till mixture thickens, frequently mixing. Allow to cool, mixing occasionally.
- Put 2/3 of mixture in another bowl. Mix orange juice concentrate in. Mix mixture from both bowls; swirling very lightly.
- Put into ice cream pop molds. Insert a stick/handle into each then freeze overnight.

266. Orange Delight

"A great dessert."
Serving: 10 slices. | Prep: 30m | Ready in: 30m

Ingredients

- 1 cup crushed vanilla wafers (about 30 wafers)
- 2 tbsps. butter, melted
- 3/4 cup orange juice
- 1/3 cup sugar
- 2 envelopes unflavored gelatin
- 1 carton (15 oz.) reduced-fat ricotta cheese
- 2 cups fat-free sugar-free vanilla yogurt
- 1 tsp. grated orange zest
- 1/8 tsp. orange extract, optional
- 1 can (15 oz.) mandarin oranges, drained
- 2 tbsps. reduced-sugar orange marmalade

Direction

- Mix butter and wafer crumbs in a bowl; press on the bottom of an ungreased 9-in. springform pan. Bake for 10 minutes at 375°. Cool on wire rack. Mix gelatin, sugar and orange juice in a saucepan; let stand for 5 minutes. Mix and cook on low heat till gelatin melts. Cool for 10 minutes.
- Meanwhile, process ricotta cheese, covered, till smooth in a food processor/blender. Add gelatin mixture, extract (optional), orange zest and yogurt; cover and process till smooth. For garnish, put aside 1/3 cup oranges. Add leftover oranges into yogurt mixture. Smear into the crust.
- Chill for at least 6 hours or overnight. Run a knife around pan's edge to loosen just before serving. Remove sides of pan. Put reserved oranges over. Melt marmalade; put on top of oranges. Refrigerate leftovers.

Nutrition Information

- Calories: 249 calories
- Total Carbohydrate: 35 g
- Cholesterol: 23 mg
- Total Fat: 8 g
- Fiber: 0 g
- Protein: 9 g
- Sodium: 184 mg

267. Orange Dream Cups

"Fun and unique dessert cup recipe with light fluffy filling."
Serving: 8 servings. | Prep: 20m | Ready in: 20m

Ingredients

- 4 large navel oranges
- 1 package (3 oz.) orange gelatin
- 1 cup boiling water
- 1-1/2 cups fat-free frozen vanilla yogurt

Direction

- Slice each orange in 1/2 widthwise, then take out the fruit carefully from both halves and leave the shells undamaged. Put aside the shells. Section the orange pulp, then cut it into cubes (get rid of the orange juice or set aside for later use).
- Dissolve the gelatin in a bowl with boiling water. Put in frozen yogurt and mix until it melts. Fold in the orange pulp. Let it chill in the fridge until it becomes thick. Scoop to the reserved orange shells, put on cover and let it freeze for three hours.

Nutrition Information

- Calories: 119 calories
- Total Carbohydrate: 28 g
- Cholesterol: 0 mg
- Total Fat: 0 g
- Fiber: 2 g
- Protein: 3 g
- Sodium: 50 mg

268. Orange Lime Gelatin Ring

"Molded gelatin ring with the tanginess of lime, orange and pineapple, filled with red grapes."
Serving: 10 servings. | Prep: 40m | Ready in: 40m

Ingredients

- 1 can (11 oz.) mandarin oranges, drained
- 1 can (20 oz.) crushed pineapple, undrained
- 2 tbsps. lemon juice
- 1 package (3 oz.) lime gelatin
- 1 package (8 oz.) reduced-fat cream cheese, cubed
- Lettuce leaves
- 2 cups seedless red grapes

Direction

- Place oranges in the bottom of a 9-in. ring mold greased with cooking spray. Freeze, covered, for 30 minutes. In the meantime, strain pineapple, saving a cup juice (remove any leftover juice or save for other uses); put pineapple aside.
- Heat up lemon juice and saved pineapple juice to a boil in a saucepan. Take off from the heat; let cool for 10 minutes. Add into a blender or food processor. Put in gelatin powder; cover and blend for half a minute or until dissolved. Put in cream cheese; cover and blend for a minute or until smooth.
- Mix in pineapple. Put into ring mold. Cover and chill for 8 hours or until set. Unmold onto a serving plate lined with lettuce. Put grapes in the center.

Nutrition Information

- Calories: 158 calories
- Total Carbohydrate: 25 g
- Cholesterol: 16 mg
- Total Fat: 5 g
- Fiber: 1 g
- Protein: 4 g
- Sodium: 126 mg

269. Orange Parfaits

""My son's fiancée wanted this recipe ever when she first tasted this citrus parfait. And followed by that, she wanted the leftovers.""
Serving: 8 servings. | Prep: 30m | Ready in: 30m

Ingredients

- 2 envelopes unflavored gelatin
- 1/2 cup orange juice
- 1 cup fat-free milk
- 1 package (8 oz.) reduced-fat cream cheese, cubed
- 1/3 cup sugar
- 1 tsp. vanilla extract
- 1/2 tsp. grated orange zest
- 1 can (11 oz.) mandarin oranges
- 1 can (20 oz.) unsweetened crushed pineapple, undrained
- 1 carton (8 oz.) reduced-fat frozen whipped topping, thawed
- 1/2 cup chocolate graham cracker crumbs (about 3 whole crackers), divided

Direction

- Mix orange juice and gelatin in a small bowl; allow it to stand for 5 minutes. Then heat milk until boiling; stir to gelatin. Slightly cool. Place to a blender; cover and blend for 30 seconds or until incorporated. Add in the orange zest, vanilla, sugar, and cream cheese; pulse until combined.
- Strain oranges, set aside the juice; reserve oranges. Add reserved juice and pineapple to gelatin mixture; pulse until smooth. Add in whipped topping then fold. In every 8 parfait glasses, put half of the oranges. Then layer with half of the gelatin mixture and 3 tbsps. of cracker crumbs. Continue layer of crumbs and gelatin; put the rest of oranges on top. Let it chill for 4 hours. Top with the rest of the crumbs.

Nutrition Information

- Calories: 277 calories

- Total Carbohydrate: 39 g
- Cholesterol: 17 mg
- Total Fat: 10 g
- Fiber: 1 g
- Protein: 6 g
- Sodium: 130 mg

270. Orange Pineapple Delight

"Sunny orange colored pudding flavored with coconut and pineapple."
Serving: 4 servings. | Prep: 5m | Ready in: 20m

Ingredients

- 1 can (8 oz.) unsweetened crushed pineapple
- 1 package (0.8 oz.) sugar-free cook-and-serve vanilla pudding mix
- 2/3 cup nonfat dry milk powder
- 1 cup orange juice
- 1/2 tsp. coconut extract
- 1/2 cup miniature marshmallows
- 1/2 cup reduced-fat whipped topping
- 4 tsps. sweetened shredded coconut, toasted

Direction

- Drain the pineapples and set aside the juices, then put aside the pineapple. Pour in enough water to the reserved juice to even 3/4 cup. Mix together the juice mixture, orange juice, milk powder and pudding mix in a saucepan. Let it cook and stir until the mixture fully boils. Take it out of the heat, then mix in coconut extract. Allow to cool for 5 minutes. Mix in marshmallows until it melts, then fold in the pineapple. Move to 4 individual serving plates. Put on cover and let it chill in the fridge for 2 hours. Put coconut and whipped topping on top as a garnish.

Nutrition Information

- Calories: 204 calories
- Total Carbohydrate: 38 g
- Cholesterol: 4 mg
- Total Fat: 2 g

- Fiber: 1 g
- Protein: 8 g
- Sodium: 238 mg

271. Orange Pumpkin Gelatin

"An easy pumpkin treat with a light taste."
Serving: 4 | Prep: 15m | Ready in: 2h15m

Ingredients

- 1 cup boiling water
- 1 (3 oz.) package orange-flavored Jell-O®
- 1/4 cup brown sugar
- 1 tsp. ground cinnamon
- 2 cups pumpkin puree
- 2/3 cup cold water

Direction

- In a bowl, stir gelatin and 1 cup of boiling water together. Whisk cinnamon and brown sugar into the mixture until sugar has dissolved. Put in cold water and pumpkin puree, then stir the mixture until smooth. Cover and refrigerate for 2 hours until set.

Nutrition Information

- Calories: 173 calories;
- Total Carbohydrate: 41.7 g
- Cholesterol: 0 mg
- Total Fat: 0.5 g
- Protein: 4.1 g
- Sodium: 86 mg

272. Orange Rosemary Sorbet

"The understated flavor of fresh rosemary gives a delightful contrast to the citrusy sorbet. Finish any meal off wonderfully with this smooth, refreshing and icy dessert from Bonnie Kinzler of New York."
Serving: 8 servings. | Prep: 15m | Ready in: 35m

Ingredients

- 1-1/2 cups water
- 1-1/2 cups sugar
- 2 to 3 fresh rosemary sprigs
- 3 cups orange juice
- 1/3 cup lemon juice

Direction

- Boil rosemary, sugar and water in a big saucepan. Leaving it uncovered, lower the heat and let it simmer for 10 minutes. Let it cool then strain and remove the rosemary. Mix in the lemon juice and orange juice. Pour the mixture into the cylinder of an ice cream freezer until it's filled two-thirds of the way. Follow the manufacturer's instructions to freeze the mixture. Before serving, leave it to ripen up in the ice-cream freezer or firm up in the refrigerator freezer for 2 to 4 hours.

Nutrition Information

- Calories: 190 calories
- Total Carbohydrate: 48 g
- Cholesterol: 0 mg
- Total Fat: 0 g
- Fiber: 0 g
- Protein: 0 g
- Sodium: 1 mg

273. Orange Tea Cake

"Sponge cake made from scratch with a touch of orange flavor."
Serving: 12 servings. | Prep: 20m | Ready in: 50m

Ingredients

- 7 large eggs
- 1-3/4 cups all-purpose flour
- 1/2 tsp. salt
- 1-1/2 cups sugar, divided
- 6 tbsps. orange juice
- 4-1/2 tsps. grated orange zest
- 3/4 tsp. confectioners' sugar

Direction

- Allow the eggs to stand for half an hour at room temperature. Sift the salt and flour, then put aside.
- Beat the yolks in a big bowl until it becomes a bit thick. Slowly add half a cup of sugar and beat it until it turns lemon-colored and thick. Blend in orange zest and juice. Put the dry ingredients into the yolk mixture and stir well.
- Beat the egg whites in a separate bowl on medium speed, until it forms soft peaks. Slowly beat in the leftover sugar, approximately a tbsp. at a time, on high until the sugar dissolves and it forms stiff glossy peaks. Fold 1/4 of the egg whites to the batter, then fold in the leftover whites.
- Gently scoop to a 10-inch tube pan that's ungreased. Use a knife to slice through the batter to release air pockets. Let it bake for 30 to 35 minutes on the lowest oven rack at 350 degrees or until the cake bounces back once pressed lightly. Instantly turn the pan upside down on a wire rack and let it fully cool, approximately an hour.
- Run a knife around the cake's sides and transfer to a serving platter. Dust confectioner's sugar on top.

Nutrition Information

- Calories: 211 calories

- Total Carbohydrate: 40 g
- Cholesterol: 124 mg
- Total Fat: 3 g
- Fiber: 1 g
- Protein: 6 g
- Sodium: 135 mg

274. Papaya Boats

""Papayas filled with walnuts, strawberries, raisins, and yogurt and with honey on top. Select ripe papayas with reddish-brown skin that is tender to the touch; don't use green papayas, as they are not yet ripe. Best flavors with organic ingredients.""
Serving: 4 | Prep: 15m | Ready in: 15m

Ingredients

- 1 cup fat-free plain yogurt
- 1/4 cup walnuts
- 1/4 cup raisins
- 1 cup chopped fresh strawberries
- 2 medium papayas, cut in half lengthwise and seeded
- 2 tbsps. honey

Direction

- Combine raisins, walnuts, and yogurt in a bowl. Add in the strawberries then fold. Scoop the mixture into the middles of the papaya halves. Top with honey then serve.

Nutrition Information

- Calories: 190 calories;
- Total Carbohydrate: 33.4 g
- Cholesterol: 1 mg
- Total Fat: 5.3 g
- Protein: 5.7 g
- Sodium: 52 mg

275. Paradise Parfaits

""Try this whipped topping and fat-free vanilla pudding flavored with instant coffee and layered with fresh strawberries for a fancy treat.""
Serving: 6 servings, about 1/2 cup each | Prep: 10m | Ready in: 1h10m

Ingredients

- 1/4 cup MAXWELL HOUSE INTERNATIONAL CAFÉ Sugar Free French Vanilla Café
- 1 Tbsp. hot water
- 2 cups cold fat-free milk
- 1 pkg. (1 oz.) JELL-O Vanilla Flavor Sugar Free Fat Free Instant Pudding
- 1/2 cup thawed COOL WHIP FREE Whipped Topping
- 1 cup sliced fresh strawberries

Direction

- 1. In a medium bowl with hot water, add flavored instant coffee and melt. Stir in pudding mix and milk; use whisk to blend for 2 minutes. Mix in COOL WHIP.
- 2. Onto each of 6 dessert glasses, put half the pudding mixture; layer and cover with strawberries. Place the rest of the pudding mixture on top.
- 3. Store in the refrigerator for at least 1 hour prior to serving.

Nutrition Information

- Calories: 90
- Total Carbohydrate: 15 g
- Cholesterol: 0 mg
- Total Fat: 1.5 g
- Fiber: 1 g
- Protein: 3 g
- Sodium: 270 mg
- Sugar: 6 g
- Saturated Fat: 1.5 g

276. Party Cranberry Salad

"For a better appearance, serve in glass bowl."
Serving: 11 | Prep: 20m | Ready in: 20m

Ingredients

- 1 (20 oz.) can crushed pineapple, drained with juice reserved
- 1 (3 oz.) package cranberry flavored Jell-O® mix
- 1 (3 oz.) package raspberry flavored Jell-O® mix
- 1 cup cold water
- 2 (16 oz.) cans whole cranberry sauce
- 1 apple - peeled, cored, and chopped
- 1/2 cup chopped walnuts
- 1/4 cup peeled, cored and sliced apple

Direction

- In a saucepan, mix together saved syrup and enough water to make 1 cup. Bring the mixture to a boil and put in raspberry gelatin and cranberry; mix until dissolved. Put in cold water and allow to cool down to room temperature.
- In a mixing bowl, combine nuts, apples, cranberry sauce and pineapple. Put into the gelatin and combine well.
- Transfer into serving dish and refrigerate until ready to serve. Top with sliced apples dipped in lemon juice to garnish.

Nutrition Information

- Calories: 245 calories;
- Total Carbohydrate: 54.2 g
- Cholesterol: 0 mg
- Total Fat: 3.5 g
- Protein: 2.5 g
- Sodium: 72 mg

277. Peanut Butter Bread Pudding

Serving: Makes 4 large or 16 small servings

Ingredients

- 2 Pullman loaves or other sweet (not sour) bread, cut into 1-inch-wide slices (remove crust if desired)
- 4 1/2 cups whole milk
- 4 1/2 cups heavy cream
- 2 cups granulated white sugar
- 2 vanilla beans, split and scraped
- 15 egg yolks
- 4 cups creamy peanut butter
- 2 cups honey
- 3 cups high-quality strawberry jam

Direction

- Boil vanilla beans, sugar and milk in heavy pot; immediately turn off. Steep vanilla beans with milk for 30 minutes. Whisk yolks till smooth; tempter hot-milk mixture into them slowly, continuously mixing. Put cream into mix immediately; put in ice bath till cool.
- Mix honey and peanut butter till homogenous with standing mixer or by hand. Keep 1/2 cup of mix to heat and serve as sauce with pudding.
- Assembling pudding: Put sliced bread in 8x10-in. metal/Pyrex pan lined with parchment paper piece to cover pan's bottom. Spread 1/2 peanut butter mixture on top then 1 cup strawberry jam. Put extra bread layer over jam; repeat layers. Finish with bread's final layer; make sure pudding is completely together by pressing down firmly on bread's top. Put 8 cups custard as follows over pudding: use wooden skewer/knife to poke holes through pudding's top to make sure entire pudding gets saturated. Put 2 cups custard over; soak in for 10 minutes. Pour 2 cups more; soak in. Repeat process till you use all the custard. Sit in the fridge for several hours – overnight; this creates a uniform pudding, or in other words, all the pieces saturated equally.

- Baking pudding: Preheat an oven to 350°F when ready to bake; use foil piece that's lightly buttered to cover pudding. Put pudding in water bath so water reaches halfway up pan's sides. Bake for an hour; check to ensure pudding is set fully. A pressed finger in center of pudding should leave dry without any custard on it. Bake for 10 minutes longer then check again if not set. Remove foil; keep baking for 20 minutes longer so top has crunchy and lovely brown crust.
- Take out of oven and water bath; refrigerate till cool. Run sharp knife around pudding edges; put pan on top. Invert it quickly; cut to 8 slices. Invert them so crust is on the top.
- Serving pudding: Preheat an oven to 400°F before serving; put pudding pieces in oven for 5 minutes to warm. Directly put warmed pudding on plate drizzled with warmed strawberry jam and warm peanut butter mixture. Immediately serve; you can serve with just a dash of confectioners' sugar or dollop of whipped cream.

Nutrition Information

- Calories: 4886
- Total Carbohydrate: 579 g
- Cholesterol: 942 mg
- Total Fat: 260 g
- Fiber: 24 g
- Protein: 101 g
- Sodium: 1348 mg
- Saturated Fat: 100 g

278. Peanut Ice Cream

"You just need several ingredients and an ice cream maker for this recipe. It's a mixture of creamy peanut butter and a nutty crunch."
Serving: 8 servings. | Prep: 15m | Ready in: 35m

Ingredients

- 2 cups fat-free half-and-half
- 1 can (14 oz.) fat-free sweetened condensed milk
- 1/2 cup reduced-fat chunky peanut butter
- 1 envelope whipped topping mix (Dream Whip)
- 1 tsp. vanilla extract

Direction

- Mix all of the ingredients together in a bowl. Put a cover on and chill for 60 minutes. Put in an ice cream freezer to freeze following the manufacturer's instructions. Let firm up in the fridge freezer or ripen in the ice cream freezer before enjoying, 2-4 hours.

Nutrition Information

- Calories: 287 calories
- Total Carbohydrate: 45 g
- Cholesterol: 3 mg
- Total Fat: 6 g
- Fiber: 1 g
- Protein: 11 g
- Sodium: 201 mg

279. Pear Cheesecake

"Pear cheesecake recipe."
Serving: 12 servings. | Prep: 20m | Ready in: 01h05m

Ingredients

- 1-1/2 cups reduced-fat graham cracker crumbs (about 8 whole crackers)
- 1 cup sugar, divided
- 1/3 cup butter, melted
- 2 cans (15 oz. each) pear halves, drained
- 3 packages (8 oz. each) cream cheese, softened
- 3 tbsps. all-purpose flour
- 2 eggs
- 1/2 cup milk
- 2 tbsps. lemon juice
- 1-1/2 tsps. grated lemon peel

Direction

- Mix together the butter, 1/4 cup of sugar and cracker crumbs in a small bowl. Press it on 1 1/2-inch up the sides and on the bottom of a 9-inch springform pan that's greased, then let it chill in the fridge for half an hour. Put the pear halves on the crust, cut side down.
- Put the leftover sugar and cream cheese in a bowl, beat until it becomes smooth. Put in flour, then beat it well. Put in eggs and beat it on low speed just until blended. Add the peel, lemon juice and milk, then beat it just until combined, then pour on top of the pears.
- Let it bake for 45 to 50 minutes at 350 degrees or until the middle becomes nearly set. Let it cool for 10 minutes on a wire rack. Run a knife around the pan's edge carefully to loosen and allow to cool for another one hour. Let it chill overnight. Take off the pan's sides. Put the leftovers in the fridge.

Nutrition Information

- Calories: 437 calories
- Total Carbohydrate: 43 g
- Cholesterol: 112 mg
- Total Fat: 27 g
- Fiber: 2 g
- Protein: 7 g
- Sodium: 330 mg

280. Pears Panos

"A tasty dessert for the autumn."
Serving: 8 | Prep: 15m | Ready in: 1h15m

Ingredients

- 4 Bosc pears, halved and cored
- 1/2 cup white sugar
- 1/4 tsp. vanilla extract
- 1/4 cup Cointreau or other orange liqueur

Direction

- In a big saucepan, place pears; add sufficient water to cover by 1 inch. Mix in sugar; heat to a boil. Without cover, cook around 1 hour until liquid is decreased into a light syrup. Take away from heat; mix in vanilla. Allow to cool just until warm. Mix in liqueur; serve.

Nutrition Information

- Calories: 123 calories;
- Total Carbohydrate: 28.6 g
- Cholesterol: 0 mg
- Total Fat: 0.1 g
- Protein: 0.3 g
- Sodium: 1 mg

281. Peppermint-kissed Fudge Mallow Cookies

"Cute and fudgy-rich chocolate cookies."
Serving: 2 dozen. | Prep: 30m | Ready in: 40m

Ingredients

- 1/3 cup reduced-fat plain yogurt
- 5 tbsps. butter, melted
- 3/4 tsp. peppermint extract
- 1 cup all-purpose flour
- 3/4 cup sugar
- 1/2 cup baking cocoa
- 1/4 tsp. salt
- 1/4 tsp. baking soda
- 12 large marshmallows, cut in half lengthwise
- CHOCOLATE GLAZE:
- 2 tbsps. semisweet chocolate chips
- 3/4 cup confectioners' sugar
- 3 tbsps. baking cocoa
- 3 tbsps. fat-free milk
- 1/4 tsp. peppermint extract
- 1/4 cup crushed peppermint candies

Direction

- Beat together the yogurt, butter and extract till well incorporated in a large bowl. Mix

together the flour, baking soda, cocoa, salt and sugar; add them into the yogurt mixture slowly and combine thoroughly.
- Drop tablespoonfuls of the mixture onto baking sheets sprayed using cooking spray. Bake for about 8 minutes at 350°. Add a marshmallow half on top of each cookie; bake until marshmallow is puffed, for another 1-2 minutes. Let them cool down for 2 minutes then take out of pans to wire racks to cool fully.
- To make glaze, melt chocolate chips in a microwave; stir till smooth. Mix together confectioners' sugar and cocoa in a small bowl. Stir milk and extract into the mix till smooth. Stir melted chocolate slowly into the mix. Drizzle on top of marshmallows; sprinkle using candies.

Nutrition Information

- Calories: 109 calories
- Total Carbohydrate: 20 g
- Cholesterol: 7 mg
- Total Fat: 3 g
- Fiber: 1 g
- Protein: 1 g
- Sodium: 60 mg

282. Picnic Berry Shortcakes

"You may prep berry sauce in advance, chilled. Assemble desert a few hours before serving."
Serving: 4 servings. | Prep: 15m | Ready in: 20m

Ingredients

- 2 tbsps. sugar
- 1/2 tsp. cornstarch
- 2 tbsps. water
- 2 cups sliced fresh strawberries, divided
- 1/2 tsp. grated lime zest
- 2 individual round sponge cakes
- 2 cups fresh blueberries
- Whipped topping, optional

Direction

- Mix cornstarch and sugar in small saucepan; mix water in. Add 1 cup strawberries and mash mixture; boil. Mix and cook till thick for 1-2 minutes; take off heat. Mix lime zest in. Put in small bowl; refrigerate till chilled, covered.
- Crosswise, cut sponge cakes in half; trim each so it fits in bottoms of 4 1/2 pint wide mouth canning jars. Mix leftover strawberries and blueberries in small bowl; put on cakes. Put sauce on top. Serve with whipped topping if desired.

Nutrition Information

- Calories: 124 calories
- Total Carbohydrate: 29 g
- Cholesterol: 10 mg
- Total Fat: 1 g
- Fiber: 3 g
- Protein: 2 g
- Sodium: 67 mg

283. Pineapple Almond Bars

"Delicious bar cookies."
Serving: 1 dozen. | Prep: 10m | Ready in: 35m

Ingredients

- 3/4 cup all-purpose flour
- 3/4 cup quick-cooking oats
- 1/3 cup packed brown sugar
- 5 tbsps. reduced-fat butter
- 1/2 tsp. almond extract
- 3 tbsps. sliced almonds
- 1 cup pineapple preserves

Direction

- Mix together the brown sugar, oats and flour in a food processor. Put on cover and process until combined. Add extract and butter, put on cover and pulse until it becomes crumbly. Take out half a cup of crumb mixture into a bowl, then mix in sliced almonds.

- Press the leftover crumb mixture in a cooking spray coated 9-inch square baking pan. Spread the preserves on top of the crust, then sprinkle the reserved crumb mixture on top. Let it bake for 25 to 30 minutes at 350 degrees or until it turns golden. Allow to cool on a wire rack.

Nutrition Information

- Calories: 166 calories
- Total Carbohydrate: 34 g
- Cholesterol: 0 mg
- Total Fat: 4 g
- Fiber: 1 g
- Protein: 2 g
- Sodium: 39 mg

284. Pineapple Orange Sherbet

"Low-fat sherbet made with an ice-cream maker."
Serving: about 2 quarts. | Prep: 15m | Ready in: 35m

Ingredients

- 3 cans (12 oz. each) orange soda
- 2 cans (8 oz. each) unsweetened crushed pineapple, undrained
- 1-1/2 cups sugar
- 1 can (12 oz.) fat-free evaporated milk
- 1/8 tsp. salt

Direction

- Mix together all ingredients in a large bowl. Fill the mixture two-thirds full into ice cream freezer cylinder; freeze following manufacturer's directions (refrigerate the rest of the mixture till ready to freeze). Pour into a freezer container; let the sherbet firm up in the refrigerator freezer for about 2-4 hours before serving.

Nutrition Information

- Calories: 175 calories
- Total Carbohydrate: 42 g
- Cholesterol: 1 mg
- Total Fat: 0 g
- Fiber: 0 g
- Protein: 3 g
- Sodium: 73 mg

285. Pineapple Pecan Cake

"Satisfyingly moist and tasty dessert, made in no time! Serve with the cream cheese on top for a full delight."
Serving: 12 | Prep: 10m | Ready in: 45m

Ingredients

- 2 cups all-purpose flour
- 2 cups white sugar
- 1 tsp. baking soda
- 2 eggs, beaten
- 1 (15 oz.) can crushed pineapple, with juice
- 1 tsp. vanilla extract
- 1 cup chopped pecans

Direction

- Turn on the oven and preheat it to 350°F (175°C). Prepare a 9x13 inch pan. Grease the pan and flour it to prevent sticking.
- Combine the flour, baking soda and sugar and sift together. Add in the vanilla, pineapple, and eggs; mix until blended. Fold in the pecans. Transfer the batter into the baking pan.
- Bake for 35 minutes in the oven, or until a toothpick poke in the center of the cake comes out clean. Allow cooling.

Nutrition Information

- Calories: 302 calories;
- Total Carbohydrate: 56.1 g
- Cholesterol: 31 mg
- Total Fat: 7.6 g
- Protein: 4.2 g
- Sodium: 117 mg

286. Pineapple Pudding

"A quick to prepare pudding recipe made with only 4 ingredients."
Serving: 6 servings. | Prep: 5m | Ready in: 5m

Ingredients

- 2 cups (16 oz.) fat-free sour cream
- 2 cans (8 oz. each) unsweetened crushed pineapple, undrained
- 1 package (1 oz.) sugar-free instant vanilla pudding mix
- 6 vanilla wafers

Direction

- Whisk the pudding mix, pineapple and sour cream in a bowl until it becomes thick and combined. Serve right away together with vanilla wafers. Put the leftovers in the fridge.

Nutrition Information

- Calories: 159 calories
- Total Carbohydrate: 31 g
- Cholesterol: 0 mg
- Total Fat: 1 g
- Fiber: 1 g
- Protein: 5 g
- Sodium: 274 mg

287. Pineapple-coconut Angel Food Cake

"Delicious cake recipe."
Serving: 16 servings. | Prep: 10m | Ready in: 45m

Ingredients

- 1 package (16 oz.) angel food cake mix
- 2 cans (8 oz. each) crushed pineapple, undrained
- 1 tsp. coconut extract
- 1 package (8 oz.) reduced-fat cream cheese
- 2 tbsps. confectioners' sugar
- 1 tsp. pineapple or orange extract
- 1-1/2 cups reduced-fat whipped topping
- 1/4 cup sweetened shredded coconut, toasted

Direction

- Mix together the coconut extract, pineapple and cake mix in a big bowl. Beat it for half a minute on low speed, then beat it for 2 minutes on medium.
- Gently scoop to 10-inch tube pan that's ungreased. Use knife to slice through the batter to release the air pockets. Let it bake for 35 to 40 minutes at 350 degrees on the lowest oven rack or until the entire surface looks dry and turns light brown in color. Instantly turn the pan upside down and let it fully cool for about an hour.
- Run a knife around the middle and side tube of the pan. Transfer the cake to a serving platter. To make the topping, beat the pineapple extract, confectioner's sugar and cream cheese in a big bowl, until it becomes smooth. Fold in the whipped topping. Frost the sides and top of the cake and sprinkle coconut on top.

Nutrition Information

- Calories: 178 calories
- Total Carbohydrate: 31 g
- Cholesterol: 8 mg
- Total Fat: 4 g
- Fiber: 1 g
- Protein: 4 g
- Sodium: 254 mg

288. Pistachio Fluff

"Fun and simple."
Serving: 14 servings. | Prep: 15m | Ready in: 15m

Ingredients

- 2 cups (16 oz.) 1% cottage cheese
- 4 cups (32 oz.) fat-free reduced-sugar vanilla yogurt, divided

- 1 package (1 oz.) sugar-free instant pistachio pudding mix
- 1 carton (8 oz.) frozen reduced-fat whipped topping, thawed
- 1 can (20 oz.) unsweetened crushed pineapple, drained
- 1 can (11 oz.) mandarin oranges, drained
- 1/2 cup halved maraschino cherries

Direction

- Process 1 cup yogurt and cottage cheese, covered, till smooth in a food processor.
- Whisk leftover yogurt and pudding mix for 2 minutes till slightly thick in a big bowl. Add cottage cheese mixture; stir well. Mix in leftover ingredients; refrigerate till serving.

Nutrition Information

- Calories: 137 calories
- Total Carbohydrate: 21 g
- Cholesterol: 3 mg
- Total Fat: 2 g
- Fiber: 0 g
- Protein: 7 g
- Sodium: 249 mg

---

289. Plum Clafouti

"This yummy plum treat with icing sugar is a family favorite. The house always smells heavenly with its cinnamon aroma."

Serving: 8 | Prep: 10m | Ready in: 1h10m

Ingredients

- 6 tbsps. white sugar, divided
- 14 Italian prune plums, halved and pitted
- 3 eggs
- 1 1/3 cups milk
- 2/3 cup all-purpose flour
- 1 1/2 tsps. grated lemon zest
- 2 tsps. vanilla
- 1 pinch salt
- 1/2 tsp. ground cinnamon

- 2 tbsps. confectioners' sugar

Direction

- Preheat oven to 190°C or 375°Fahrenheit. In a ten-inch pie plate, spread butter and sprinkle the bottom with a tbsp. of sugar.
- Assemble the plum halves on the pie plate cut-side down until it covers the bottom. Coat 2tbsp sugar over the plums. Mix in salt, remaining 3tbsp sugar, vanilla, eggs, cinnamon, milk, lemon zest, and flour together in a blender for 2mins until smooth; pour over the plums.
- Place the pie plate in preheated oven and bake for 50-60mins until light brown and firm. Let it cool for 5mins then slice. Sprinkle confectioners' sugar on top to serve.

Nutrition Information

- Calories: 186 calories;
- Total Carbohydrate: 34.9 g
- Cholesterol: 73 mg
- Total Fat: 3.1 g
- Protein: 5.6 g
- Sodium: 63 mg

---

290. Plum Dumplings

"This delicious entree from Istria can also be a side dish."

Serving: 10 | Prep: 1h30m | Ready in: 2h15m

Ingredients

- 25 Italian prune plums
- 3 tbsps. sugar
- 2 large potatoes, peeled and quartered
- Dough:
- 2 1/2 cups all-purpose flour
- 1 tsp. sugar
- 1/2 tsp. baking powder
- 1/2 tsp. salt
- 3 egg yolks
- 2 tbsps. shortening or butter, softened
- Sauce:

- 1/2 cup butter
- 1 1/2 cups dark brown sugar
- 1/4 cup fine dry bread crumbs

Direction

- Slice the plums open early in half then take out the pit. Put 1/3tsp sugar in each plum hollow, then close it. Place the closed plum in a bowl then set aside.
- In a pot, put potatoes then pour in enough water to cover; boil. Cook the potatoes until tender; drain. Let the potatoes cool. With a potato masher or fork, mash the cooled potatoes until you have a cup of mashed potatoes. Let it stand and keep the potatoes warm.
- For the dough, sift salt, flour, baking powder, and sugar together on a breadboard; form a well in the middle of the mixture. Put in shortening, egg yolks, and a cup of mashed potatoes then mix until it forms into a smooth and flexible dough.
- Once well-kneaded, roll the dough on a floured breadboard to a quarter-inch thick. Using a biscuit cutter, cut dough into four-inch circles. With a dough round in your hand, put one whole pitted plum in the middle. Top with another round dough then press the edges together to seal. Avoid making leaks to prevent the plum from coming out while cooking.
- Boil a big pot of salted water; add in dumplings. Boil slightly for 10mins.
- Prepare the sauce. On medium heat, melt butter in a big skillet then mix in brown sugar. If preferred, mix in some of the juice from pitted plums. Mix in a few bread crumbs to make sauce thick.
- Once cooked, take the dumplings out of the boiling water. Transfer to the big skillet; flip dumplings to coat. Serve hot dumplings with sauce on top.

Nutrition Information

- Calories: 519 calories;
- Total Carbohydrate: 94.3 g
- Cholesterol: 86 mg
- Total Fat: 14.1 g
- Protein: 7.2 g
- Sodium: 236 mg

291. Plum Flummery

"A delicious fruity mousse with plum tang."
Serving: 5 | Prep: 15m | Ready in: 3h50m

Ingredients

- 2 cups plums, pitted and sliced
- 1 tbsp. water (optional)
- 1 (.25 oz.) package unflavored gelatin
- 1/2 cup hot water
- 1/2 cup white sugar
- 2 tbsps. lemon juice
- 1/2 cup evaporated milk

Direction

- Into saucepan over medium-low heat, put plums, place cover, and let simmer for 5 to 10 minutes, mixing from time to time, till plums are tender. In case mixture turns extremely thick or begins to burn, put 1 tbsp. water. Take off heat, and let cool.
- In bowl, dissolve gelatin in half cup hot water, and mix in lemon juice, sugar and cooled plums. Stir till sugar and gelatin have dissolved. Refrigerate plum mixture to chill for 30 minutes till it starts to thicken. In mixing bowl using electric mixer, beat evaporated milk till thick, then into plum mixture, slowly scoop whipped milk. Whip once more using electric mixer till dessert is well blended and fluffy. Refrigerate for a minimum of 3 hours prior to serving.

Nutrition Information

- Calories: 148 calories;
- Total Carbohydrate: 30.6 g
- Cholesterol: 7 mg
- Total Fat: 2.1 g
- Protein: 3.4 g

- Sodium: 30 mg

292. Poached Pears With Orange Cream

"A sophisticated and easy to prepare dessert with a touch of orange."
Serving: 2 servings. | Prep: 10m | Ready in: 55m

Ingredients

- 2 firm medium pears
- 1-1/2 cups water
- 1 cup dry red wine or red grape juice
- 1/2 cup sugar
- 2 tsps. vanilla extract
- 1/4 cup reduced-fat sour cream
- 2 tsps. confectioners' sugar
- 1/2 tsp. grated orange zest
- 1/8 tsp. orange extract
- Additional grated orange zest, optional

Direction

- Core pears from the base and leave the stems undamaged. Take off the skin from the pears and slice it a quarter inch from the base to make it level, if needed. Put the pears on their sides in a big saucepan. Add vanilla, sugar, wine and water, then boil. Lower the heat and let it simmer for 35 to 40 minutes with cover, flipping once, until the pears become nearly tender. To make the color and flavor more intense, leave the fruit in the cooking liquid and let it chill in the fridge overnight. In the meantime, mix together the extract, orange zest, confectioner's sugar and sour cream. Let it chill in the fridge until ready to serve.
- Use a slotted spoon to take out the pears and pat it dry. If it's still warm, let it cool to room temperature. Get rid of the cooking liquid. Put the pears on the dessert plates. Serve together with orange cream and put extra grated orange zest on top, if preferred.

Nutrition Information

- Calories: 239 calories
- Total Carbohydrate: 46 g
- Cholesterol: 10 mg
- Total Fat: 3 g
- Fiber: 5 g
- Protein: 3 g
- Sodium: 23 mg

293. Poached Pears With Wine Vinaigrette

"Drizzle this yummy red wine vinaigrette over poached pears for a delicious meal!"
Serving: 4 | Prep: 25m | Ready in: 1h55m

Ingredients

- 6 medium Bosc pears, peeled with stems intact
- 1 cup white wine
- 2 cups water
- 2 tbsps. sugar
- 1/2 vanilla bean, halved lengthwise
- 2 whole star anise pods
- 1 small cinnamon stick
- 1 lemon, zested
- 1 orange, zested
- 1/4 cup walnut oil
- 1/4 cup red wine vinegar
- salt and freshly ground black pepper to taste

Direction

- Remove the bottom part of the pears and place them in an upright position at the bottom of a big pot. Put in the water and wine and set the heat to high. Dredge with star anise, orange and lemon peels, sugar, cinnamon stick, and vanilla bean. Let the mixture boil then lower the heat to medium-low setting; let it simmer for 20-25 minutes. Remove the pot from heat and let it cool down fully. Set aside 1/4 cup of the poaching liquid. Put the poached pears in a covered bowl and keep in the fridge.

- Crush 2 poached pears using a food processor or a blender. Transfer the crushed poached pears in a big bowl. Mix in the red wine vinegar, reserved poaching liquid, and walnut oil. Put pepper and salt to taste. Cover the mixture and keep in the fridge.
- Put the remaining poached pears into solo bowls and drizzle the prepared sauce on top.

Nutrition Information

- Calories: 357 calories;
- Total Carbohydrate: 50.6 g
- Cholesterol: 0 mg
- Total Fat: 14 g
- Protein: 1.2 g
- Sodium: 48 mg

294. Power Bars

"Delicious and easy alternative recipe to power bars."
Serving: 24

Ingredients

- 1 cup white sugar
- 1 cup light corn syrup
- 3/4 cup reduced fat peanut butter
- 4 cups wheat and barley nugget cereal (e.g. Grape-Nuts™)

Direction

- Use foil to line the one 9x13-inch pan and spritz it with nonstick cooking spray.
- In a saucepan, boil the peanut butter, syrup and sugar for 1 minute. It should not be more than a minute, or the bars will become impossible to eat. Put in the grape nuts and mix. Instantly spread in the prepped pan. Allow to cool and slice it into bars. This will be a great snack.

Nutrition Information

- Calories: 183 calories;
- Total Carbohydrate: 37.2 g
- Cholesterol: 0 mg
- Total Fat: 3.2 g
- Protein: 4.4 g
- Sodium: 173 mg

295. Power Cookies

"Delicious, low in fat, high-protein and high fiber cookies recipe."
Serving: 18 | Prep: 15m | Ready in: 30m

Ingredients

- 4 cups rolled oats
- 1 (15 oz.) can cannellini beans, drained and rinsed
- 1/2 cup white sugar
- 1/2 cup brown sugar
- 1 tsp. vanilla extract
- 1 tsp. baking powder
- 1 tsp. baking soda
- 1 tsp. ground cinnamon
- 1/2 cup chopped pitted dates
- 1/2 cup flaked coconut
- 1/2 cup raisins
- 1/2 cup chopped walnuts

Direction

- Set an oven to preheat to 165°C (325°F), then grease the cookie sheets. In a blender, grind the oats until it looks like coarse flour.
- Mash the beans in a medium bowl until it forms a smooth paste. Stir in vanilla, brown sugar and white sugar until well combined. Mix together the cinnamon, baking soda, baking powder and ground oats, then blend into the bean mixture. Stir in walnuts, raisins, coconut and dates. Drop the dough onto the prepped cookie sheet by heaping spoonfuls.
- Let it bake in the preheated oven for 10-15 minutes until it becomes golden. Allow to cool for 5 minutes on the baking sheets, then transfer to the wire racks to completely cool.

Nutrition Information

- Calories: 180 calories;
- Total Carbohydrate: 33.3 g
- Cholesterol: 0 mg
- Total Fat: 4 g
- Protein: 4.1 g
- Sodium: 147 mg

296. Pretzel Strawberry Dessert

"Let's cook a wonderful dessert!"
Serving: 18 servings. | Prep: 30m | Ready in: 30m

Ingredients

- 2-2/3 cups crushed pretzels (10 oz.)
- 1 cup butter, melted
- 1 package (8 oz.) cream cheese, softened
- 1 cup sugar
- 1 carton (8 oz.) frozen whipped topping, thawed
- 1 can (20 oz.) crushed pineapple
- 2 packages (3 oz. each) strawberry gelatin
- 2 packages (10 oz. each) frozen sliced sweetened strawberries, thawed

Direction

- Combine butter and pretzels in a bowl. Press onto the bottom of an oiled baking dish, about 13x9 inches. Bake at 350° until set, about 8 to 10 mins. Place on wire rack to cool. Beat sugar and cream cheese in a bowl until they become smooth. Then fold in the whipped topping and spread over the cooled crust. Place in the refrigerator until chilled.
- Drain the pineapple, saving the juice; put pineapple aside. If necessary, pour water into pineapple juice to measure one cup; mix into the gelatin mixture. Place in the refrigerator until set partially. Mix in the strawberries and reserved pineapple. Spoon over the filling carefully. Refrigerate, covered, until firm, about 3 to 4 hours.

Nutrition Information

- Calories: 363 calories
- Total Carbohydrate: 49 g
- Cholesterol: 41 mg
- Total Fat: 18 g
- Fiber: 1 g
- Protein: 4 g
- Sodium: 592 mg

297. Pudding Fruit Salad

"Serve this homemade fruit cocktail as a great side dish."
Serving: 8 | Prep: 10m | Ready in: 35m

Ingredients

- 1 (29 oz.) can pear slices, drained and cut into bite-size pieces
- 1 (28 oz.) can sliced peaches, drained and cut into bite-size pieces with 1 cup liquid reserved
- 1 (20 oz.) can pineapple tidbits, drained
- 1 (4.6 oz.) package non-instant vanilla pudding mix

Direction

- In a serving bowl, combine together pineapple, peaches and pears.
- In a small saucepan, stir pudding mix into reserved liquid from peaches on moderately low heat, then cook and stir for 5 minutes, until the mixture is bubbly and pudding has fully dissolved. Drizzle pudding mixture over fruit mixture and stir to coat.
- Chill salad for a minimum of 20 minutes, until totally chilled.

Nutrition Information

- Calories: 199 calories;
- Total Carbohydrate: 51 g
- Cholesterol: 0 mg
- Total Fat: 0.2 g
- Protein: 1.3 g
- Sodium: 130 mg

298. Pumpkin Angel Food Cake

"This pumpkin cake is great when top with whipped topping and cinnamon."
Serving: 14 servings. | Prep: 15m | Ready in: 55m

Ingredients

- 1 cup canned pumpkin
- 1 tsp. vanilla extract
- 1/2 tsp. ground cinnamon
- 1/2 tsp. ground nutmeg
- 1/4 tsp. ground cloves
- 1/8 tsp. ground ginger
- 1 package (16 oz.) angel food cake mix
- 14 tbsps. reduced-fat whipped topping
- Additional ground cinnamon, optional

Direction

- Mix ginger, cloves, nutmeg, cinnamon, vanilla and pumpkin in a large bowl. Prepare cake mix as directed on the package. Fold 1/4 of the batter into pumpkin mixture; fold gently in the rest of the batter. Scoop gently into a clean and dry 10-in. tube pan. Using a knife, cut through batter to get rid of air pockets.
- Bake at 350° on the lowest oven rack until top turns golden brown and when lightly touched, cake springs back and entire top appears dry for 38-44 minutes. Turn the pan upside down immediately; cool completely for about 1 hour.
- Run a knife around side and center tube of the pan. Transfer the cake to a serving plate. Decorate each slice with a tbsp. of whipped topping; dust with cinnamon if preferred.

Nutrition Information

- Calories: 151 calories
- Total Carbohydrate: 33 g
- Cholesterol: 0 mg
- Total Fat: 1 g
- Fiber: 1 g
- Protein: 3 g
- Sodium: 264 mg

299. Pumpkin Pecan Frozen Yogurt

"This recipe is tasty yet very easy to make with fat-free frozen yogurt."
Serving: 8 servings. | Prep: 10m | Ready in: 10m

Ingredients

- 1 quart fat-free frozen vanilla yogurt, softened
- 1/2 cup canned pumpkin
- 1/3 cup packed brown sugar
- 3/4 tsp. pumpkin pie spice
- 1/4 cup chopped pecans, toasted

Direction

- Mix the first 4 ingredients together in a big bowl. Remove to a freezer container and freeze until eating. Sprinkle pecans over each serving.

Nutrition Information

- Calories: 161 calories
- Total Carbohydrate: 30 g
- Cholesterol: 2 mg
- Total Fat: 3 g
- Fiber: 1 g
- Protein: 5 g
- Sodium: 69 mg

300. Pumpkin Protein Cookies

"Sugar-free cookie recipe that are great for breakfast."
Serving: 14 | Prep: 15m | Ready in: 20m

Ingredients

- 3/4 cup SPLENDA® Granular
- 1 cup rolled oats
- 1 cup whole wheat flour
- 1/2 cup soy flour
- 1 3/4 tsps. baking soda
- 1/2 tsp. baking powder

- 1/2 tsp. salt
- 2 tsps. ground cinnamon
- 1 tsp. ground nutmeg
- 1/2 cup pumpkin puree
- 1 tbsp. canola oil
- 2 tsps. water
- 2 egg whites
- 1 tsp. molasses
- 1 tbsp. flax seeds (optional)

Direction

- Set an oven to 175°C (350°F) to preheat.
- Whisk together the nutmeg, cinnamon, salt, baking powder, baking soda, soy flour, wheat flour, oats and Splenda(R) in a big bowl. Stir in molasses, egg whites, water, canola oil and pumpkin. If preferred, mix in flax seeds. Roll into 14 big balls and flatten on a baking tray.
- Bake in the preheated oven for 5 minutes. Avoid overbaking; the cookies will become very dry if overbaked.

Nutrition Information

- Calories: 85 calories;
- Total Carbohydrate: 13.1 g
- Cholesterol: 0 mg
- Total Fat: 2.2 g
- Protein: 4.2 g
- Sodium: 284 mg

301. Quinoa Pudding

"A high-protein dish and vegan!"
Serving: 6 | Prep: 5m | Ready in: 40m

Ingredients

- 1 cup quinoa
- 2 cups water
- 2 cups apple juice
- 1 cup raisins
- 2 tbsps. lemon juice
- 1 tsp. ground cinnamon, or to taste
- salt to taste
- 2 tsps. vanilla extract

Direction

- Thoroughly rinse quinoa in a sieve; drain. Put quinoa into medium saucepan with water; boil on high heat. Use lid to cover pan; lower heat. Simmer for 15 minutes till quinoa is tender and all water is absorbed.
- Mix in salt, cinnamon, lemon juice, raisins and apple juice; cover pan. Simmer for 15 minutes. Mix in vanilla extract and serve warm.

Nutrition Information

- Calories: 202 calories;
- Total Carbohydrate: 42.6 g
- Cholesterol: 0 mg
- Total Fat: 1.9 g
- Protein: 4.4 g
- Sodium: 8 mg

302. Raspberry Cream Cake

"An appealing dessert loaded with chocolate glaze, fresh raspberries, vanilla cream, and golden cake."
Serving: 14 slices. | Prep: 20m | Ready in: 50m

Ingredients

- 1 package yellow cake mix (regular size)
- 1/4 tsp. baking soda
- 1-1/3 cups water
- 4 large egg whites
- 2 tbsps. unsweetened applesauce
- 1-1/3 cups cold fat-free milk
- 1 package (1 oz.) sugar-free instant vanilla pudding mix
- 3/4 tsp. vanilla extract
- 1-1/2 cups fresh raspberries, divided
- 1/2 cup fat-free hot fudge ice cream topping
- 1 tbsp. light corn syrup

Direction

- Mix baking soda and cake mix in a large bowl. Add applesauce, egg whites, and water; whisk

- for half a minute at low speed. Whisk for 2 minutes at medium speed.
- Add into 2 greased 9-inch round baking pans. Bake at 350 degrees until a toothpick comes out clean when inserted into the center, for 28-32 minutes. Allow to cool for 10 minutes, then transfer from the pans onto wire racks to cool completely.
- For the filling: Beat vanilla, pudding mix, and milk for 2 minutes in a large bowl; allow to stand until soft-set, for 2 minutes.
- On a serving plate, arrange 1 cake layer. Spread the pudding mixture over; dust with 3/4 cup of the raspberries. Add the rest of the cake layer on top. Mix corn syrup and ice cream topping; whisk until smooth. Spread over the top of the cake and allow the glaze to drip over the sides. Top with the rest of berries.

Nutrition Information

- Calories: 215 calories
- Total Carbohydrate: 42 g
- Cholesterol: 0 mg
- Total Fat: 4 g
- Fiber: 2 g
- Protein: 4 g
- Sodium: 388 mg

303. Raspberry Cream Pie

"It's fresh, luscious and beautiful."
Serving: 8 servings. | Prep: 25m | Ready in: 25m

Ingredients

- 3 whole graham crackers, crushed
- 3 whole chocolate graham crackers, crushed
- 1 tbsp. sugar
- 1/4 cup reduced-fat stick margarine, melted
- 1 package (.3 oz.) sugar-free raspberry gelatin
- 1/3 cup boiling water
- 1 package (8 oz.) reduced-fat cream cheese
- 1 tsp. vanilla extract
- 2 cups reduced-fat whipped topping
- 2-1/2 cups fresh raspberries or blackberries

Direction

- Combine margarine, sugar and graham cracker crumbs in a bowl. Press up sides and onto bottom of an unoiled 9-in. pie plate. Bake for 8 to 10 mins at 375°, until set. Place on wire rack to cool.
- Dissolve the gelatin in the boiling water in a bowl. Let cool to room temperature.
- Combine vanilla and cream cheese in a bowl until well blended. Beat the gelatin mixture gradually into the cream cheese mixture. Fold in the whipped topping. Place into the crust. Sprinkle with the raspberries. Place in the refrigerator for at least 120 mins.

Nutrition Information

- Calories: 209 calories
- Total Carbohydrate: 20 g
- Cholesterol: 16 mg
- Total Fat: 11 g
- Fiber: 3 g
- Protein: 5 g
- Sodium: 196 mg

304. Raspberry Whip

"It's great after a heavy meal."
Serving: 6 servings. | Prep: 15m | Ready in: 15m

Ingredients

- 1 package (.3 oz.) sugar-free raspberry gelatin
- 1 cup boiling water
- 2/3 cup cold water
- 1 cup (8 oz.) vanilla yogurt
- 1 cup fresh or frozen unsweetened raspberries, drained, divided

Direction

- Dissolve gelatin in a bowl of boiling water. Stir in the cold water. Refrigerate for 30 to 45 mins, covered, until set partially. Put in yogurt. Beat

for 2 to 3 mins on medium speed until foamy and light. Place in the refrigerator for 15 mins.
- Portion 2/3 cup of raspberries into 6 dessert dishes. Add about a half cup of gelatin mixture and the remaining raspberries over top each. Place in the refrigerator until enjoying.

Nutrition Information

- Calories: 48 calories
- Total Carbohydrate: 8 g
- Cholesterol: 2 mg
- Total Fat: 1 g
- Fiber: 1 g
- Protein: 3 g
- Sodium: 65 mg

305. Raspberry-filled Meringue Torte

"Fail-proof light meringue recipe."
Serving: 10 servings. | Prep: 30m | Ready in: 60m

Ingredients

- 6 egg whites
- 1/4 tsp. cream of tartar
- 1-1/2 cups sugar
- 1 cup sweetened shredded coconut
- 1/2 cup cornstarch
- FILLING:
- 2 packages (10 oz. each) frozen sweetened raspberries
- 3 tbsps. cornstarch
- 2 tbsps. sugar
- 1 carton (8 oz.) frozen reduced-fat whipped topping, thawed
- 10 fresh raspberries

Direction

- Use parchment paper to line the baking trays and trace the five 7 1/2-inch rounds on the paper, then put aside.
- Beat the cream of tartar and egg whites in a big bowl on medium speed, until it forms soft peaks. Slowly beat in the sugar, 1 tbsp at a time, on high speed until the sugar dissolves and it forms stiff glossy peaks. Mix together the cornstarch and coconut and fold it into the meringue.
- On the prepped pans, evenly spread the meringue on top of each round, then let it bake for half an hour at 300 degrees or until it turns light golden and becomes firm. Allow to cool for 5 minutes. Take out the meringues from the baking trays gently, then transfer to wire racks to let it fully cool.
- In the meantime, drain the raspberries and set aside the juice. Put aside the berries. Pour enough water into the juice to get 2 cups. Mix together the sugar and cornstarch in a small saucepan and mix in the raspberry liquid until it becomes smooth, then boil. Let it cook and stir for 2 minutes or until it becomes thick. Let it fully cool. Fold in the raspberries that were sweetened.
- To assemble, on a serving plate, put 1 meringue, then put 3/4 cup of raspberry filling and put 2/3 cup of whipped topping on top. Redo the process thrice more. Put the leftover layer of meringue and whipped topping on top. Prior to serving, let it chill in the fridge for 1 hour. Put fresh berries on top as a garnish, then use serrated knife to slice it.

Nutrition Information

- Calories: 332 calories
- Total Carbohydrate: 66 g
- Cholesterol: 0 mg
- Total Fat: 6 g
- Fiber: 3 g
- Protein: 3 g
- Sodium: 59 mg

306. Raspberry-topped Cream Tarts

"With a beautiful look, these tarts bring off delicious tastes of raspberries, cream cheese and tortilla crusts."
Serving: 16 servings. | Prep: 40m | Ready in: 40m

Ingredients

- 1 tbsp. brown sugar
- 1/4 tsp. ground cinnamon
- 1/8 tsp. ground nutmeg
- 4 flour tortillas (8 inches)
- Warm water
- 1 package (8 oz.) reduced-fat cream cheese, softened
- 3 tbsps. sugar
- 1 to 2 tbsps. fat-free milk
- 1/2 tsp. almond extract
- 1 cup fresh raspberries

Direction

- Mix together nutmeg, cinnamon and brown sugar in a bowl; put aside. Using a 3 1/2-in. biscuit cutter, slice tortillas; get rid of the excess. Brush warm water over both sides of tortillas rounds. Coat the tops with cooking spray; scatter brown sugar mixture over top. Press tortillas into ungreased muffin cups.
- Bake in 350-degree oven until the tortillas are light brown, about 12 to 15 minutes. Transfer to a wire rack to cool.
- Mix together almond extract, milk, sugar and cream cheese in a small bowl; stir thoroughly. Spoon mixture into the shells; add raspberries on top. Keep leftovers refrigerated to store.

Nutrition Information

- Calories: 93 calories
- Total Carbohydrate: 13 g
- Cholesterol: 8 mg
- Total Fat: 3 g
- Fiber: 1 g
- Protein: 3 g
- Sodium: 108 mg

307. Real German Baked Apples

"A very delicious Baked Apple."
Serving: 4 | Prep: 20m | Ready in: 28m

Ingredients

- 1 egg white
- 1 tsp. white sugar
- 1 tsp. ground cinnamon
- 2 tsps. raisins
- 1 tsp. crushed toffee candy
- 4 large Red Delicious apples, cored

Direction

- Preheat an oven to 190°C (or 375°F). Arrange cored apples upright in a shallow baking dish.
- Beat egg white in medium bowl till it holds a firm peak. Scatter in sugar, and beat just a little more. Mix in toffee, raisins and cinnamon until equally blended. Scoop into apples cores.
- Bake for 5 to 10 minutes without cover until meringue crisps. Cool a little prior to serving.

Nutrition Information

- Calories: 132 calories;
- Total Carbohydrate: 32.9 g
- Cholesterol: < 1 mg
- Total Fat: 0.8 g
- Protein: 1.5 g
- Sodium: 22 mg

308. Red, White And Blueberry Pie

""Berries create a beautiful dress-up for this creamy pie.""
Serving: 8 servings. | Prep: 20m | Ready in: 20m

Ingredients

- 2 oz. white baking chocolate, melted
- One 9-inch graham cracker crust (about 6 oz.)
- 3/4 cup sliced fresh strawberries
- 1 package (8 oz.) cream cheese, softened

- 3/4 cup confectioners' sugar
- 3/4 cup 2% milk
- 1 package (3.3 oz.) instant white chocolate pudding mix
- 1 cup whipped topping
- 8 fresh strawberries, halved lengthwise
- 1 cup fresh blueberries

Direction

- Arrange melted chocolate onto the bottom and sides of the crust; spread. Cover with sliced strawberries.
- Beat confectioners' sugar and cream cheese in a bowl, till smooth; slowly beat in milk. Include in pudding mix; whisk on low speed for around 2 minutes, till thickened. Arrange over the strawberries and spread out.
- Garnish the pie with halved strawberries, blueberries and whipped topping. Keep in a refrigerator till serving.

Nutrition Information

- Calories: 383 calories
- Total Carbohydrate: 50 g
- Cholesterol: 30 mg
- Total Fat: 19 g
- Fiber: 1 g
- Protein: 4 g
- Sodium: 395 mg

309. Refreshing Cranberry Ice

"Let's try something different!"
Serving: 7 cups. | Prep: 20m | Ready in: 03h20m

Ingredients

- 4 cups fresh or frozen cranberries
- 3 cups water
- 1-1/8 tsps. unflavored gelatin
- 1 cup cold water
- 2-1/2 cups sugar
- 1 cup orange juice
- 1/4 cup lemon juice
- 1/2 cup heavy whipping cream

Direction

- Boil water and cranberries in a large saucepan. Lower the heat to medium and cook, uncovered, until berries pop. Discard from heat.
- Sprinkle the cold water in a bowl with gelatin; allow to stand 5 mins. In the meantime, strain the cranberries into a large bowl through the food mill, remove skin and seeds. Put in softened gelatin, lemon juice, orange juice and sugar; stir until the gelatin dissolves. Mix in cream. Transfer to a 13-inch x 9-inch dish. Freeze, covered, until firm, about 3 to 4 hours.

Nutrition Information

- Calories: 191 calories
- Total Carbohydrate: 42 g
- Cholesterol: 12 mg
- Total Fat: 3 g
- Fiber: 1 g
- Protein: 1 g
- Sodium: 4 mg

310. Rhubarb Shortcake Dessert

"The most requested dessert."
Serving: 12 servings. | Prep: 30m | Ready in: 01h45m

Ingredients

- 2 cups all-purpose flour
- 2 tbsps. sugar
- 1 cup cold butter
- FILLING:
- 6 large egg yolks
- 2 cups sugar
- 1/4 cup all-purpose flour
- 1/4 tsp. salt
- 5 cups chopped fresh or frozen rhubarb, thawed
- 1 cup half-and-half cream
- 2 tsps. grated orange zest

- MERINGUE:
- 6 large egg whites
- 2 tsps. vanilla extract
- Dash salt
- 3/4 cup sugar
- 2 tbsps. finely chopped walnuts

Direction

- Mix sugar and flour; cut butter in till crumbly. Press into a 13x9-inch greased baking dish. Allow to bake for 10 to 15 minutes at 350° till slightly browned. Let cool.
- Whisk egg yolks in a bowl; put salt, flour and sugar. Mix in orange zest, cream and rhubarb; put on top of crust. Allow to bake for 50 minutes to an hour at 350° till an inserted knife in the middle comes out clean.
- Whisk the salt, vanilla and egg whites in a big bowl on medium speed till soft peaks create. Slowly whisk in sugar, a tbsp. at a time, till stiff peaks create. Quickly scatter on top of hot filling, securing edges; scatter nuts on top. Bake for 12 to 15 minutes more till slightly browned. Allow to cool for a minimum of 1-hour prior serving. Chill the remaining.

Nutrition Information

- Calories: 490 calories
- Total Carbohydrate: 69 g
- Cholesterol: 157 mg
- Total Fat: 21 g
- Fiber: 2 g
- Protein: 7 g
- Sodium: 260 mg

311. Rich Caramel Pecan Bars

"These scrumptious bars are made with wonderful blend of pecans, chocolate and caramel."
Serving: 6 dozen. | Prep: 5m | Ready in: 15m

Ingredients

- 1-1/2 cups crushed vanilla wafers (about 45 wafers)
- 1/4 cup butter, melted
- 2 cups (12 oz.) semisweet chocolate chips
- 1 cup chopped pecans
- 1 jar (12 oz.) caramel ice cream topping

Direction

- Mix together butter and wafer crumbs in a small bowl. Pat mixture in a 13x9-inch baking pan coated with grease. Garnish with pecans and chocolate chips. Warm caramel topping in a small microwavable bowl until heated. Glaze onto the top.
- Bake at 350 degrees to melt the chips, about 8 to 12 minutes. Place on a wire rack to cool.

Nutrition Information

- Calories: 62 calories
- Total Carbohydrate: 8 g
- Cholesterol: 2 mg
- Total Fat: 4 g
- Fiber: 1 g
- Protein: 1 g
- Sodium: 31 mg

312. Rich Chocolate Snack Cake

"Tasty chocolate dessert that's light and rich tasting."
Serving: 12 servings. | Prep: 15m | Ready in: 45m

Ingredients

- 2 eggs plus 2 egg whites
- 2/3 cup unsweetened applesauce
- 1/3 cup canola oil
- 2 oz. semisweet chocolate, melted
- 2 tsps. vanilla extract
- 1 cup all-purpose flour
- 1 cup sugar
- 1/3 cup baking cocoa
- 1 tsp. baking powder
- 1/2 tsp. salt
- 6 cups frozen vanilla yogurt

Direction

- Beat the egg whites and the eggs in a bowl. Add vanilla, chocolate, oil and applesauce, then stir well. Mix together the dry ingredients and slowly add into the egg mixture just until blended.
- Pour into a cooking spray coated 9-inch springform pan. Let it bake for 30 to 35 minutes at 350 degrees or until an inserted toothpick exits clean. Allow to cool on a wire rack. Run a knife carefully around the pan's edge, then take out the sides of the pan. Slice it into wedges and serve together with frozen yogurt.

Nutrition Information

- Calories: 290 calories
- Total Carbohydrate: 48 g
- Cholesterol: 36 mg
- Total Fat: 9 g
- Fiber: 1 g
- Protein: 6 g
- Sodium: 177 mg

313. Rosemary Pineapple Upside-down Cake

"Mouthwatering pineapple upside-down cake sprinkled with rosemary."
Serving: 8 servings. | Prep: 15m | Ready in: 50m

Ingredients

- 1 tbsp. plus 1/4 cup butter, softened, divided
- 1/3 cup packed brown sugar
- 1 tsp. minced fresh rosemary
- 6 canned unsweetened pineapple slices, drained
- 2/3 cup sugar
- 1 large egg
- 1 tsp. vanilla extract
- 1-1/4 cups all-purpose flour
- 1-1/4 tsps. baking powder
- 1/8 tsp. salt
- 1/2 cup fat-free milk
- Fresh rosemary sprigs, optional

Direction

- Melt a tbsp. of butter, then pour it in a 9-inch round baking pan. Sprinkle rosemary and brown sugar on top. Put slices of pineapple on top and put aside.
- Cream the leftover butter and sugar in a small bowl, then beat in vanilla and egg. Mix together the salt, baking powder and flour, then add it to the creamed mixture alternating with milk. Scoop on top of the pineapple.
- Let it bake for 35 to 40 minutes at 350 degrees, until an inserted toothpick in the middle exits clean. Allow to cool for 5 minutes on a wire rack. Run a knife around the pan's edge, then turn the cake upside down on a serving platter. Let it fully cool. If preferred, put rosemary sprigs on as garnish.

Nutrition Information

- Calories: 264 calories
- Total Carbohydrate: 45 g
- Cholesterol: 46 mg
- Total Fat: 8 g
- Fiber: 1 g
- Protein: 3 g
- Sodium: 207 mg

314. Shudderuppers

"Caramel added to s'mores."
Serving: 20 | Prep: 1m | Ready in: 1h3m

Ingredients

- 1 (14 oz.) package individually wrapped caramels, unwrapped
- 1 (10.5 oz.) package large marshmallows

Direction

- Build a good fire and allow the wood to burn down to coals. It will take around 1 hour.

- On a stick, thread a marshmallow, followed by the caramel candy in front of the marshmallow. Let it roast on top of the coals from the fire, until you reach your preferred doneness in marshmallow, yet not on fire. Pull up the marshmallow above the caramel so that it will be placed inside. Allow to cool, then enjoy.

Nutrition Information

- Calories: 122 calories;
- Total Carbohydrate: 27 g
- Cholesterol: 1 mg
- Total Fat: 1.6 g
- Protein: 1.2 g
- Sodium: 60 mg

315. Silky Lemon Pie

"This tasty dessert is requested often."
Serving: 8 servings. | Prep: 25m | Ready in: 55m

Ingredients

- 1 cup all-purpose flour
- 1 tsp. sugar
- 1/4 tsp. salt
- 3 tbsps. canola oil
- 1 tbsp. butter, melted
- 2 to 3 tbsps. cold water
- FILLING:
- 1-3/4 cups sugar
- 1/2 cup lemon juice
- 1 tbsp. grated lemon peel
- 1/2 tsp. salt
- 3 egg whites
- 1 package (8 oz.) reduced-fat cream cheese, cubed
- 2 eggs
- 1 tsp. confectioners' sugar

Direction

- Combine salt, sugar and flour in large bowl. Stir in butter and oil with a fork until crumbly. Pour in enough water gradually until the dough holds together. Then roll out to 11-inch circle between the plastic wrap. Place in freezer 10 mins. Discard the top sheet of the plastic wrap from the pastry; turn onto a 9-inch pie plate coated with the cooking spray. Discard the remaining plastic wrap. Then trim pastry to 1/2-inch beyond the pie plate edge; flute the edges. Let chill. Combine salt, lemon peel, juice and sugar in small saucepan. Boil. Lower the heat and cook while stirring until the sugar dissolves. Let cool 10 to 15 mins. Beat cream cheese and egg whites in small bowl until they become smooth. Beat in the eggs. Beat in the lemon mixture gradually. Transfer to the crust. Bake for 30 to 35 mins at 350°, until set. Place on wire rack to cool for 60 mins. Sprinkle the confectioners' sugar over. Place the leftovers in refrigerator.

Nutrition Information

- Calories: 356 calories
- Total Carbohydrate: 59 g
- Cholesterol: 67 mg
- Total Fat: 10 g
- Fiber: 1 g
- Protein: 8 g
- Sodium: 376 mg

316. Simple Broiled Grapefruit

"Fresh fruit is the main ingredient in this recipe. You will have an energetic and bright day after taking a bite."
Serving: 4 | Prep: 5m | Ready in: 10m

Ingredients

- 2 grapefruit, cut in half
- 6 tbsps. brown sugar

Direction

- Turn on the oven's broiler to preheat and place the oven rack about 6 inches from the heat source.

- Set grapefruit halves, cut sides up, on a baking sheet; scatter with about 1 1/2 tbsp. of brown sugar.
- Broil the grapefruit until the brown sugar has melted and started to bubble, about 3 to 8 minutes. Allow to cool for a few minutes before enjoying this warm meal.

Nutrition Information

- Calories: 137 calories;
- Total Carbohydrate: 35 g
- Cholesterol: 0 mg
- Total Fat: 0 g
- Protein: 1 g
- Sodium: 6 mg

317. Simple Strawberry Sherbet

"An accidental recipe."
Serving: 12 | Prep: 15m | Ready in: 13h15m

Ingredients

- 3/4 cup white sugar
- 1/4 cup milk (optional)
- 1/4 cup lime juice
- 2 quarts fresh strawberries, mashed
- 1 egg white

Direction

- Mix together the sugar, milk, and lime juice in a bowl. Mix mashed strawberries into the mixture.
- In a ceramic, metal, or glass bowl, beat the egg white till it can hold stiff peaks. Fold the egg white into the strawberry-lime mixture. Transfer the mixture into a freezer-safe container. Use plastic wrap to cover.
- Freeze till almost firm for about 2 hours. Take it out of freezer and stir thoroughly to break up any chunks. Take it back to the freezer for 3 hours, stir once every hour. Freeze till firm for about 8 hours to overnight.

Nutrition Information

- Calories: 86 calories;
- Total Carbohydrate: 21 g
- Cholesterol: < 1 mg
- Total Fat: 0.4 g
- Protein: 1.2 g
- Sodium: 8 mg

318. Slow Cooker Baked Apples

"An easy slow cooker dessert recipe."
Serving: 6 servings. | Prep: 25m | Ready in: 04h25m

Ingredients

- 6 medium tart apples
- 1/2 cup raisins
- 1/3 cup packed brown sugar
- 1 tbsp. grated orange zest
- 1 cup water
- 3 tbsps. thawed orange juice concentrate
- 2 tbsps. butter

Direction

- Core and peel the top 1/3 of every apple, if preferred. Mix together the orange zest, brown sugar and raisins, then scoop into the apples. Put it in a 5-quart slow cooker.
- Pour the water surrounding the apples. Drizzle orange juice concentrate on top, then dot it using butter. Put on cover and let it cook for 4 to 5 hours on low or until the apples become tender.

Nutrition Information

- Calories: 203 calories
- Total Carbohydrate: 44 g
- Cholesterol: 10 mg
- Total Fat: 4 g
- Fiber: 4 g
- Protein: 1 g
- Sodium: 35 mg

319. Slow-cooked Bread Pudding

"Hearty and warm dessert."
Serving: 8 servings. | Prep: 15m | Ready in: 03h15m

Ingredients

- 4 whole wheat bagels, split and cut into 3/4-inch pieces
- 1 large tart apple, peeled and chopped
- 1/2 cup dried cranberries
- 1/4 cup golden raisins
- 2 cups fat-free milk
- 1 cup egg substitute
- 1/2 cup sugar
- 2 tbsps. butter, melted
- 1 tsp. ground cinnamon
- 1 tsp. vanilla extract
- Confectioners' sugar

Direction

- Mix raisins, cranberries, apple and bagels in 3-qt. slow cooker coated in cooking spray. Whisk vanilla, cinnamon, butter, sugar, egg substitute and milk in a big bowl; put on bagel mixture. Mix to combine; press bagels down gently into milk mixture.
- Cover; cook for 3-4 hours on low till inserted knife in middle exits clean. Dust confectioners' sugar on servings if desired.

Nutrition Information

- Calories: 231 calories
- Total Carbohydrate: 45 g
- Cholesterol: 9 mg
- Total Fat: 3 g
- Fiber: 4 g
- Protein: 8 g
- Sodium: 257 mg

320. Sparkling Grapefruit Pie

"Indian River pink pomelo is used in this recipe. It's served together with whipped cream."
Serving: 8 | Prep: 20m | Ready in: 1day4h30m

Ingredients

- 1 (9 inch) pie crust, baked
- 4 pink grapefruit
- 1/2 cup white sugar
- 1 tbsp. cornstarch
- 3/4 cup grapefruit juice
- 1 (3 oz.) package strawberry flavored Jell-O®

Direction

- Peel the grapefruit, remove all the pith. Slice into bite-sized pieces. Drain for 4 or more hours in a strainer, save the juice. (You can do this the day before.)
- In a small saucepan, mix the 3/4 cup juice, cornstarch, and sugar; if the saved juice does not fill 3/4 cup, top it off with water. Heat up to a boil. Mix in strawberry gelatin. Let it rest until slightly cool.
- Distribute grapefruit in the bottom of the baked crust and spread gelatin on top of the fruit. Refrigerate for a few hours or overnight.

Nutrition Information

- Calories: 235 calories;
- Total Carbohydrate: 46.3 g
- Cholesterol: 0 mg
- Total Fat: 5.4 g
- Protein: 2.8 g
- Sodium: 145 mg

321. Spice Bars

"Delicious, chewy, and spicy cookie bars."
Serving: 30 | Prep: 15m | Ready in: 45m

Ingredients

- 3/4 cup shortening

- 3/4 cup white sugar
- 1/4 cup honey
- 1/4 cup molasses
- 2 tsps. baking soda
- 1 tsp. ground cinnamon
- 1 tsp. ground ginger
- 1/2 tsp. ground cloves
- 2 1/2 cups all-purpose flour
- 3/4 cup raisins (optional)
- 1 cup confectioners' sugar
- 3 tbsps. milk
- 1/2 tsp. vanilla extract

Direction

- Preheat the oven to 175°C or 350°Fahrenheit. Lightly oil a 9-in x 13-in baking dish.
- Cream shortening and white sugar together in a medium bowl; fold in honey and molasses. Sieve cloves, flour, baking soda, ginger, and cinnamon together. Mix flour mixture and creamed mixture together until well combined; fold in raisins.
- Evenly spread the batter in the baking dish. Bake in the preheated oven for 20-30mins until golden brown and the surface is dry and smooth to the touch.
- For the icing, combine vanilla, milk, and confectioners' sugar together in a smaller bowl. Spread icing over the warm spice bars; cool. Cut bars then serve.

Nutrition Information

- Calories: 148 calories;
- Total Carbohydrate: 24.8 g
- Cholesterol: < 1 mg
- Total Fat: 5.3 g
- Protein: 1.3 g
- Sodium: 86 mg

322. Spice Crumb Cake

"Old-fashioned cake recipe."
Serving: 18 servings. | Prep: 15m | Ready in: 50m

Ingredients

- 3 cups all-purpose flour
- 2 cups packed brown sugar
- 2 tsps. baking soda
- 2 tsps. each ground cinnamon, nutmeg and cloves
- 1 tsp. salt
- 1 cup shortening
- 2 eggs
- 2 cups buttermilk
- 2 tbsps. molasses

Direction

- Mix together the salt, spices, baking soda, brown sugar and flour in a bowl, then slice in the shortening until the mixture looks like coarse crumbs. Take out and reserve 1 cup for the topping. Beat the molasses, buttermilk and eggs in a separate bowl, then add into the leftover flour mixture and stir well.
- Pour in a 13x9-inch baking pan that's greased. Sprinkle reserved topping on top and let it bake for 35 to 40 minutes at 350 degrees or until an inserted toothpick in the middle exits clean. Allow to cool on a wire rack.

Nutrition Information

- Calories: 291 calories
- Total Carbohydrate: 43 g
- Cholesterol: 26 mg
- Total Fat: 21 g
- Fiber: 1 g
- Protein: 4 g
- Sodium: 326 mg

323. Spiced Fruit Bake

"An easy to make compote made with canned fruits and spiced with nutmeg and cinnamon."
Serving: 8 servings. | Prep: 5m | Ready in: 30m

Ingredients

- 1 can (20 oz.) unsweetened pineapple chunks
- 1 can (15 oz.) reduced-sugar apricot halves
- 1 can (15 oz.) pear halves in juice
- 1/4 cup packed brown sugar
- 1 tbsp. butter, melted
- 1/4 tsp. ground cinnamon
- 1/4 tsp. ground nutmeg
- 1/2 cup vanilla yogurt

Direction

- Let the fruits drain and set aside 3/4 cup of juice in total. In a 2-quart baking dish, place the fruit.
- Mix together the reserved juice, nutmeg, cinnamon, butter and brown sugar in a small bowl and pour on top of the fruit. Let it bake for 25 to 30 minutes at 350 degrees without cover or until it becomes heated through. Serve it using a slotted spoon.
- Put 1 tbsp of yogurt on top of each serving.

Nutrition Information

- Calories: 132 calories
- Total Carbohydrate: 30 g
- Cholesterol: 5 mg
- Total Fat: 2 g
- Fiber: 1 g
- Protein: 1 g
- Sodium: 30 mg

324. Spiced Pear Cake

"Delicious cake recipe made with convenient mix."
Serving: 14 servings. | Prep: 20m | Ready in: 01h20m

Ingredients

- 1 can (15 oz.) pear halves in juice
- 1 package white cake mix (regular size)
- 1 large egg
- 2 large egg whites
- 1/4 cup reduced-fat sour cream
- 1/4 cup packed brown sugar
- 1/4 tsp. ground cinnamon
- 1/8 tsp. ground nutmeg
- 2 tsps. confectioners' sugar

Direction

- Use cooking spray to coat a 10-inch fluted tube pan, then dust it using flour and put aside. Let the pears drain and set aside the juice. Chop the pears and put it in a big bowl. Pour in the reserved pear juice, then add the succeeding 7 ingredients. Beat it for half a minute on low speed, then beat it for 2 minutes on high. Pour into the prepped pan.
- Let it bake for 60 to 65 minutes at 350 degrees or until an inserted toothpick in the middle exits clean. Allow to cool for 10 minutes prior to taking it out of the pan and transferring to wire rack to let it fully cool. Dust confectioner's sugar on top.

Nutrition Information

- Calories: 207 calories
- Total Carbohydrate: 40 g
- Cholesterol: 16 mg
- Total Fat: 4 g
- Fiber: 1 g
- Protein: 3 g
- Sodium: 268 mg

325. Spiced Pineapple Pumpkin Delight

"A light and refreshing substitution for the pumpkin pie."
Serving: 2

Ingredients

- 3/4 tsp. unflavored gelatin
- 1/3 cup unsweetened apple juice
- 1 cup pumpkin puree
- 1 tbsp. pumpkin pie spice
- 2 tsps. white sugar
- 1 tsp. honey
- 1 cup crushed pineapple

Direction

- Beat apple juice and gelatin together in a small bowl. In a larger bowl filled with hot water, arrange the bowl of gelatin and apple juice and stir until the gelatin dissolves.
- Combine the gelatin mixture, honey, sugar, spice, and pumpkin together.
- In the bottom of custard cups, place 1/4 of the mixture. Put 1/4 cup of pineapple on top; then repeat the layers. Before serving, chill for an hour.

Nutrition Information

- Calories: 156 calories;
- Total Carbohydrate: 38.9 g
- Cholesterol: 0 mg
- Total Fat: 0.6 g
- Protein: 2.3 g
- Sodium: 7 mg

326. Stewed Holiday Fruit

"Fruity concoction made with fresh bananas, prunes and dried apricots with a drizzle of marmalade sauce and sweet cider."
Serving: 4 servings. | Prep: 15m | Ready in: 25m

Ingredients

- 12 dried apricots
- 12 pitted dried plums
- 1-1/2 cups apple cider or unsweetened apple juice
- 2 cinnamon sticks (3 inches)
- 8 whole cloves
- 2 whole allspice berries
- 1/4 cup orange marmalade
- 2 tsps. lemon juice
- 1 tsp. butter
- 2 medium firm bananas, sliced
- 2 tbsps. sliced almonds, toasted

Direction

- Mix together the initial 6 ingredients in a small saucepan, then boil. Take it out of the heat and let it chill in the fridge overnight with cover.
- Strain the cider and set aside the liquid. Put the plums and apricots aside. Get rid of the spices. Mix together the reserved cider, butter, lemon juice and marmalade in a small saucepan, then boil and mix it continuously. Allow to cool. Split the bananas, plums and apricots among the serving plates and drizzle the cooled sauce on top. Sprinkle almonds on top.

Nutrition Information

- Calories: 259 calories
- Total Carbohydrate: 61 g
- Cholesterol: 3 mg
- Total Fat: 3 g
- Fiber: 5 g
- Protein: 2 g
- Sodium: 26 mg

327. Strawberry Almond Pastries

"Dessert pastries that are crisp and light and made with suitable phyllo dough."
Serving: 1 dozen. | Prep: 25m | Ready in: 40m

Ingredients

- 12 sheets phyllo dough (14 inches x 9 inches)
- 1 jar (10 oz.) strawberry all-fruit spread
- 1/4 cup slivered almonds

Direction

- On a work surface, put 1 sheet of phyllo dough with the long side towards you, then use cooking spray to spritz the dough. Layer 2 sheets more and spritz it in between. Spread 1/2 of the fruit spread on top of the dough to within half an inch of the edges. Sprinkle 1/2 of the almonds on top.
- Roll it up the jelly-roll style, beginning with the long side, then use water to moisten the edges and press for it to seal. Slice it into 3 pieces. Redo the process thrice more with the leftover ingredients.
- Put the pieces on a cooking spray coated baking tray, cut side down and place it an inch apart. Use cooking spray to spritz the tops lightly. Let it bake for 12 to 15 minutes at 375 degrees or until it turns golden brown. Transfer to wire racks to let it cool.

Nutrition Information

- Calories: 101 calories
- Total Carbohydrate: 19 g
- Cholesterol: 0 mg
- Total Fat: 2 g
- Fiber: 1 g
- Protein: 1 g
- Sodium: 51 mg

328. Strawberry Cheesecake Torte

""I got this tasty dessert recipe from one of my friends at a party.""
Serving: 12 servings. | Prep: 30m | Ready in: 55m

Ingredients

- 1 package (16 oz.) angel food cake mix
- 1 tbsp. confectioners' sugar
- 1 package (.3 oz.) sugar-free strawberry gelatin
- 1/2 cup boiling water
- 1/4 cup seedless strawberry jam
- 1 package (8 oz.) reduced-fat cream cheese, cubed
- 1/3 cup fat-free milk
- 2 tbsps. lemon juice
- 3 cups reduced-fat whipped topping
- 1 package (3.4 oz.) instant cheesecake or vanilla pudding mix
- 1 cup sliced fresh strawberries
- 1 kiwifruit, peeled, halved and sliced
- 1-1/2 tsps. grated lemon peel

Direction

- Use ungreased parchment paper to line a 15x10x1-in. baking pan. Following the package instructions, prepare cake mix properly. Evenly spread the batter into the prepared pan. Bake at 350° till the top slightly turns brown, or for 24-26 minutes. Sprinkle sugar over a baking sheet lined with waxed paper. Invert the cake onto the baking sheet immediately. Peel off the parchment paper gently; allow to cool completely.
- In boiling water, dissolve gelatin. Mix in jam till melted. Poke the cake, using a fork, at 1/2-in. intervals. Use the gelatin mixture to brush; chill for 10 minutes.
- Beat lemon juice, milk and cream cheese in a bowl, till smooth. Beat in pudding mix and whipped topping. Reserve 1 cup. In the corner of a plastic bag or pastry, cut a small hole; insert a large star tip. Fill the pudding mixture into the bag.
- Trim the edges of the cake. Cut into three equal rectangles widthwise; arrange one on a

serving plate. In the center, spread 1/2 cup of the reserved pudding mixture. Pipe the mixture around the top edge of the cake. Repeat the layer. Place the third cake layer on top. Pipe the pudding mixture along the top edges. Fill fruit into the center. Sprinkle lemon peel over. Place in the refrigerator for storage.

Nutrition Information

- Calories: 284 calories
- Total Carbohydrate: 51 g
- Cholesterol: 11 mg
- Total Fat: 6 g
- Fiber: 1 g
- Protein: 6 g
- Sodium: 427 mg

329. Strawberry Chiffon Pie

"The creamy strawberry chiffon pies are ready under 10 mins."
Serving: Makes 8 servings, one slice each. | Prep: 10m | Ready in: 5h10m

Ingredients

- 2/3 cup boiling water
- 1 pkg. (4-serving size) JELL-O Strawberry Flavor Gelatin
- ice cubes
- 1/2 cup cold water
- 1-1/2 tsp. grated lime zest
- 2 Tbsp. lime juice
- 2 cups thawed COOL WHIP Whipped Topping
- 8 strawberries, finely chopped
- 1 ready-to-use graham cracker crumb crust (6 oz.)

Direction

- In large bowl, stir the boiling water into the dry gelatin mix until it is completely dissolved, about at least 2 mins. Put enough ice cubes into the cold water to measure one cup. Put into the gelatin; then stir until the ice

is completely melted. Mix in lime juice and zest.
- Put in the whipped topping; then use a wire whisk to stir until well blended. Mix in the strawberries. Place in the refrigerator until the mixture will mound and is thick, or about 60 mins. Spoon into the crust.
- Place in the refrigerator for at least 4 hours or overnight. Keep all the leftovers in the refrigerator.

Nutrition Information

- Calories: 200
- Total Carbohydrate: 29 g
- Cholesterol: 0 mg
- Total Fat: 9 g
- Fiber: 1 g
- Protein: 2 g
- Sodium: 135 mg
- Sugar: 19 g
- Saturated Fat: 6 g

330. Strawberry Italian Ice

"This dish is ready in 45 mins or less."
Serving: Serves 2

Ingredients

- 1 pint fresh strawberries, trimmed
- 1/4 cup sugar
- 2 tsps. fresh lemon juice
- 2 cups ice cubes (about 11)

Direction

- In the freezer, place 9 or 10-inch metal cake pan. Blend lemon juice, sugar and strawberries in a blender, until the sugar dissolves and the mixture become smooth. Put in the ice cubes and blend the mixture until it becomes smooth and pour it into the cooled pan. Let the mixture freeze for 30-40 minutes or until it turns frozen around the edge yet is still soft in the middle. Mix in the strawberry ice, then use fork to mash the frozen parts and scoop it into two bowls.

Nutrition Information

- Calories: 155
- Total Carbohydrate: 39 g
- Total Fat: 1 g
- Fiber: 4 g
- Protein: 1 g
- Sodium: 12 mg
- Saturated Fat: 0 g

331. Strawberry Pie Mousse

"A strawberry pie recipe with less calories."
Serving: 8 servings. | Prep: 20m | Ready in: 20m

Ingredients

- 4 cups fresh or frozen unsweetened strawberries
- 1/2 cup sugar
- 1 package (1 oz.) sugar-free instant vanilla pudding mix
- 1 carton (8 oz.) frozen reduced-fat whipped topping, thawed

Direction

- Process sugar and strawberries till smooth, covered, in food processor. Strain then discard seeds. Put strawberry mixture back in food processor and add pudding mix; process till smooth, covered.
- Put in big bowl; fold whipped topping in. Put in dessert dishes; refrigerate till serving.

Nutrition Information

- Calories: 145 calories
- Total Carbohydrate: 27 g
- Cholesterol: 0 mg
- Total Fat: 3 g
- Fiber: 2 g
- Protein: 0 g
- Sodium: 148 mg

332. Strawberry Raspberry Trifle

"A low-fat trifle."
Serving: 14 servings. | Prep: 20m | Ready in: 20m

Ingredients

- 3 cups cold fat-free milk
- 2 packages (1 oz. each) sugar-free instant white chocolate pudding mix
- 1 prepared angel food cake (8 to 10 oz.), cut into 1-inch cubes
- 3 cups sliced fresh strawberries
- 3 cups fresh raspberries
- 1 carton (8 oz.) frozen reduced-fat whipped topping, thawed
- 3 whole strawberries, quartered

Direction

- Whisk pudding mix and milk for 2 minutes in big bowl; it will be thick.
- Put 1/3 cake cubes in 3 1/2-qt. glass serving bowl/trifle bowl. Put 1/3 pudding, 1 cup sliced strawberries, 1 1/2 cups raspberries then 1/3 whipped topping. Layer with 1/3 pudding and cake, 1 cup strawberries then 1/3 whipped topping.
- Put leftover cake, pudding, raspberries, strawberries then whipped topping over; garnish using quartered strawberries. Immediately serve/cover then chill till serving.

Nutrition Information

- Calories: 0g sugar total.

333. Strawberry Rhubarb Tart

"This tart is great to enjoy in spring. The crust is made with oats."
Serving: 12 servings. | Prep: 60m | Ready in: 01h20m

Ingredients

- 1/2 cup old-fashioned oats, toasted
- 2/3 cup all-purpose flour
- 1/4 cup sugar
- 1 tsp. grated lemon zest
- 3/4 tsp. baking powder
- 1/4 tsp. salt
- 2 tbsps. canola oil
- 3 tbsps. whole milk
- 1/2 tsp. vanilla extract
- FILLING:
- 3-1/2 cups sliced fresh strawberries, divided
- 2 cups sliced fresh or frozen rhubarb
- 1/4 cup sugar
- 1/2 tsp. grated lemon zest
- 5 tsps. cornstarch
- 1 tbsp. cold water
- 4 tsps. currant jelly, melted

Direction

- In a food processor, finely grind oats. Put in a big bowl; add salt, baking powder, lemon zest, sugar, and flour. Gradually pour in oil, whisking until the mixture looks like coarse crumbs. Mix together vanilla and milk, then mix into the flour mixture, 1 tbsp. each time, until the mixture turns into a ball.
- Invert the dough onto a surface scattered with flour; knead 7-8 times. Put the pastry between waxed paper sheets, then roll out until fitting a 9-inch removable-bottomed fluted tart pan. Oil the tart pan, then lightly press the pastry into the pan. Use heavy-duty foil with double thickness to line the pastry shell. Bake for 12 minutes at 350°. Peel off the foil, then bake until turning light brown, about another 8-12 minutes. Put on a wire rack to cool.
- To prepare the filling, in a big saucepan, mix together lemon zest, sugar, rhubarb, and 1 cup strawberries. Let sit for 30 minutes.
- Stir and cook over medium-low heat until the rhubarb is soft but remains shape, about 8-10 minutes. Mix together water and cornstarch until smooth, then mix into the fruit mixture. Boil it; stir and cook until thickened, about 2 minutes. Add to a bowl, then put waxed paper on the surface to cover. Chill for 1-2 hours.
- Spread into the crust with the filling right before eating. Top with the leftover strawberries. Brush jelly over.

Nutrition Information

- Calories: 0g sugar total.

334. Strawberry Shortcake With Balsamic

"A low-calorie angel food cake topped with strawberries soaked in balsamic vinegar and black pepper."
Serving: 4 | Prep: 10m | Ready in: 20m

Ingredients

- 2 cups sliced strawberries
- 1/4 cup balsamic vinegar
- 1 tbsp. white sugar
- 1 pinch ground black pepper
- 4 slices angel food cake
- 1/2 cup whipped cream

Direction

- Preheat the outdoor grill for medium heat and grease grate lightly.
- In a bowl, mix black pepper, sugar, balsamic vinegar and strawberries; allow to marinate for 10 to 15 minutes.
- On the prepped grill, grill angel food cake slices for 3 to 5 minutes on every side till toasted.
- To 4 dessert plates, put the cake and set marinated strawberries on top and liquid and a spoonful of whipped cream.

Nutrition Information

- Calories: 141 calories;
- Total Carbohydrate: 29.3 g
- Cholesterol: 6 mg
- Total Fat: 2.2 g
- Protein: 2.6 g
- Sodium: 227 mg

335. Strawberry-banana Ice Cream

"This strawberry ice cream is so delightful."
Serving: about 3 quarts. | Prep: 15m | Ready in: 35m

Ingredients

- 6 eggs
- 2 cups sugar
- 4 cups half-and-half cream
- 1 can (14 oz.) sweetened condensed milk
- 1-1/2 tsps. vanilla extract
- Red food coloring, optional
- 1 carton (8 oz.) frozen whipped topping, thawed
- 1 package (16 oz.) frozen unsweetened whole strawberries, coarsely chopped
- 2 medium firm bananas, sliced
- 1 cup chopped pecans, toasted

Direction

- Combine sugar and eggs in a heavy saucepan. Put in cream gradually. Cook while stirring over low heat until the mixture coats back of the metal spoon and reaches 160°. Discard from the heat. Quickly place the pan in a bowl of ice water to cool and stir about 2 mins. If desired, stir in food coloring, milk and vanilla. Press the plastic wrap onto the surface of the mixture. Place in the refrigerator for several hours or overnight.
- Fold the whipped topping into the cream mixture. Then fold in pecans, bananas and strawberries. Fill 2/3 full with cylinder of the ice cream freezer; then freeze following the manufacturer's instructions. Place the remaining mixture in refrigerator until ready to freeze. Let it firm up in refrigerator freezer or ripen in ice cream freezer about 2 to 4 hours. Serve.

Nutrition Information

- Calories: 245 calories
- Total Carbohydrate: 32 g
- Cholesterol: 68 mg
- Total Fat: 12 g
- Fiber: 1 g
- Protein: 4 g
- Sodium: 50 mg

336. Striped Fruit Pops

"Luscious and delicious frosty treats with peaches, kiwifruit, and strawberries plus the natural sweetness of honey."
Serving: 1 dozen. | Prep: 15m | Ready in: 15m

Ingredients

- 3/4 cup honey, divided
- 2 cups sliced fresh strawberries
- 12 plastic cups or Popsicle molds (3 oz. each)
- 12 plastic cups or Popsicle molds (3 oz. each)
- 6 kiwifruit, peeled and sliced
- 12 Popsicle sticks
- 1-1/3 cups sliced fresh ripe peaches

Direction

- Process strawberries and a quarter cup honey in a blender, covered, until combined. Transfer to molds or cups. Place in the freezer for half an hour until solid.
- Process kiwi and a quarter cup honey in a blender, covered, until combined. Pour over the firm strawberry layer; put in Popsicle sticks. Place in the freezer until solid.
- Repeat the process with the remaining honey and peaches; transfer on top of the kiwi layer. Place in the freezer until solid.

Nutrition Information

- Calories: 106 calories
- Total Carbohydrate: 27 g
- Cholesterol: 0 mg
- Total Fat: 0 g
- Fiber: 2 g
- Protein: 1 g
- Sodium: 1 mg

337. Sugarless Rice Pudding

"This yummy rice pudding doesn't take me a long time to prepare.""
Serving: 6 servings. | Prep: 10m | Ready in: 10m

Ingredients

- 2 cups cold 2% milk
- 1 package (1 oz.) sugar-free instant vanilla pudding mix
- 1/4 tsp. vanilla extract
- 2 cups cold cooked rice

Direction

- Stir pudding mix and milk together in a mixing bowl until slightly thickened, about 2 minutes. Mix in vanilla until well combined. Mix in rice. Serve right away or chill, covered.

Nutrition Information

- Calories: 115 calories
- Total Carbohydrate: 20 g
- Cholesterol: 7 mg
- Total Fat: 2 g
- Fiber: 0 g
- Protein: 4 g
- Sodium: 241 mg

338. Summer Berry Compote

"A delectable dessert with fresh summer berries."
Serving: 5 | Prep: 10m | Ready in: 30m

Ingredients

- 1 pint strawberries, quartered
- 1 pint blueberries, rinsed and drained
- 1 pint fresh blackberries, rinsed and drained
- 1 pint fresh raspberries
- 1 pint red currants
- 1 tbsp. white sugar
- 3 tbsps. chopped fennel greens

Direction

- Mix together currants, raspberries, blackberries, blueberries and strawberries in a large bowl. Top with a sprinkle of sugar and slowly mix in fennel. Put into refrigerator for about 20 minutes. Serve cold.

Nutrition Information

- Calories: 138 calories;
- Total Carbohydrate: 33.5 g
- Cholesterol: 0 mg
- Total Fat: 1.1 g
- Protein: 2.7 g
- Sodium: 4 mg

339. Summer Berry Parfait With Yogurt And Granola

""Enjoy this big parfait using frozen or fresh blueberries, also try adding fresh strawberries."
Serving: 1 | Prep: 10m | Ready in: 10m

Ingredients

- 3/4 cup sliced strawberries
- 3/4 cup blueberries
- 1 (6 oz.) container vanilla yogurt
- 1 tbsp. wheat germ
- 1/2 banana, sliced
- 1/3 cup granola

Direction

- Make layers of quarter cup strawberries, quarter cup blueberries, one third container yogurt, 1/3 tbsp. wheat germ, 1/3 of sliced banana, and two tbsp. granola in a large bowl. Continue making the parfait by repeating layers until all ingredients are used up.

Nutrition Information

- Calories: 520 calories;
- Total Carbohydrate: 86.9 g
- Cholesterol: 8 mg
- Total Fat: 13.5 g
- Protein: 18.3 g
- Sodium: 126 mg

340. Sunny Sponge Cake

"Tender and moist golden cake with mild orange flavor and light texture."
Serving: 12 servings. | Prep: 40m | Ready in: 60m

Ingredients

- 6 large egg whites
- 3 large egg yolks
- 1-1/2 cups all-purpose flour
- 1-1/4 tsps. baking powder
- 1/4 tsp. salt
- 1 cup sugar, divided
- 2 tsps. hot water
- 1/2 cup orange juice, warmed
- 1-1/4 tsps. vanilla extract
- 3/4 tsp. grated orange zest
- 1/4 tsp. grated lemon zest
- 3/4 cup reduced-fat whipped topping

Direction

- Allow the egg yolks and egg whites to stand at room temperature for half an hour. Sift together the salt, baking powder and flour, then put aside.
- Beat the egg yolks in a big bowl, until it turns a bit thick. Slowly add hot water and 3/4 cup sugar, then beat it until it turns pale yellow and becomes thick. Blend in the lemon and orange zests, vanilla and orange juice. Put the reserved flour mixture into the egg yolk mixture.
- Beat the egg whites in a separate bowl on medium speed using clean beaters, until it forms soft peaks. Slowly beat in the sugar, approximately a tbsp. at a time, on high until the sugar dissolves and forms stiff glossy peaks. Fold 1/4 of egg whites into the batter and fold in the leftover whites.
- Scoop the batter to a 10-inch tube pan that's ungreased. Let it bake for 25 to 30 minutes at 350 degrees on the lowest rack or until the cake bounces back once pressed lightly. Instantly turn the pan upside down and let it fully cool. Run a knife around the middle and sides of the tube pan. Turn the cake upside down on a serving plate. Top it with whipped topping, then serve.

Nutrition Information

- Calories: 160 calories
- Total Carbohydrate: 31 g
- Cholesterol: 53 mg
- Total Fat: 2 g
- Fiber: 0 g
- Protein: 431 g
- Sodium: 103 mg

341. Sweet And Silky Strawberry Sorbet

"While other homemade sorbets turn to a frosty slush, this recipe yields a melt-in-your-mouth sorbet because it is thickened before storing in the freezer. I couldn't find the recipe that's perfect for me so I made my own and this soft strawberry sorbet can compete with any store-bought brands. It's even more amazing because this sorbet can be prepared using a regular freezer if you don't have an ice cream machine handy."

Serving: 4 | Prep: 15m | Ready in: 2h30m

Ingredients

- 1 lb. ripe strawberries, hulled and chopped
- 1/2 cup white sugar
- 1 pinch salt
- 1 1/2 tsps. cornstarch
- 1 1/2 tsps. cold water
- 3 tbsps. lemon juice

Direction

- Puree berries in the food processor until they are a smooth consistency. In a big saucepan, mix together sugar, salt and the pureed berries. Heat to a simmer until all ingredients melt. Meanwhile, beat together cornstarch and cold water; then pour into heated berry mixture, stirring while pouring. Take the pan off the heat and add the lemon juice in. Let mixture cool a bit; then refrigerate for 2 hours until chilled.
- Put mixture in an ice cream machine and follow manufacturer's directions to freeze.

Nutrition Information

- Calories: 140 calories;
- Total Carbohydrate: 35.6 g
- Cholesterol: 0 mg
- Total Fat: 0.3 g
- Protein: 0.8 g
- Sodium: 1 mg

342. Sweet Grilled Peaches

""A nice recipe to make use of fresh peaches.""
Serving: 4 | Prep: 5m | Ready in: 15m

Ingredients

- 1 (16 oz.) package frozen peach slices
- 1/2 cup honey
- 2 tbsps. cinnamon

Direction

- Preheat a grill for medium heat.
- On a large piece of aluminum foil, arrange preaches. Hold in all of the peaches with two pieces, if needed, without spillage. Drizzle with honey, sprinkle cinnamon on top. Close up the foil; tightly seal.
- Put the foil packet into the prepared grill; cook while turning once halfway through, about 10 minutes. Open the packet carefully. Serve.

Nutrition Information

- Calories: 244 calories;
- Total Carbohydrate: 64.9 g
- Cholesterol: 0 mg
- Total Fat: 0.2 g
- Protein: 1 g
- Sodium: 9 mg

343. Sweetheart Red Cake

"A family favorite."
Serving: 12 servings. | Prep: 25m | Ready in: 50m

Ingredients

- 6 tbsps. butter, softened
- 1-3/4 cups sugar
- 1 large egg
- 2 large egg whites
- 1/4 cup unsweetened applesauce
- 1 bottle (1 oz.) red food coloring
- 1 tsp. white vinegar
- 1 tsp. vanilla

- 2-1/2 cups cake flour
- 1 tsp. salt
- 1 tsp. baking soda
- 1 tsp. baking cocoa
- 1-1/4 cups buttermilk
- FROSTING:
- 1-1/2 cups sugar
- 4 large egg whites
- 1/4 cup water
- 1/2 tsp. cream of tartar
- 1 tsp. vanilla extract
- Pink gel food coloring

Direction

- Use cooking spray then flour to coat 2 round 9-in. baking pans. Cream sugar and butter till crumbly for 2 minutes in a bowl. One by one, add egg whites and egg; beat well after each. Beat in vanilla, vinegar, food coloring and applesauce. Mix cocoa, baking soda, salt and flour. Alternately with buttermilk, add to creamed mixture. Put in prepped pans; bake it at 350° till inserted toothpick in middle exits clean for 25-30 minutes. Cool for 10 minutes. Transfer from pans onto wire racks; fully cool.
- Frosting: Beat cream of tartar, water, egg whites and sugar with a portable mixer for 1 minute on low speed in a heavy saucepan; beat at low speed on low heat for 8-10 minutes till frosting reaches 160°. Put into heavy-duty stand mixer's bowl. Add vanilla; beat at high speed for 7 minutes till frosting makes stiff peaks. Remove 1/2 cup frosting and tint pink. Spread leftover frosting between layers and on sides and top of cake. On top of cake, pipe pink hearts.

Nutrition Information

- Calories: 373 calories
- Total Carbohydrate: 75 g
- Cholesterol: 34 mg
- Total Fat: 7 g
- Fiber: 1 g
- Protein: 5 g
- Sodium: 419 mg

344. Swirled Chocolate Peanut Butter Cake

""A delicious and quick-to-make cake dessert.""
Serving: 18 servings. | Prep: 35m | Ready in: 01h10m

Ingredients

- 1 package chocolate cake mix (regular size)
- 1-1/4 cups water
- 1/2 cup reduced-fat sour cream
- 2 large egg whites
- 1 package (8 oz.) reduced-fat cream cheese
- 1 large egg, lightly beaten
- 1/2 cup sugar
- 1/2 cup reduced-fat creamy peanut butter
- 1/4 cup fat-free milk

Direction

- Beat egg whites, sour cream, water and cake mix together in a large bowl on medium speed for 2 minutes. Use cooking spray to coat a 9x13-in. baking pan; dust with flour. Transfer the batter into the pan.
- Beat together milk, peanut butter, sugar, egg and cream cheese in a small bowl till smooth. Drop over the batter by tablespoonfuls; use a knife to swirl. Bake at 350° till a toothpick turns out clean when inserted into the center, about 35-40 minutes. Place on a wire rack to cool. Keep any leftovers in the refrigerator.

Nutrition Information

- Calories: 225 calories
- Total Carbohydrate: 32 g
- Cholesterol: 23 mg
- Total Fat: 9 g
- Fiber: 1 g
- Protein: 6 g
- Sodium: 289 mg

345. Thumbprint Cookies

Ingredients

- 1 package cream cheese 8oz
- 3/4 cup butter
- 1 cup sugar
- 2 tsps. vanilla
- 2.25 cups flour
- 1/2 tbsp. baking soda
- 1 cup finely chopped pecans
- 1 jar jam or preserves

Direction

- Let it bake for 8 minutes at 350 degrees. Add the jam and let it bake for 8 minutes.
- Combine all the ingredients except for the jam.
- Dab on the tray and press in the middle.
- Add the jam halfway through the baking process.

346. Trail Mix Clusters

"These delicious snack with dried fruit and nuts is a heart-healthy treat."
Serving: 4 dozen. | Prep: 20m | Ready in: 25m

Ingredients

- 2 cups (12 oz.) semisweet chocolate chips
- 1/2 cup unsalted sunflower kernels
- 1/2 cup salted pumpkin seeds or pepitas
- 1/2 cup coarsely chopped cashews
- 1/2 cup coarsely chopped pecans
- 1/4 cup sweetened shredded coconut
- 1/4 cup finely chopped dried apricots
- 1/4 cup dried cranberries
- 1/4 cup dried cherries or blueberries

Direction

- Liquefy chocolate chips in a big microwave-safe bowl; mix till smooth. Mix in the rest of the ingredients.
- Onto baking sheets lined with waxed paper, drop mixture by tablespoonfuls. Chill till firm. Keep in the refrigerator in an airtight container.

Nutrition Information

- Calories: 79 calories
- Total Carbohydrate: 8 g
- Cholesterol: 0 mg
- Total Fat: 6 g
- Fiber: 1 g
- Protein: 2 g
- Sodium: 26 mg

347. Triple Berry Sorbet

""For a light and refreshing dessert, I would recommend this tart sorbet!""
Serving: 8 | Prep: 10m | Ready in: 4h30m

Ingredients

- 1 3/4 cups white sugar
- 1 3/4 cups water
- 2 cups fresh or frozen cranberries
- 1 (12 oz.) package frozen unsweetened raspberries
- 1 1/2 cups cherry juice
- 1/2 cup lime juice
- 2 tbsps. frozen orange juice concentrate

Direction

- In a saucepan over medium heat, boil the water and sugar until the sugar dissolves. Stir in the cranberries and cook for 5 minutes then add the raspberries. Let it simmer until the raspberries have turned soft and the cranberries pop, about 5 minutes. Use a strainer or sieve to strain the mixture and get rid of the pulp. Keep the mixture in the fridge for 2 hours then add the orange juice concentrate, lime juice and cherry juice. Fill an ice cream maker up with the mixture and follow the manufacturer's directions to freeze. Fit the sorbet into a freezer container and freeze until the sorbet turns firm, about 2 hours. Before serving, make sure to get the sorbet out 10 minutes in advance.

Nutrition Information

- Calories: 238 calories;
- Total Carbohydrate: 60.9 g
- Cholesterol: 0 mg
- Total Fat: 0.1 g
- Protein: 0.8 g
- Sodium: 9 mg

348. Triple Orange Fluff

"It's refreshing, light and very delicious."
Serving: 15 servings. | Prep: 15m | Ready in: 15m

Ingredients

- 1 package (.3 oz.) sugar-free orange gelatin
- 1 cup boiling water
- 1 pint orange sherbet, softened
- 1 carton (8 oz.) frozen reduced-fat whipped topping, thawed
- 1 prepared angel food cake (8 to 10 oz.), cut into 1-inch pieces
- 1 can (15 oz.) mandarin oranges, drained

Direction

- Dissolve the gelatin powder in a large bowl of boiling water. Mix in sherbet. Place in the refrigerator until set partially. Fold in the whipped topping. Put the cake pieces into a 13x9 inches dish. Top the cake with oranges. Top with the gelatin mixture. Refrigerate, covered, until firm, about 4 hours.

Nutrition Information

- Calories: 0g sugar total.

349. Tropical Delight Sherbet

"This delicious dessert has a tropical vibe to it."
Serving: 4 | Prep: 15m | Ready in: 4h40m

Ingredients

- 1/3 cup water
- 1/3 cup white sugar
- 1/2 fresh pineapple, chopped
- 1 cup orange juice
- 1 cup fresh strawberries
- 1 mango, peeled and chopped
- 3/4 cup whole milk
- 1 tbsp. lime juice
- 1 tsp. coconut extract

Direction

- In a small saucepan, mix together sugar with water over medium heat. Heat up, mixing occasionally about 5 minutes until the sugar is dissolved. Take simple syrup off from heat.
- In a blender, mix together milk, mango, strawberries, orange juice and pineapple; puree until smooth. Put in coconut extract, lime juice, and simple syrup; puree until smooth.
- Put the blended mixture into an ice cream maker and freeze about 20 minutes, according to manufacturer's instructions. Pour into an airtight container and freeze about 4 hours until firm.

Nutrition Information

- Calories: 245 calories;
- Total Carbohydrate: 57.2 g
- Cholesterol: 5 mg
- Total Fat: 2 g
- Protein: 3.3 g
- Sodium: 22 mg

350. Tropical Mango Mousse

"A refreshing recipe that takes only 5 minutes to prepare!"
Serving: 6

Ingredients

- 2 mangos - peeled, seeded, and cubed
- 1 banana
- 2/3 cup nonfat plain yogurt
- 2 tsps. honey
- 6 cubes ice
- 1 tsp. vanilla extract

Direction

- Mix vanilla extract, ice cubes, honey, yogurt, bananas and mangoes till smooth in blender; refrigerate for 3 hours then put in individual dishes. Serve.

Nutrition Information

- Calories: 87 calories;
- Total Carbohydrate: 20.5 g
- Cholesterol: < 1 mg
- Total Fat: 0.3 g
- Protein: 2.1 g
- Sodium: 23 mg

351. Tutti-frutti Angel Food Cake

"Feathery-light cake that's made from scratch."
Serving: 12 servings. | Prep: 20m | Ready in: 55m

Ingredients

- 1-1/2 cups egg whites (about 10)
- 1-1/4 tsps. cream of tartar
- 1/2 tsp. salt
- 1 tsp. vanilla extract
- 1/2 tsp. almond extract
- 1 to 2 drops red food coloring, optional
- 1-1/2 cups sugar
- 1-1/4 cups cake flour
- 1 cup finely chopped mixed candied fruit

Direction

- In a big bowl, put the egg whites and allow to stand for half an hour at room temperature, then put aside.
- Add food coloring, if preferred, salt, extracts and cream of tartar into the egg whites and beat it on medium speed, until it forms soft peaks. Slowly add the sugar, approximately 2 tbsp at a time, then beat it on high until the sugar dissolves and forms stiff glossy peaks. Slowly fold in the flour mixture, approximately half a cup at a time, then fold in the candied fruit.
- Lightly scoop to a 10-inch tube pan that's ungreased. Use a knife to slice through the batter to release air pockets. Let it bake for 35 to 40 minutes at 375 degrees on the lowest oven rack or until the entire surface looks dry and turns light brown in color. Instantly turn the pan upside down and let it fully cool for about an hour.
- Run a knife around the middle and side tube of the pan. Transfer the cake to a serving platter.

Nutrition Information

- Calories: 226 calories
- Total Carbohydrate: 53 g
- Cholesterol: 0 mg
- Total Fat: 0 g
- Fiber: 2 g
- Protein: 4 g
- Sodium: 169 mg

352. Ultimate Chocolate Cake

"What's better than a dessert that contains less fat? Try out this chocolate cake that has a moist and soft texture and a rich flavor of semisweet chocolate chips."
Serving: 12 servings. | Prep: 15m | Ready in: 60m

Ingredients

- 1 package devil's food cake mix (regular size)

- 1 package (1.4 oz.) sugar-free instant chocolate pudding mix
- 1 cup (8 oz.) fat-free sour cream
- 1/2 cup unsweetened applesauce
- 1/2 cup water
- 2 eggs
- 1/2 cup egg substitute
- 1/2 cup semisweet chocolate chips
- 1-1/2 tsps. confectioners' sugar

Direction

- Mix together the first 7 ingredients in a bowl and stir thoroughly. Mix in chocolate chips. Use cooking spray to coat and flour to dust a fluted tube pan of 10 inches; pour in the batter.
- Bake in 350-degree oven until a toothpick is clean when coming out of the middle of the cake, about 45 to 50 minutes. Allow to cool in pan for 10 minutes, then transfer from pan to a wire rack to cool fully. Sprinkle confectioners' sugar on top.

Nutrition Information

- Calories: 266 calories
- Total Carbohydrate: 41 g
- Cholesterol: 62 mg
- Total Fat: 9 g
- Fiber: 2 g
- Protein: 6 g
- Sodium: 520 mg

353. Upside-down Peach Cake

"A famous upside-down cake recipe."
Serving: 8 servings. | Prep: 15m | Ready in: 60m

Ingredients

- 3/4 cup butter, softened, divided
- 1/2 cup packed brown sugar
- 2 cups sliced peeled fresh peaches
- 3/4 cup sugar
- 1 egg
- 1 tsp. vanilla extract
- 1-1/4 cups all-purpose flour
- 1-1/4 tsps. baking powder
- 1/4 tsp. salt
- 1/2 cup milk

Direction

- Melt a quarter cup of butter, then pour in a 9-inch round baking pan that's ungreased. Sprinkle brown sugar on top. Lay out the slices of peach on top of the sugar in a single layer.
- Cream the leftover butter and sugar in a big bowl, until it becomes fluffy and light. Beat in the vanilla and egg. Mix together the salt, baking powder and flour, then add it to the creamed mixture alternately with the milk and beat it well after every addition. Scoop on top of the peaches.
- Let it bake for 45 to 50 minutes at 350 degrees or until an inserted toothpick in the middle exits clean. Allow to cool for 10 minutes prior to turning it upside down on a serving plate. Serve while still warm.

Nutrition Information

- Calories: 386 calories
- Total Carbohydrate: 53 g
- Cholesterol: 75 mg
- Total Fat: 19 g
- Fiber: 1 g
- Protein: 4 g
- Sodium: 347 mg

354. Valentine Strawberry Shortcake

"A wonderful strawberry recipe."
Serving: 2 servings. | Prep: 30m | Ready in: 45m

Ingredients

- 1/4 cup fat-free plain yogurt
- 2 tbsps. reduced-fat sour cream
- 2 tbsps. confectioners' sugar

- 1/4 tsp. rum extract
- 1 pint fresh strawberries, sliced, divided
- SHORTCAKE:
- 2/3 cup all-purpose flour
- 2 tbsps. whole wheat flour
- 2 tbsps. plus 1/2 tsp. sugar, divided
- 3/4 tsp. baking powder
- 1/4 tsp. baking soda
- 1/8 tsp. salt
- 5 tbsps. cold butter
- 1/3 cup buttermilk

Direction

- Mix extract, confectioners' sugar, sour cream and yogurt in small bowl. Mash 1/2 cup strawberries in small bowl; mix into yogurt mixture. Cover then refrigerate.
- Mix salt, baking soda, baking powder, 2 tbsp. sugar and flour in another bowl. Cut butter in till mixture looks like coarse crumbs. Mix buttermilk in till you make a sticky soft dough. Knead dough gently 10 times on floured surface. Gently pat/roll to 1/2-in. thick circle. Use 3 1/2-in. cutter to cut 2 heart shapes out.
- Put on greased baking sheet; sprinkle leftover sugar on top. Bake for 12-14 minutes till golden brown at 400°. Transfer to wire rack; slightly cool. Assembling: Split shortcakes in half. Put cake bottoms onto dessert plates then spread yogurt mixture on. Top with leftover strawberries then shortcake tops.

Nutrition Information

- Calories: 445 calories
- Total Carbohydrate: 75 g
- Cholesterol: 33 mg
- Total Fat: 12 g
- Fiber: 5 g
- Protein: 10 g
- Sodium: 560 mg

355. Vanilla Berry Parfaits

""Simple and luscious, this is an awesome combination of yogurt and berries! You can create a thin layer of granola or graham crackers in each berry/vanilla layer if you want. That adds it a bit more crunch.""
Serving: 2 | Prep: 5m | Ready in: 5m

Ingredients

- 2 (8 oz.) containers vanilla yogurt
- 1 (10 oz.) package frozen mixed berries
- 2 tbsps. crushed graham crackers
- 1/8 tsp. ground nutmeg

Direction

- In two small glasses, layer a yogurt to cover the bottoms. Then add berries to cover top layer. Continue until both glasses are full, finishing with a fruit layer. Top and sprinkle with nutmeg and graham crackers.

Nutrition Information

- Calories: 354 calories;
- Total Carbohydrate: 69.4 g
- Cholesterol: 11 mg
- Total Fat: 3.7 g
- Protein: 13.6 g
- Sodium: 186 mg

356. Very Berry Parfaits

""Chopped chocolatey sandwich cookies with coconut, yogurt and fresh berries make these simple yet delicious dessert parfaits.""
Serving: Makes 6 servings, 2/3 cup each. | Prep: 15m | Ready in: 15m

Ingredients

- 2 cups assorted fresh berries (sliced strawberries, raspberries and blueberries)
- 2 cups vanilla low-fat yogurt
- 1/4 cup BAKER'S ANGEL FLAKE Coconut

- 12 OREO Cookies, coarsely chopped, divided

Direction

- 1. Toss berries with coconut and yogurt until coated evenly.
- 2. Set aside 1/2 cup of the chopped cookies for decorating. In six 6-8-oz. parfait glasses or dessert dishes, layer the rest of the chopped cookies and yogurt mixture.
- 3. Serve right away. Alternately, store in the refrigerator, covered, for 1 hour. Dust evenly with the reserved chopped cookies just prior to serving.

Nutrition Information

- Calories: 230
- Total Carbohydrate: 36 g
- Cholesterol: 5 mg
- Total Fat: 8 g
- Fiber: 3 g
- Protein: 5 g
- Sodium: 190 mg
- Sugar: 26 g
- Saturated Fat: 3 g

357. Walnut Raisin Apple Cookies

"These chunky cookies are perfect for taking to potlucks."
Serving: 4 dozen. | Prep: 20m | Ready in: 35m

Ingredients

- 1/4 cup butter, softened
- 1 cup packed brown sugar
- 2 eggs
- 1/4 cup unsweetened apple juice
- 1/4 tsp. lemon extract
- 1-1/2 cups all-purpose flour
- 1 cup quick-cooking oats
- 1 tsp. ground cinnamon
- 3/4 tsp. baking soda
- 3/4 tsp. salt
- 1/4 tsp. ground nutmeg
- 1/8 tsp. ground cloves
- 1-1/2 cups chopped peeled tart apple
- 1 cup raisins
- 1/2 cup chopped walnut

Direction

- Cream brown sugar and butter in a big bowl for 2 minutes, until crumbly. Put in one egg at a time while beating well after each addition. Put in lemon extract and apple juice. Mix together cloves, nutmeg, salt, baking soda, cinnamon, oats and flour, then put into the creamed mixture gradually and blend well. Fold in walnuts, raisins and apples.
- Drop onto ungreased baking sheets by rounded tablespoonfuls spacing 2 inches apart. Bake at 350 degrees until brown slightly, about 11 to 13 minutes. Transfer to wire racks.

Nutrition Information

- Calories: 139 calories
- Total Carbohydrate: 24 g
- Cholesterol: 23 mg
- Total Fat: 4 g
- Fiber: 1 g
- Protein: 2 g
- Sodium: 143 mg

358. Walnut Streusel Coffee Cake

"This Streusel Coffee cake will surprise your guests with a nutty filling."
Serving: 12 servings. | Prep: 20m | Ready in: 01h05m

Ingredients

- 1 cup chopped walnuts
- 1/2 cup packed brown sugar
- 2 tbsps. butter, melted
- 1/2 tsp. ground cinnamon
- COFFEE CAKE:
- 4 eggs, separated
- 1 cup butter, softened
- 1-3/4 cups sugar

- 1 tsp. vanilla extract
- 3 cups all-purpose flour
- 2 tsps. baking powder
- 1/2 tsp. baking soda
- 1/4 tsp. salt
- 1 cup (8 oz.) sour cream
- 2 tsps. confectioners' sugar

Direction

- Combine cinnamon, butter, brown sugar and walnuts in a small bowl.
- Bring egg whites into a large bowl; allow to sit at room temperature for half an hour. Start preheating the oven to 350 degrees. Prepare a 10" fluted tube pan coated with cooking spray and dusted with flour.
- Beat sugar and butter until fluffy and light in a large bowl. Slowly put in egg yolks. Beat vanilla into the mixture. Stir salt, baking soda, baking powder and flour in a separate bowl; alternately add to creamed mixture with sour cream, beating thoroughly after adding another.
- Beat egg whites using clean beaters on medium speed to form firm peaks. Fold into the batter.
- Transfer 1/2 of the batter into greased and floured pan; pour walnut mixture on top. Add the rest of the batter. Bake for 45 to 55 minutes until a toothpick slid into the middle comes out with no streaks of batter. Let cool for 10 minutes, then transfer to a wire rack to cool thoroughly. Sprinkle confectioners' sugar on top.

Nutrition Information

- Calories: 540 calories
- Total Carbohydrate: 65 g
- Cholesterol: 128 mg
- Total Fat: 29 g
- Fiber: 2 g
- Protein: 8 g
- Sodium: 323 mg

359. Warm Banana Pudding

"Pudding recipe made with reduced-fat ingredients and sugar substitute with soft layer of vanilla wafer and a top similar to meringue."
Serving: 6 servings. | Prep: 30m | Ready in: 45m

Ingredients

- Sugar substitute equivalent to 1/2 cup sugar
- 1/2 cup sugar, divided
- 3 tbsps. cornstarch
- 2 cups fat-free milk
- 2 eggs, separated
- 2 tbsps. butter
- 1 tsp. vanilla extract
- 2 large ripe bananas, sliced
- 1 tsp. lemon juice
- 12 reduced-fat vanilla wafer

Direction

- Mix together the cornstarch, a quarter cup of sugar and sugar substitute in a big saucepan. Slowly mix in the milk until it becomes smooth, then boil and mix continuously. Let it cook and stir until it becomes thick. Take it out of the heat. Mix a little amount of hot filling to the egg yolks, then put it all back into the pan and mix continuously. Gently boil, then cook and stir for 2 minutes. Take it out of the heat, then mix in vanilla and butter.
- Pour 1/2 of the pudding in a 1-quart baking dish that's ungreased. Toss the bananas together with lemon juice, then layer it on top of the pudding. Lay out the vanilla wafers on top of the bananas in a single layer, then pour the leftover pudding on top of the wafers.
- Beat the egg whites in a big bowl on medium speed, until it forms soft peaks. Beat in the leftover sugar, a tbsp. at a time, on high until the sugar dissolves and forms stiff glossy peaks. Evenly spread the meringue on top of the pudding and let it bake for 12 to 15 minutes at 350 degrees without cover or until it turns golden brown in color. Put the leftovers in the fridge.

Nutrition Information

- Calories: 239 calories
- Total Carbohydrate: 45 g
- Cholesterol: 72 mg
- Total Fat: 5 g
- Fiber: 1 g
- Protein: 6 g
- Sodium: 116 mg

360. Warm Blackberry Cobbler

"Fat-free yogurt and egg whites make this classic dish become lighter to eat."
Serving: 8 servings. | Prep: 15m | Ready in: 45m

Ingredients

- 5 cups fresh or frozen blackberries
- 3/4 cup sugar
- 2 tbsps. all-purpose flour
- 1 tbsp. lemon juice
- 1 tsp. grated lemon peel
- 1 tsp. vanilla extract
- TOPPING:
- 1 cup all-purpose flour
- 1/2 tsp. baking powder
- 1/2 tsp. baking soda
- 2 egg whites
- 1/2 cup fat-free plain yogurt
- 2 tbsps. butter
- 2 tbsps. lemon juice
- 1 tsp. vanilla extract
- 1/2 cup reduced-fat whipped topping

Direction

- Mix vanilla, lemon peel, lemon juice, flour, sugar and blackberries together in a large bowl. Spoon into a baking dish of 11x7 inches greased with cooking spray; put aside.
- To make topping, mix baking soda, baking powder and flour together in a small bowl. In a separate bowl, mix vanilla, lemon juice, butter, yogurt and egg whites together; stir into the dry ingredients just until moistened.
- Drop tablespoonfuls of the yogurt mixture over blackberry mixture. Bake in the oven at 400° until the topping is golden and filling is bubbly, about 30 minutes. Serve together with whipped topping.

Nutrition Information

- Calories: 232 calories
- Total Carbohydrate: 47 g
- Cholesterol: 8 mg
- Total Fat: 4 g
- Fiber: 5 g
- Protein: 4 g
- Sodium: 145 mg

361. Warm Chocolate Almond Pudding

"This recipe is what I think of when I crave something chocolatey and creamy. Serve warm with a blob of whipped topping."
Serving: 8 servings. | Prep: 10m | Ready in: 10m

Ingredients

- 1/2 cup sugar
- 1/3 cup baking cocoa
- 2 tbsps. cornstarch
- 2 cups fat-free milk
- 1 egg, lightly beaten
- 1/4 tsp. vanilla extract
- 1/4 to 1/2 tsp. almond extract
- 1/4 cup reduce-fat whipped topping

Direction

- Mix cornstarch, cocoa and sugar in a saucepan. Whip in egg and milk. Cook and mix over medium heat until mixture comes to a boil. Let it boil for 1 minute. Take it off the heat; mix in extracts. Serve while it's still warm. Top with whipped topping.

Nutrition Information

- Calories: 205 calories

- Total Carbohydrate: 40 g
- Cholesterol: 56 mg
- Total Fat: 3 g
- Fiber: 2 g
- Protein: 7 g
- Sodium: 83 mg

362. Warm Chocolate Melting Cups

"Light cake desserts."
Serving: 10 servings. | Prep: 20m | Ready in: 40m

Ingredients

- 1-1/4 cups sugar, divided
- 1/2 cup baking cocoa
- 2 tbsps. all-purpose flour
- 1/8 tsp. salt
- 3/4 cup water
- 3/4 cup plus 1 tbsp. semisweet chocolate chips
- 1 tbsp. brewed coffee
- 1 tsp. vanilla extract
- 2 large eggs
- 1 large egg white
- Sliced fresh strawberries, optional

Direction

- Mix together the salt, flour, cocoa and 3/4 cup sugar in a small saucepan. Slowly mix in the water, then boil. Let it cook and stir until it becomes thick or for 2 minutes. Take it out of the heat and mix in vanilla, coffee and chocolate chips, until it becomes smooth. Move to a big bowl.
- Beat the egg white and eggs in a separate bowl, until it turns a bit thick. Slowly put in the leftover sugar and beat it until it turns lemon-colored and thick, then fold into the chocolate mixture.
- Move to 10 cooking spray coated 4-oz. ramekins. In the baking pan, put the ramekins, then pour an inch of boiling water into the pan. Let it bake for 20 to 25 minutes at 350 degrees without cover or just until the middle becomes set. If preferred, put strawberries on top as a garnish, then serve right away.

Nutrition Information

- Calories: 197 calories
- Total Carbohydrate: 37 g
- Cholesterol: 42 mg
- Total Fat: 6 g
- Fiber: 2 g
- Protein: 3 g
- Sodium: 51 mg

363. Watermelon Ice Cream (sugar-free)

"Sugar-free and milk-free ice cream recipe."
Serving: 3 | Prep: 10m | Ready in: 10m

Ingredients

- 1 banana
- 1 cup frozen diced watermelon
- 1/2 cup frozen mango chunks
- 1/4 cup frozen strawberries
- 1/4 cup almonds (optional)
- 1 tsp. hemp seeds, or to taste (optional)

Direction

- In a high-powered blender, put the banana, then add hemp seeds, almonds, strawberries, mango and watermelon. Blend until the mixture becomes creamy and smooth.

Nutrition Information

- Calories: 147 calories;
- Total Carbohydrate: 20.9 g
- Cholesterol: 0 mg
- Total Fat: 6.8 g
- Protein: 3.8 g
- Sodium: 2 mg

364. White Chip Cranberry Blondies

"Tasty blondies made with pecans, white chips, dried cranberries and applesauce."
Serving: 20 bars. | Prep: 15m | Ready in: 30m

Ingredients

- 2 eggs
- 1/4 cup canola oil
- 1/4 cup unsweetened applesauce
- 1-1/2 tsps. vanilla extract
- 1-1/3 cups all-purpose flour
- 2/3 cup packed brown sugar
- 1 tsp. baking powder
- 1/2 tsp. salt
- 1 cup dried cranberries, divided
- 1/2 cup white baking chips
- 1/2 cup chopped pecans

Direction

- Beat the vanilla, applesauce, oil and eggs in a big bowl. Mix together the salt, baking powder, brown sugar and flour, then mix it into the egg mixture until combined. Mix in half a cup of cranberries (the batter will get thick).
- Spread it in a cooking spray coated 13x9-inch baking pan. Put the leftover cranberries, pecans and chips on top, then press down the toppings gently.
- Let it bake for 15 to 20 minutes at 350 degrees or until an inserted toothpick in the middle exits clean. Allow to cool on a wire rack. Slice it into bars.

Nutrition Information

- Calories: 154 calories
- Total Carbohydrate: 22 g
- Cholesterol: 22 mg
- Total Fat: 7 g
- Fiber: 1 g
- Protein: 2 g
- Sodium: 92 mg

365. White Chocolate Cranberry Cookies

"Cookies with cranberries and white chocolate are the best. Its color can bring the holiday feel to your mind as well"
Serving: 2 dozen. | Prep: 20m | Ready in: 30m

Ingredients

- 1/3 cup butter, softened
- 1/2 cup packed brown sugar
- 1/3 cup sugar
- 1 large egg
- 1 tsp. vanilla extract
- 1-1/2 cups all-purpose flour
- 1/2 tsp. salt
- 1/2 tsp. baking soda
- 3/4 cup dried cranberries
- 1/2 cup white baking chips

Direction

- Beat sugars and butter in a large bowl until crumbly, for 2 minutes. Beat in vanilla and egg. Combine baking soda, salt and flour; gently put into butter mixture and blend well. Mix in chips and cranberries.
- Drop 2 inches apart on baking sheets covered with cooking spray by heaping tablespoonfuls. Bake at 375° until turn to light brown, about 8-10 minutes. Allow to cool for 1 minute before taking out to wire racks.

Nutrition Information

- Calories: 113 calories
- Total Carbohydrate: 18 g
- Cholesterol: 16 mg
- Total Fat: 4 g
- Fiber: 0 g
- Protein: 1 g
- Sodium: 109 mg

Index

A

Allspice, 10, 27, 94, 98, 108-109, 131, 172

Almond, 3-4, 6-7, 10-11, 37, 43-46, 61, 66, 70, 72-73, 81, 85-86, 92, 124, 131-133, 137, 142, 151, 163, 172-173, 184, 189-190

Almond extract, 10, 43-46, 61, 66, 70, 85, 92, 124, 137, 151, 163, 184, 189

Almond milk, 37

Anise, 156

Apple, 3-7, 11-18, 20-22, 29, 31-32, 37-40, 47-49, 64-66, 80, 83-84, 87, 97-98, 100-101, 108-111, 113, 130, 137, 139, 141, 148, 160, 163, 168-169, 172, 187

Apple juice, 20, 31, 37, 137, 160, 172, 187

Apple sauce, 130

Apricot, 3, 18-20, 87, 135, 140-141, 171-172, 182

B

Bagel, 169

Baking, 10, 15-20, 22-24, 26-27, 31-35, 37-61, 64-68, 70-79, 82-85, 88, 90, 92-96, 99-104, 107-114, 116-120, 123-127, 129-130, 132-135, 137-142, 149-152, 154-155, 157-163, 165-166, 168, 170-171, 173, 176, 179, 181-182, 185-191

Baking powder, 15, 18, 23-24, 26-27, 33-34, 38-42, 46-48, 55, 57-60, 66-68, 72, 74-77, 96, 100, 102, 107-108, 111-113, 116, 119, 123, 126, 130, 132, 134-135, 139, 154-155, 157, 159-160, 165-166, 176, 179, 185-186, 188-189, 191

Balsamic vinegar, 88, 176

Banana, 3-7, 22, 24-30, 38, 58, 60-63, 80, 87, 90-92, 94-95, 108, 123-124, 133, 137, 141, 172, 177-179, 184, 188, 190

Barley, 114, 157

Beans, 32-33, 148, 157

Beef, 98

Berry, 3-7, 11, 30-31, 33, 66, 68, 70-71, 81, 84, 88, 91, 109, 113, 121, 135, 151, 161-164, 172, 178, 180, 182, 186-187

Biscotti, 4, 55, 76

Black beans, 32-33

Black pepper, 156, 176

Blackberry, 5, 7, 11, 30-31, 88, 108-109, 161, 178, 189

Blueberry, 3-6, 11, 22-23, 30-31, 33-37, 40, 80-81, 84, 88, 102, 112, 114-115, 135, 151, 163-164, 178-179, 182, 186

Bran, 3, 26

Brandy, 131-132

Bread, 3, 6, 27, 35, 120, 148, 155, 169

Brown rice, 106

Brown sugar, 12, 17-18, 20-21, 23, 26-27, 31-32, 35, 37-38, 40-42, 45-47, 50, 54, 59, 64, 68-69, 71, 73-74, 80, 83, 94-103, 107, 109-111, 114, 117, 121, 123-124, 126-128, 130-131, 134, 136-137, 139-140, 142, 145, 151, 155, 157, 159, 163, 166-168, 170-171, 185, 187-188, 191

Butter, 4-7, 10, 12-13, 15-16, 18-19, 21-23, 26-36, 38-41, 44-51, 53-57, 59, 64-69, 71-80, 82-83, 85, 90, 92-93, 95-97, 100-111, 113, 115-119, 124, 126-132, 135, 138-140, 143, 148-151, 154-155, 157-158, 164-169, 171-172, 180-182, 185-189, 191

Buttermilk, 3, 27-28, 34, 38-39, 51, 74, 77, 124-125, 129-130, 132, 135, 170, 181, 186

C

Cake, 3-7, 10-11, 15-17, 19, 22, 27-28, 33-34, 38-41, 43-44, 46, 51-52, 58, 66, 73-74, 76-79, 85-86, 91, 95-96, 99, 104-105, 111-112, 114, 117-120, 122, 124-126, 129-130, 132, 134, 146, 151-153, 159-161, 165-166, 170-171, 173-176, 179-181, 183-187, 190

Candied peel, 98

Cannellini beans, 157

Caramel, 4, 6, 15, 37-38, 49, 65, 78-79, 165-167

Carrot, 3-4, 10, 38-39, 41-42, 85, 99

Carrot cake, 3-4, 10, 38, 41, 85

Cashew, 6, 133, 142, 182

Cayenne pepper, 21

Celery, 32, 69

Champagne, 3, 43

Cheese, 3, 5, 10-11, 17, 19, 29, 33-34, 38, 43-46, 49-50, 52, 57, 61, 66, 78, 83-84, 90-92, 105, 109-110, 115, 117, 120, 128, 135-136, 138, 142-144, 149-150, 152-154, 158, 161, 163-164, 167, 173, 181-182

Cherry, 3-4, 32, 43-45, 67, 70, 86,

95-96, 125, 131-132, 137, 139, 154, 182

Chips, 22, 32-33, 42, 47, 49-50, 55, 57-58, 67, 71-72, 75-77, 83-84, 96, 101-103, 120, 123-124, 127-128, 136, 150-151, 165, 182, 184-185, 190-191

Chocolate, 3-7, 22, 32-33, 39, 42, 44, 47, 49-58, 60-62, 67-68, 70-78, 81, 83-86, 92-96, 99, 101-105, 120, 123-124, 126-128, 130, 136, 138, 144, 150-151, 160-161, 163-166, 175, 181-182, 184-185, 189-191

Chocolate cake, 3-5, 7, 44, 51, 58, 73, 85, 99, 105, 181, 184

Chocolate mousse, 4, 52, 54, 56

Cider, 18, 23, 172

Cinnamon, 4-5, 10, 12-19, 21-27, 29-30, 32-33, 35, 38-39, 41-42, 46-48, 55, 59, 64, 68-71, 82-85, 93-100, 103-104, 107-109, 111-114, 117, 120, 130-131, 136-137, 139-141, 145, 154, 156-157, 159-160, 163, 169-172, 180, 187-188

Citrus fruit, 10-11

Cloves, 10, 24, 27, 32, 41, 47-48, 64, 82-83, 85, 93-94, 98, 103-104, 112, 130, 137, 159, 170, 172, 187

Cocktail, 84, 91, 158

Cocoa butter, 181

Cocoa powder, 21, 29, 32-33, 44, 51, 54, 60, 74, 76-77, 81, 102-103, 106

Coconut, 3-6, 10, 38-39, 45-46, 61-62, 72-73, 77, 106, 109, 125-128, 131-132, 138-139, 142, 145, 153, 157, 162, 182-183, 186-187

Coconut milk, 45-46

Coconut oil, 77, 142

Coffee, 3-5, 7, 32-34, 54, 62-63, 74, 76, 93, 95-96, 147, 187, 190

Coffee granules, 76

Coffee liqueur, 54

Condensed milk, 44, 46, 177

Corn syrup, 37-38, 47, 52, 59, 67-68, 74, 89, 96, 113, 124-126, 131-132, 137, 157, 160-161

Cottage cheese, 115, 120, 153-154

Crackers, 36, 53, 57, 94, 105, 120, 128, 136, 144, 149, 161, 186

Cranberry, 3-4, 6-7, 32, 55, 59, 64-71, 87, 96, 102, 110-111, 123-124, 148, 164, 169, 182, 191

Cranberry sauce, 65-67, 148

Cream, 3-7, 10-12, 15, 17, 19, 25, 27-30, 32-34, 36, 38-41, 43-44, 49-52, 54-58, 60-63, 65-66, 70, 72, 74-84,

86–88, 90–93, 97, 100, 105, 109–111, 113, 116–120, 122–125, 127–129, 132–138, 140–142, 144, 146, 148–150, 152–153, 156, 158, 160–167, 169–171, 173, 176–177, 180–188, 190

Cream cheese, 10–11, 17, 19, 29, 33–34, 38, 43–44, 49–50, 52, 57, 61, 66, 78, 83–84, 90–92, 105, 109–110, 117, 120, 128, 135–136, 138, 142, 144, 149–150, 152–153, 158, 161, 163–164, 167, 173, 181–182

Cream of tartar, 27–28, 36, 52, 54, 56, 60–61, 72, 86, 117–118, 124–125, 127–128, 133, 141, 162, 181, 184

Crisps, 163

Crumble, 4, 71, 100, 105, 112

Curd, 117–118

Currants, 141, 178

Custard, 3, 5, 24–26, 36, 115–116, 135, 148–149, 172

D

Dab, 182

Dark chocolate, 4, 74, 85

Date, 3, 28–29, 46, 108, 157

Dried apricots, 18, 140, 172, 182

Dried cherries, 70, 139, 182

Dried fruit, 96, 114, 182

Dried mixed fruit, 114

Dulce de leche, 71

Dumplings, 6, 154–155

E

Egg, 8, 10, 15–17, 19, 22–24, 26–29, 31–36, 38–42, 44–61, 64–68, 70, 72–79, 83–86, 92, 95–96, 99–106, 111–112, 114, 116–121, 123–133, 135–137, 139–142, 146, 148–150, 152, 154–155, 160, 162–171, 177, 179–181, 184–185, 187–191

Egg white, 10, 26–28, 33–34, 36, 41, 47, 50–52, 54–57, 60–61, 64, 70, 72–73, 75–76, 78, 83–86, 96, 99, 103, 111, 116–118, 120, 123–128, 130–133, 139, 141–142, 146, 160, 162–163, 165–168, 171, 179–181, 184, 188–190

Egg yolk, 27–28, 36, 55, 78, 85, 102, 132, 135–137, 142, 148, 154–155, 164–165, 179, 188

Elderberries, 83

Evaporated milk, 21, 24, 29, 35, 51, 67, 81, 86, 94–95, 152, 155

F

Fat, 5, 10-175, 177-191

Fennel, 178

Fig, 4, 84

Fish, 8

Flour, 10, 12-13, 15-18, 20-24, 26-29, 32-35, 38-42, 44-48, 50-51, 53-60, 64-72, 74-77, 80, 82-83, 85, 92-96, 99-105, 107-109, 111-114, 116-121, 123-132, 134-135, 139-140, 142, 146, 149-152, 154-155, 157, 159-160, 163-167, 170-171, 176, 179, 181-182, 184-191

Flour tortilla, 163

Fruit, 4-6, 10-11, 20, 26, 30-31, 42, 48-49, 65, 69, 71, 84, 87-89, 91, 96-98, 110, 114, 118, 135, 137, 139-141, 143, 156, 158, 167, 169, 171-174, 176-177, 182, 184, 186

Fruit salad, 4, 6, 48, 89, 137, 158

Fudge, 3-6, 47, 51, 67, 78-79, 93, 130, 134, 150, 160

G

Ginger, 3-5, 23-24, 27, 65, 80, 82-83, 93-94, 99, 104, 136-137, 159, 170

Gingerbread, 4, 65, 94

Grain, 16

Grape juice, 156

Grapefruit, 6, 10-11, 60, 167-169

Grapefruit juice, 60, 169

Grapes, 48-49, 87, 144

Ground ginger, 23-24, 27, 65, 82, 93-94, 99, 104, 136, 159, 170

Guava, 5, 98

H

Heart, 181-182, 186

Honey, 3, 5, 11-12, 24-25, 30, 59, 87, 97, 102-103, 110-112, 114, 133, 147-148, 170, 172, 177, 180, 184

I

Ice cream, 4-7, 12, 15, 25, 39, 50-51, 58, 62, 65, 78, 80-82, 97, 110-111, 116, 122-123, 133, 136, 142, 146, 149, 152, 160, 165, 177, 180, 182-183, 190

Icing, 142, 154, 170

Icing sugar, 154

J

Jam, 148-149, 173, 182

Jelly, 4, 43, 62, 79, 98, 173, 176

K

Kumquat, 3, 40

L

Lamb, 6, 137

Lemon, 3-6, 10-16, 18, 21, 23, 25, 29, 31, 33-37, 42-44, 46, 57-58, 60, 65, 68-69, 80-83, 85, 87-88, 93, 97-98, 107, 109-111, 114-120, 125, 128-129, 138, 140-141, 144, 146, 148-150, 154-156, 160, 164, 167, 172-174, 176, 179-180, 187-190

Lemon curd, 117-118

Lemon juice, 13-16, 18, 21, 23, 25, 29, 31, 35-37, 44, 57-58, 60, 68-69, 87-88, 97, 107, 109-110, 115-117, 119-120, 125, 128, 138, 144, 146, 148-150, 155, 160, 164, 167, 172-174, 180, 188-189

Lemonade, 4, 81-82, 89-90, 115-116

Lettuce, 69, 144

Lime, 5-6, 10-11, 31, 48, 114, 122-123, 134, 144, 151, 168, 174, 182-183

Lime juice, 31, 48, 122, 134, 168, 174, 182-183

Liqueur, 54, 81, 90, 150

M

Macadamia, 123

Macaroon, 3, 46

Mandarin, 4, 63, 86, 91, 114, 137, 143-144, 154, 183

Mango, 7, 183-184, 190

Maple syrup, 23, 26, 37, 84, 133

Margarine, 45, 78, 94-95, 139-140, 161

Marmalade, 30-31, 73, 143, 172

Marshmallow, 49-50, 75, 79, 87, 130, 145, 150-151, 166-167

Mayonnaise, 69

Meat, 8

Melon, 48, 89, 105, 112, 122

Meringue, 3-6, 28, 36, 52-54, 56, 60-61, 117-118, 127, 133, 141, 162-163, 165, 188

Milk, 8, 11, 15, 18-19, 21-27, 29, 32-39, 41-42, 44-46, 49-58, 61-64, 66-67, 70-71, 74-75, 78-83, 85-86, 89-95, 104-106, 108-109, 111, 113, 115-116, 118, 121, 127-132, 134-135, 137-140, 144-145, 147-152, 154-155, 160-161, 163-164, 166, 168-170, 173, 175-178, 181, 183, 185, 188-190

Milk chocolate, 32

Mincemeat, 5, 98

Mint, 4, 31, 48, 50, 53, 63, 81, 91, 119, 122, 125

Mixed berries, 88, 186

Molasses, 65, 93-94, 104, 130, 160, 170

N

Nectarine, 48-49

Noodles, 19

Nut, 8, 27, 31, 39, 48, 58, 67, 72-73, 95, 114, 123, 126-127, 134, 148, 157, 165, 182

Nutmeg, 13-14, 16-17, 21-22, 24, 27, 29, 32, 35, 41-42, 46, 59, 66, 68, 70-71, 82-83, 85, 99, 107-108, 112, 130-131, 136-137, 139, 159-160, 163, 170-171, 186-187

O

Oatmeal, 3-6, 12, 47, 68, 70, 103, 112, 139-140

Oats, 12-13, 20-21, 25-29, 35, 38, 42, 45, 47-48, 59, 64, 68-73, 80, 96-97, 100, 103-104, 106, 108, 114, 123, 127, 138-140, 151, 157, 159-160, 176, 187

Oil, 10, 16-17, 20, 23-24, 27-28, 32-34, 38, 42, 47-48, 53-54, 58-59, 61, 66-67, 70, 72-74, 76-78, 96, 98, 108, 112-116, 122, 124, 126-127, 130, 134, 142, 156-157, 160, 165-167, 170, 176, 191

Orange, 4, 6-7, 10-11, 19-20, 27-31, 38-40, 48-49, 51, 59-60, 63-68, 71-73, 79-81, 84, 86, 89-91, 98, 103, 108-109, 114, 121, 125, 137, 141-146, 150, 152-154, 156, 164-165, 168, 172, 179, 182-183

Orange juice, 20, 29-30, 39-40, 48-49, 59-60, 66-68, 71-73, 79, 89-90, 98, 103, 108-109, 114, 125, 142-146, 164, 168, 179, 182-183

Orange liqueur, 90, 150

P

Pancakes, 74, 110

Papaya, 6, 147

Parfait, 3-7, 31, 80-81, 123, 135, 144, 147, 178-179, 186-187

Passion fruit, 49

Pastry, 4, 6, 14-15, 18, 24, 44-45, 60-61, 69, 77, 82, 84, 101, 107, 109-110, 121, 131, 133, 136, 167, 173, 176

Peach, 3-5, 7, 22-23, 59, 64, 87, 89, 107, 158, 177, 180, 185

Peanut butter, 4-7, 51, 78, 92, 96-97, 106, 128, 140, 148-149, 157, 181

Peanuts, 78

Pear, 3-6, 23, 48, 69, 72-73, 87, 128-129, 149-150, 156-158, 171

Pecan, 5-6, 22-23, 32, 44, 47, 49, 66-67, 71, 73, 75, 95-97, 117, 130-131, 134, 152, 159, 165, 177, 182, 191

Peel, 3, 10-12, 18, 22, 33-34, 40, 43, 46, 48, 52, 65, 73, 80-81, 83, 87, 98, 109-111, 116, 119-120, 125, 128-129, 139, 141, 149-150, 156, 167-169, 173-174, 176, 189

Pepper, 21, 156-157, 176

Pie, 3-6, 12-14, 18, 23-24, 28-29, 33, 35-36, 43-45, 53, 57, 60, 62, 64-65, 69, 81-82, 86, 88-89, 93, 95, 101, 109-110, 117, 119, 121, 128, 131, 134, 136-138, 154, 159, 161, 163-164, 167, 169, 172, 174-175

Pineapple, 3-4, 6, 22, 32, 38-39, 41-42, 62, 67, 69, 71, 85, 87, 90-92, 94-95, 122, 137, 144-145, 148, 151-154, 158, 166, 171-172, 183

Pineapple juice, 62, 144, 158

Pistachio, 4-6, 55, 90, 97, 153-154

Pizza, 5, 135

Plantain, 98

Plum, 6, 154-155, 172

Pomelo, 169

Poppy seeds, 71, 117

Pork, 65

Potato, 5, 103, 121, 131, 155

Praline, 4, 65

Preserves, 5, 98, 135, 151-152, 182

Prune, 27, 75-76, 85, 140-141, 154, 172

Pulse, 12, 36, 64, 88, 98, 144, 151

Pumpkin, 3, 6, 12, 23-24, 121, 136-137, 145, 159-160, 172, 182

Pumpkin seed, 182

Q

Quinoa, 3, 6, 37, 160

R

Raisins, 10, 16-19, 22, 26-27, 31-32, 41-42, 47-48, 85, 96-99, 101, 103-104, 106, 131-132, 139, 141, 147, 157, 160, 163, 168-170, 187

Raspberry, 4-6, 11, 30-31, 56-57, 64-65, 84, 88, 90, 92, 118, 135, 148, 160-163, 175, 178, 182, 186

Red wine, 156-157

Red wine vinegar, 156

Rhubarb, 4-6, 82, 95-96, 110, 164-165, 176

Rice, 3, 5-6, 16, 21, 38, 49, 59, 72, 96, 106, 127, 139, 178

Rice flour, 139

Rice pudding, 3, 5-6, 21, 106, 139, 178

Ricotta, 143

Rosemary, 6, 146, 166

Rum, 54, 186

S

Salad, 3-4, 6, 32, 42, 48, 67, 69, 79, 87, 89, 91, 137, 148, 158

Salt, 10, 13-15, 17-18, 20, 22-27, 32-36, 38-42, 44-48, 50, 52-54, 57-61, 65-68, 70-72, 74-78, 83, 88-89, 92-96, 98, 102-104, 106-113, 115-127, 129-137, 139-140, 142, 146, 150-152, 154-157, 160, 164-167, 170, 176, 179-181, 184-188, 190-191

Sea salt, 24-25

Seeds, 24-25, 57, 71, 89-90, 109, 114, 117, 133, 160, 164, 175, 182, 190

Shortbread, 88, 116, 138

Soda, 10, 17, 20, 22, 27, 32, 34, 38-39, 41-42, 44, 47-48, 50, 53-54, 58, 60, 65, 68, 70, 72, 74, 76-77, 83, 85, 93-96, 99-104, 109, 112, 114, 116, 119, 123-127, 129-130, 132, 135, 139-140, 150-152, 157, 159-160, 170, 181-182, 186-189, 191

Sorbet, 3, 5-7, 11-12, 68, 97, 122, 141, 146, 180, 182-183

Soup, 4-6, 48, 83, 112, 140

Spices, 10, 16, 24, 130-131, 136, 170, 172

Sponge cake, 6, 146, 151, 179

Star anise, 156

Stock, 13

Strawberry, 3-7, 26, 30-31, 43, 70, 81, 84, 87-88, 90-92, 95-96, 107, 110, 120-122, 135-136, 141, 147-149, 151, 158, 163-164, 168-169, 173-180, 183, 185-186, 190

Strawberry jam, 148-149, 173

Sucralose, 100

Suet, 98

Sugar, 5, 7, 10-24, 26-191

Sunflower seed, 114

Sweet potato, 5, 103, 121, 131

Sweets, 120

Syrup, 12, 14, 23-24, 26, 37-38, 47, 52, 59, 67-68, 74, 84, 88-89, 95-96, 113, 124-126, 131-133, 137, 148, 150, 157, 160-161, 183

T

Tapioca, 13, 108–109, 140–141

Tea, 6, 146

Tempura, 3, 28

Tequila, 5, 122

Toffee, 163

Tomato, 5, 98

Turkey, 68

V

Vanilla extract, 10–11, 16–17, 19–22, 24–29, 32–33, 35–39, 41, 44–47, 49–50, 52–61, 66–70, 72, 74–75, 77–79, 83, 85–86, 92, 96, 99–106, 108, 111, 117–121, 123–124, 126–127, 129–135, 138, 142, 144, 149–150, 152, 156–157, 159–161, 165–166, 169–170, 176–179, 181, 184–185, 188–191

Vegan, 160

Vegetable oil, 32, 38, 58, 72, 108, 114

Vegetable shortening, 79

Vegetables, 42

Vinegar, 18, 23–24, 42, 52, 88, 98, 129, 156–157, 176, 180–181

W

Waffles, 74

Walnut, 7, 10, 17, 22, 38, 41, 47, 64–66, 69, 72, 78–79, 84–85, 92, 95, 100–101, 103–104, 106, 112, 114, 127–128, 147–148, 156–157, 165, 187–188

Walnut oil, 156

Watermelon, 7, 190

Whipping cream, 51, 74, 116, 137, 164

White chocolate, 4, 7, 51, 53, 76, 93, 164, 175, 191

White sugar, 12–15, 19, 21, 26, 32, 35–36, 40–41, 44–45, 49, 51, 63, 68–69, 71, 76, 83, 85, 87–89, 95–98, 100–107, 113, 122, 136–137, 139–141, 148, 150, 152, 154–155, 157, 163, 168–170, 172, 176, 178, 180, 182–183

White wine, 114, 122, 156

Wine, 6, 114, 122, 156–157

Z

Zest, 27–28, 30–31, 35, 38–40, 51, 60, 64, 79, 84, 121–123, 142–144, 146, 151, 154, 156, 164–165, 168, 174, 176, 179

Conclusion

Thank you again for downloading this book!

I hope you enjoyed reading about my book!

If you enjoyed this book, please take the time to share your thoughts and post a review on Amazon. It'd be greatly appreciated!

Write me an honest review about the book – I truly value your opinion and thoughts and I will incorporate them into my next book, which is already underway.

Thank you!

If you have any questions, **feel free to contact at:** mshealthy@mrandmscooking.com

Ms. Healthy

www.MrandMsCooking.com

Printed in Great Britain
by Amazon